Al,

Thank you so much for all your time and insight for this book.

All the best,

Carl

FRENZY

FRENZY

BUBBLES, BUSTS, AND
HOW TO COME OUT AHEAD

CARL HAACKE

First published 2004 by
PALGRAVE MACMILLAN™
175 Fifth Avenue, New York, N.Y. 10010 and
Houndmills, Basingstoke, Hampshire, England RG21 6XS.
Companies and representatives throughout the world.

PALGRAVE MACMILLAN is the global academic imprint of the Palgrave
Macmillan division of St. Martin's Press, LLC and of Palgrave Macmillan
Ltd. Macmillan® is a registered trademark in the United States, United
Kingdom and other countries. Palgrave is a registered trademark in the
European Union and other countries.

ISBN 1-4039-6131-X

Library of Congress Cataloging-in-Publication Data
Haacke, Carl.
Frenzy : bubbles, busts and how to come out ahead / by Carl Haacke.
    p.   cm.
  Includes bibliographical references and index.
  ISBN 1–4039–6131-X
  1. Speculation.   2. Stocks—Prices.   3. Investment analysis.
4. Financial crises—History.   5. Internet industry—Finance.   I. Title.

HG6015.H28 2004
332.6—dc22

                                                                200404470

A catalogue record for this book is available from the British Library.

Design by Letra Libre, Inc.

First edition: December 2004
10 9 8 7 6 5 4 3 2 1

Printed in the United States of America.

Dedicated to Anna, Matthew and Evan

CONTENTS

ACKNOWLEDGEMENTS

THIS BOOK HAS BEEN AN INCREDIBLE OPPORTUNITY and experience to talk with some of the greatest business leaders about one of the most remarkable periods in business history, how it relates to past bubbles, and what lessons can be learned for the future.

As a result, this book simply would not have been possible without the help of nearly 100 people, many of whom took time out of their busy schedules to talk with me in great detail for hours and at times over many conversations. This entire book is a reflection of my gratitude to the seriousness of purpose and honesty with which each of these individuals approached our discussions. Others provided detailed and extremely helpful comments on the text and helped hone some ideas that are presented. I would like to thank Kurt Abrahamson, Michael Armstrong, William Baumol, Scott Bertetti, Tom Bingham, Peter Bisson, John Bogle, Don Cassidy, Robert Clauser, Evan Cohen, David Collis, John Conner, Mark Cuban, Andrew D'Ambrosio, Maziar Delaeli, Gene DeRose, Dave Dorman, Steve Dow, Bill Draper, Tim Draper, Barry Eggars, Stuart Ellman, Dan Estabrook, Bob Feldman, Alan Fields, Steve Friedman, Tom Flynn, John Fontana, Aram Fuchs, Fred Giudfredda, Fred Gluck, Josh Grotstein, John Koskinen, Mark Hagan, Bill Hambrecht, Paul Harrington, Bill Janeway, Paul Johnson, John Jones, Terrel Jones, Bob Kagle, Habib Kairuz, Craig Kanarick, Will Lansing, Bob Latta, Al Leach, Steven Leslie, Jim Lesserson, Roger McNamee, Roger Meznick, Mark Moradian, Mike Moritz, Chip Morris, Tim Mulony, Martin Neisenholz, Evan Neufield, Dan Nordstromm, Terry Odean, Andrew Odlyzko, Alan Patricof, Michele Peluso, Stephen Penmen, Tom

Perkins, Will Porteous, Jesse Reyes, Jay Ritter, Ross Ruben, Edmund
Sanctis, Eric Schoenberg, Rob Shepardson, Clay Shirky, Al Sikes, Marc
Singer, Peter Sisson, Kevin Slavin, Amy Snyder, Pete Solvik, Lenny
Stern, Ross Stevens, Tony Sun, David Turnbull, Troy Tyler, Don Valen-
tine, Hal Varian, Mark Walsh, Dan Weiner, Ron Weissman, Geoff Yang,
Marty Yuckovitch, Strauss Zelnick. There are a number of people who I
also wish to thank who contributed substantively to this book but who
wish to remain anonymous.

It is worth noting that legal investigations into various activities in investment banks and mutual funds made many people uncomfortable or
unable to speak on the record. Their input, nonetheless, contributed
greatly to the approach and general content of the book on a wide range
of issues. The treatment in this book of unethical and illegal activities
were drawn exclusively from the public record.

I would also like to thank my editor Toby Wahl for taking a chance
on a first-time author.

Finally, a special gratitude must go to my wife Anna for putting up
with long hours of my writing, interviewing, editing, my new sons Evan
and Matthew for providing inspiration, and my mother Linda, father
Hans, and brother Paul all a lifetime of support.

INTRODUCTION

THE BUBBLE OF THE 1990S, DESPITE THE HYPE, was not primarily driven by the Internet. It was driven by human nature. Bubbles are created by human impulses that transcend the Internet, the 1990s, the twentieth century, or the United States. We frequently create bubbles when we are presented with an extraordinary and incalculable opportunity and wild uncertainty. We become seized by frenzy. Creative imagination runs wild. Throughout history, the promise of a glorious new world seizes us, setting in motion a cascade of great opportunities and disastrous investments. At the same time, bubbles are not simply "irrational exuberance." They are fueled by a complex human dynamic that warps how we perceive information and respond to competitive pressures.

We normally try to understand the economy by tracking the numbers—profits, GDP, stock prices, the unemployment rate, inflation. However, using these indicators *exclusively* is like trying to understand how a car works just by looking at a speedometer and odometer. *Frenzy* opens the hood and inspects the engine to reveal the core human machinery of the economy that leads to bubbles. It answers the perennial question: *What were people thinking?* Frenzy focuses on three types of investors—venture capitalists who start new companies, corporations who acquire start-ups and launch internal initiatives and stock pickers.

In the aftermath of the Internet bubble, the lesson is not that reason will thankfully always prevail in the long run. The lesson is that bubbles are inevitable. Bubbles and the frenzy that drives them are a basic feature of human and economic activity. They are not rare, once-in-a-lifetime events. They occur all the time. Certainly, bubbles as big as the Internet bubble are extremely uncommon. But on smaller scales, they are everywhere. For centuries, human beings have been captivated by wild manias of enthusiasm when a new, wondrous, and unknown opportunity is introduced—a new market to explore, a new technology, a new product. So far, we have created technology bubbles with the introductions of new innovations such as canals, railways, autos, radios, high technology companies in the 1960s, personal computers, biotech, and many other innovations, each of which seems to transform business capacity, commerce, or social activities. We have also created bubbles based on financial arrangements such as leveraged buyouts (LBOs) in the 1980s. Real-estate bubbles occur frequently all over the world. Even single firms such as Long Term Capital Management featured bubble dynamics. New markets in other countries can create bubbles as well. During the early part of the 1990s, the Asian Tiger countries such as Thailand and Indonesia suffered from bubble dynamics in what became known as the "Asian Miracle." The Miracle ended with the Asian Economic Crisis of 1997, causing dramatic upheaval in the region and threatening the global economy. As of the writing of this book, there is likely a bubble in China, driven by the excitement that the country will quickly become the world's biggest economy with a billion customers.

Since the 1950s at least, there have been very few years of economic growth that did not generate a bubble in some industry, some new market opportunity, or some country. Four years after the Internet bubble burst in March 2000, insiders and outsiders have worried about many smaller bubbles in hedge funds, exchange traded funds, biotechnology, outsourcing, nanotechnology, social networking platforms, oil prices, real estate in numerous parts of the world, and plasma screens. In each of these cases, participants have said *this is like the Internet in 1999.* The frenzy operates similarly in small and big market opportunities. This means that the risks and opportunities of bubbles are ever present. It is comforting, for some, to view bubbles as unusual events caused by the irrational behavior of human beings that interrupts normal, rational economic functioning. But the reality is that since human beings are the engine that drives the economy, bubbles must be accepted as a normal consequence of economic behavior.

Commenting on bubbles and busts, Alan Greenspan, Chairman of the U.S. Federal Reserve Bank, said in 1999, "What is so intriguing is that this type of behavior has characterized human interaction with little appreciable difference over the generations. Whether Dutch tulip bulbs or Russian equities, the market price patterns remain much the same."[1]

The Internet bubble was probably the *second* largest in history. It was likely smaller than the railway mania that overtook Great Britain in 1840s, when, by some accounts, investment in railways consumed 5 percent of the entire country's economic production—equivalent to investing more than $500 billion in the United States today. Size does matter. Big bubbles have widespread effects. The Internet bubble had dramatic global effects, both on the way up and on the way down. When big bubbles crash, like the Internet bubble, the Asian Miracle, the roaring 20s, the go-go years of the 1960s, long-term capital management, they can be very destabilizing to the global economy By contrast, something like the biotech bubble is narrowly focused on a specific sector, and many never knew that it was going on.

As Mark Twain, aptly noted, "History does not repeat itself, but it rhymes."

It is hard to understand the nuanced human decision-making and competitive pressures that build into a frenzy when looking at events that happened decades or centuries ago. There are some historical records that illustrate some of these dynamics, but the passage of time now prevents us from talking in depth with the key decision makers about what they were thinking, how they perceived information, and what the pressures on them were to make different kinds of investments. The advantage of the Internet bubble is that we can talk to many of the decision makers to derive a relatively clear picture of what was going on. The period serves as a great lab experiment, shining giant Klieg lights on our brains and our behavior in the marketplace. Furthermore, since the Internet bubble was so big, even small decisions making patterns had a big impact, thus enabling us to see them, whereas they may not have been observable in smaller bubbles.

The Internet bubble had special features, of course: it occurred during the longest economic expansion in history; individual participation in the stock market grew to record levels; the new technology driving the bubble seemed to touch every aspect of our lives from supply chain management to dating; and venture capitalists played a much larger role in the "new economy" than they had in the past. Deregulation in the telecommunications industry, Y2K, and low inflation also created some unique conditions. Despite all of it, though, the Internet bubble followed some fairly classic patterns. The Internet was new, but the human forces behind it were not.

Despite all the bubbles that occurred in the past, many more lie ahead of us. We do not learn from history. The next one may not be as large as the Internet bubble or may not take over as much of the economy, but whatever its size or the opportunity that sparks it, the next bubble will tap into many of the same motivations that warped so many decisions during the 1990s. In fact, as the pace of technological innovation increases, as global capital markets make it easier for more people to invest in these innovations, and as the venture capital industry continues to grow in scale and scope, bubbles may be even more common in the future than they were in the past.

As a result, it is now more important than ever that we improve our understanding of how human behavior creates unsustainable investment bubbles that can crash with devastating consequences. We must be able to manage these wild swings more effectively, or we will continue to be the victims of market upheavals rather than their masters. While a few lucky investors manage to make a lot of money during bubbles, many investors—from individuals to venture capitalists to business managers—make bad decisions that end up wasting money and destroying value.

With more insight into the human dimension of bubbles, we can become more effective at managing the whirlwinds of innovative change. We can formulate better decisions, better investments, and better visions for the future. We can avoid the systemic traps that emerge during bubbles and lead to confusion, missteps, wasted investment, and misdirected strategies. With a better understanding of the dynamics of bubbles, we can recognize them sooner and manage money better when they inflate and lose less money when they burst.

While bubble dynamics appear to have many similarities, it turns out that there are at least two distinct types of bubbles throughout history. One type of bubble is the purely speculative bubble. This type exists in a liquid marketplace like a stock market or currency exchange. The speculative bubble does not produce anything in the real sectors of the economy. Investors are simply buying and selling assets, trying to take advantage of souring prices. They are driven by pure speculation that prices will continue to raise and the hope of "getting rich fast." Historically, this is most vividly illustrated by the Dutch Tulip Mania of the 1630s. At the time, rare breeds of tulips, which had been coveted by the upper classes, were widely traded in early versions of the stock market. The value of the tulips skyrocketed as the general public became enraptured with owning one of these artifacts and becoming rich overnight. Tulip mania was a pure asset bubble. The stock market bubbles of the 1920s, 1960s, 1980s, and 1990s also had aspects of a speculative bubble since a fair number of shares were traded strictly for their speculative value.

The second type of bubble, the business investment bubble, does not rely exclusively on a speculative drive. Investment bubbles emerge when some new technology or market opportunity seems to demonstrate a huge but unquantifiable potential for growth and profit. Mixed in with the rush to strike it rich is also the excitement and dream of transforming and improving the world. Railways, radios, the go-go years of the 1960s, personal computers, the Asian Tigers, and the Internet all rested on such a transformative vision. Despite the insane valuations that these bubbles may engender, something substantial is created along the way. Real businesses are built. Some investors can speculate on soaring prices during these bubbles. Many investors, however, such as those who finance start-ups or corporations who invest in new initiatives or purchase other companies cannot time the market because they cannot get in and out of the market quickly. They are making longer-term investments with business goals. Moreover, investment bubbles are fueled not just by asset traders, but by large corporations and financiers of young start-ups. Speculation is simple, business investment is far more complex. Investment bubbles do not burst because the innovative visionaries are proven entirely wrong. They burst because investors believed in exaggerated ideas of the profits these nascent technologies could generate and how long it would take to achieve them. In the end, over many years, significant aspects of the initial vision become reality—with some surprises along the way.

To be sure, investment bubbles also create speculative behavior. Investment bubbles and speculative bubbles work together and reinforce each other in a vicious cycle. Investment activity for railways, radio, personal computers, and the Internet all featured speculative behavior. With so much uncertainty surrounding the new technologies, investors have a very hard time distinguishing speculative stocks from investments in real business potential.

The life cycle of an investment bubbles seem to be quite regular. Before bubbles can inflate, there are fragmented efforts and experiments at solving old problems and creating new inventions. Tinkerers and entrepreneurs are always at work, more often than not in obscurity. Sometimes they find success, and every once in a while, they hit on an explosive opportunity that puts them in the center of an emergent bubble.

Bubbles often begin with a big bang, where an innovation makes a significant number of people very wealthy very quickly or captures the attention of a large number of investors. A consensus then forms that "This is the next big thing." The general public, normally engrossed in varied fields of business, is compelled to stop and take notice of the astonishing new opportunity. Progressively, more investors get swept away by the frenzy to take advantage of the incredible returns.

Bubbles create two powerful distortions that ripple through the economy on a massive scale. They distort information and they warp competition. Bubbles cloud our ability to perceive information effectively. Similar to looking at our reflection in a crystal ball or soap bubble, our perception of reality becomes warped during investment bubbles. Information is always limited when investment opportunities are evaluated. Many facts are simply not knowable. Traditional analysis tries to make educated guesses based on industry experience and knowledge. However, because the opportunities are so new during investment bubbles, there is very little historic experience that can inform good decision-making. Descriptions of euphoric scenarios dominate words of caution, as the press repeatedly tells captivating stories about stunning IPOs and brilliant visionaries who make vast sums of money.

The longer the bubble lasts, the more likely it is that skeptics will be perceived as wrong-headed because the stock market and corporations repeatedly seem to generate real data that confirm the visionaries' projections. As time goes by, a growing number of wary investors start believing the hype—they become *converted*. After all, for how many years can someone keep repeating that prices are too high and companies over-valued, only to be contradicted by the reality of prices doubling within a few months?

Increasingly, the normal discipline of analyzing investment opportunities is lost as unexpected opportunities suddenly appear to become viable and valuable. As a result, unsustainable companies get funded, planting the early seeds of destruction of the bubble. These bad investments in poorly conceived start-ups lay in wait, like time bombs waiting to explode. With so much uncertainty, investors and business managers become desperate for insight. Whom can they trust to provide real information when everything seems to have changed? The experts who emerge may or may not have any special insight, but their actions and comments are actively watched for signals pointing to where the good investment opportunities can be found. Many investors and business managers follow their lead. But the ripple effects that these experts, such as venture capitalist, analysts, and technology gurus, have when they place their imprimatur on a new business are disproportionate to the true insight they provide.

At the same time, regardless of one's perception of the merits of the investment opportunities, powerful competitive incentives and pressures make it extremely difficult to resist the lure of the bubble. Greed is a powerful force. These incentives attract hordes of new people to the market who jump in to capture the incredible profits that seem so easy. As a result, too many copy-cat start-ups emerge for too small a customer market. The market becomes saturated, becoming increasingly unsustainable and insuring that the bubble is going to end. Investor enthusiasm drives far too much money to chase too few real opportunities.

The pressures force many investors to warp their normal decision-making and even skeptics begin to capitulate and play the game, many despite their better judgment. Eventually, the risks of being wrong with the crowd become easier to manage than being correct but standing alone, resisting the mania.

With so much money being generated during bubbles, the perception emerges among venture capitalists, heads of start-ups, and corporations that money will be endlessly available, further enabling bad business practices.

Perceptions and pressures affect individuals in every investment decision they make during bubbles. These micro-level forces multiplied across the marketplace affect the economy as a whole. The race to chase the highest returns creates a spiraling of capital away from "old economy" investments, increasingly focused on the red-hot sectors of the "new economy." The inflow of money into these funds and companies creates incredible demand and further inflates prices.

For all the hype and exaggerated valuations that bubbles create, they also inflate real fundamentals. Start-ups need people and machines and offices. They buy advertising and hire consultants. Corporations launch expensive initiatives. All of these activities create some real demand, and sometimes they generate real profits. The trouble is, they are all built on bubble demand and bubble companies, which will quickly fall away when the bubble bursts.

The end of bubbles does not usher in the decline of the innovations that sparked them. Nor do bubbles burst because the visionaries are proven entirely wrong. They burst because of investors' exaggerated expectations for the profits that can be made from these innovations and how fast they will develop. The rapid speed of a revolution slows to the more gradual but substantial pace of transformation. As quickly as new technologies arrive, old technologies take a long time to fade away. In the long run, many features of the Internet vision will be proven correct, but it will take twenty years rather than two. Other unexpected uses will emerge as providing great benefits.

The social and economic benefits of bubbles last forever. The railroad, the radio, cars, television, computers, the Internet have all thoroughly transformed the economy and social interaction. The bubbles in emerging markets such as the Asian Tiger countries and now China have lifted millions of people from poverty and created powerful global businesses.

Bubbles usher in momentous change, but they do not represent the entire journey. It is the road to get there that is so bumpy and it is our driving skills that need improving to avoid continuing wreckage.

ONE

PERCEPTIONS (SEEING IS BELIEVING)

All truth passes through three stages. First, it is ridiculed. Second, it is violently opposed. Third, it is accepted as being self-evident.

—Arthur Schopenhauer

FROM FRAGMENTATION TO BUBBLE FORMATION

Most bubbles start "when someone makes a bunch of money," said Tom Perkins frankly. "We think it is very important to be first. But it is tricky because if you are too early there is no market and you're just spending money and you've educated the rest of the world about what you are doing. If you are too late it is worse because then everybody is in it and you'll never get out in time."[1]

Perkins has a lot of experience with bubbles as one of a handful of the elder statesmen who built the venture capital industry. Perkins himself began in the late 1960s by inventing one of the first commercializable lasers that cut the cost from thousands to about $300. A small-scale laser bubble ensued as investors began to imagine all the wonderful possibilities for laser technology. Since then Perkins as lived through bubbles in computers, PCs, biotech, and now the Internet.

The Netscape IPO was the catalytic event that ignited the Internet bubble. It was the first widely noticeable grand money making opportunity. On August 8, 1995, 8.5 million shares of Netscape Communications was released into the public market in the company's initial public offering, a little more than a year after it was founded. The day started off like any other day, but when these shares were sprinkled like fairy dust into the market, they created a magical and explosive reaction. Netscape's price started at $14 and closed at $58.25, reaching a market value of $1 billion.

In its fullness, Netscape transformed the market by making 3 important opportunities appear extremely easy on a mass scale. It made the Internet easy to use for the everyday consumer. It made it easy for nearly any entrepreneur to start a company simply by creating a website. And it made it seemingly easy to make a lot of money very quickly. (In the end, each of these things would prove far more difficult than imagined.)

Prior to that day, awareness of the emerging information superhighway was limited to a small group who saw intriguing potential for interactive media and new forms of communication. After the IPO, it was recognized as an emerging industry in which an entrepreneur or an investor could become very, very rich. The power of such a tremendous IPO was stunning and rippled through the markets. Venture Capitalists, investors, newly minted MBAs, and bankers all took notice. Some thought it was lunacy, while others saw their opportunity.

Regarding the Netscape IPO, Jim Clark said, "Barksdale [CEO of Netscape] and I both felt that an IPO was as much a marketing event as a financial event, so it was just as important to price the stock where it would express the quality of the company, sell well, and create buzz as it was to reward the new shareholders with something that went up, showing that they had made the right decision."[2] They succeeded on a scale far beyond simply Netscape. They ignited the global frenzy.

Before Netscape and its predecessor, Mosaic, "cyberspace," as it was called at the time, the Internet was extremely hard to use. It was a purely text-based information exchange, and strange codes were required to navigate the information superhighway. While there already seemed great possibilities for sharing information, it had not yet been demonstrated that cyberspace could deliver as a technology, much less as an investment. If VCRs are hard enough for consumers to use, FTP commands, the strange commands used to get access to the information, were far more cumbersome. The World Wide Web at this point was largely inhabited by university professors, researchers, and computer buffs.

"The Internet was nowhere," remembered an investment banker directly involved with some of the most prominent Internet IPOs. "You just had a lot of interesting innovation. Not directly related to the Internet, but underpinnings."[3]

There had been numerous fragmented efforts to bring interactive media to the general public. They were driven by dreams that interactive communication had the potential for changing human behavior. IBM and Sears joined forces to produce Prodigy, H&R Block created CompuServe, News Corp had Delphi Internet, Apple developed eWorld, Bell Atlantic promoted Stargazer, and AT&T had PersonaLink. Time Warner launched an interactive TV initiative. These were serious companies all taking a stab at the next frontier, and all of them failed. But like most failures, they were not all wasted efforts. They taught valuable lessons. Perhaps more importantly, they also prevented a bubble from forming. Big public failures such as these keep people guessing about what the next big opportunity will be. The guessing keeps the market fragmented between the people who believe, the people who don't, and those who do not even know what is happening. Among private investors, only the bravest and personally connected would put their money into these infant experiments. (This is also the time when some of the most sophisticated venture capitalists made their most important investments.) For companies, these ventures represent R&D attempts to push the envelope, and possible failure is an expected part of the process. For the job seekers, the talent pool, there is no compelling reason to jump on board a vessel that could easily sink tomorrow without some sense that tremendous opportunities also exist. This fragmentation undermines the momentum that is necessary for bubbles to form. Without a consensus that any of these efforts is the next big opportunity, too few investors get involved to create much excitement, much less the mass frenzy that characterizes bubbles.

Fragmented efforts speckle the sweep of history. For the radio mania, the tinkerers of that period were primarily Guglielmo Marconi, Professor Reginald Fessenden, and Lee De Forest. Through competing demonstrations and public efforts they battled over whether the signal for radio transmission would be based on an electric spark or continuous wave.

For Marconi, an inventor of an early radio, one demonstration of his radio at the America's Cup yacht race in October 1899 attracted early attention. Using his radio he provided the *New York Herald* with real-time reports on the race. These early radios could not transmit signals over distances longer than 30 miles. Fassenden in turn was working in the U.S. Weather Bureau in an effort to demonstrate the practical benefits of the radio and then later struck out on his own by forming the National Electric Signalling Company (NESCO).

Fassenden demonstrated what would be considered the first real radio broadcast on Christmas Day 1906 for the industry press and representatives from AT&T. The initial view of the commercial application was connecting individuals. AT&T immediately thought that it was a threat to their long distance telephone service. At the time, radio broadcast from one point to many had not yet been considered.

De Forest launched the Wireless Telegraph Company of America in 1901 and tried to emulate Marconi by transmitting signals for the America's Cup race that year. The two inventors competed head-to-head in that race. Macroni was commissioned by the Associated Press to cover the race and De Forest by the Publisher's Press Association. By 1902, De Forest's company was valued at $3 million or equivalent to $200 million in 2002 dollars. Shortly thereafter, while the inventions had not yet proven commercially viable, they did generate enough attention to continue the flow of investors seeking a "piece of the action." By 1904 De Forest's company, now called American De Forest Wireless Telegraph Company, was valued at $15 million or $1 billion in 2002 dollars.

The beginning of the auto boom was also marked initially by experimentation and uncertainty about the core technology. While the Internet emerged as the leading platform for interactive media, in the early 1990s it was not clear whether the ruling technology would become the CD-ROM, interactive television or whether the leading companies would be computer companies or phone companies. Similarly, the initial technological foundations for cars could have been steam, electric power, or the now pervasive petrol-powered internal combustion engine. It was also not clear whether the leading companies would be in the United States or Europe. The first workable gasoline-powered automobile was built in Germany in 1885 by Karl Benz and Gottlieb Daimler. Charles and Frank Duryea built the first in the United States in 1893.

Early entrants had various backgrounds in engineering ranging from bicycles, horse-drawn carriages, and wagons, to stationary gas engines or metal fabricators. In 1897, for example, the Pope Manufacturing Company of Hartford began to produce electric and gas, and historically was the largest producer of bicycles.

SKEPTICS

Investors and entrepreneurs who are involved in the early experiments continue with their activity, as they did before any bubble, not knowing that they will soon enter the vortex of hysteria. The experiments that do end up leading to great change and wealth creation are typically met with stiff skepticism if not outright hostility. The early years of cyberspace suffered from the same doubts, "Aside from the infrastructure and [Internet] access providers, it isn't clear that we are missing very many business opportunities at the moment," said Jon Feiber, general partner at Mohr, Davidow Ventures. "While we continually need to explore value added opportunities or changes in the use of the Internet that create opportunities, VCs don't generally bet on sociological change and fundamental evolution in the way people operate—it's hard to predict when these changes will happen, and we need an entry and an exit!"[4] said another VC.

The historical record of skeptical industry leaders proven wildly wrong is remarkable:

- "What could be more palpably absurd than the prospect held of locomotives traveling twice as fast as stagecoaches."—The Quarterly Review, March 1825.
- "That any general system of conveying passengers would . . . go at a velocity exceeding ten miles per hour, or thereabouts, is extremely improbable."—Thomas Tredgold (British Railroad designer), *Practical Treatise on Railroads and Carriages,* 1835.
- "The 'telephone' has too many shortcomings to be seriously considered a means of communication."—Western Union Internal Memo, 1876.
- "Heavier-than-air flying machines are impossible."—Lord Kelvin, President, Royal Society, 1895.

- "This wireless music box has no imaginable commercial value. Who would pay for a message sent to nobody in particular?"—David Sarnoff's associates in response to his urgings for investment in radio in the 1920s.
- "Who the hell wants to hear actors talk?"—Harry M. Warner, Warner Bros., 1927.
- "There is no reason for any individuals to have a computer in their home."—Ken Olsen, President, Chairman and Founder of DEC, 1977

Each of these remarkable technologies faced hostility among the industry leaders of its day. The pattern is a sign that experts are fairly bad at recognizing possibilities in the uncertain future. Each of these technologies were so new, and proposed so much change, that many found it evidently hard to imagine how it will translate into reality. Bubbles are created on the enthusiasm that a rapid revolution is underway. They crash on the excesses that occur and the reality that it takes a long time and a lot of work to deliver on the promises of remarkable vision.

Consensus and Vision

A boom cannot become a bubble without a critical mass of opinion makers who agree that they have found the next great frontier. There are always entrepreneurs and business people looking for new ways to make money or new technologies that satisfy consumers' needs, demands, and desires. There are always investors with cash in hand ready to take a chance on innovation. The media is always ready to hype the next big thing. Bubbles start only when something seizes the imagination of enough people, when something breaks away from the millions of fragmented efforts by creating so much money that the markets, entrepreneurs, business people, and media all stop what they are doing and take notice—and then rush in to get their piece of the action in the next big thing.

It takes a little more than a single event to inflate a legitimate bubble. The Netscape IPO pushed the emerging Internet into the mainstream. It created awareness of the Internet on a mass scale but it also ushered in a succession of IPOs whose remarkable first day returns reinforced the potential opportunities and kept the momentum building.

On April 12, 1996, one of these IPOs—Yahoo!—did more than perhaps any of the others to build the mystique surrounding the Internet that anyone could start an Internet company and become rich. Unlike Netscape, which required sophisticated programming skills to create its product, Yahoo! started as a hobby of two electrical engineering students. Twenty-four months after they casually started cataloguing their favorite Internet sites, they had become millionaires. This made them heroes of the New Economy. This fed the interest and emotions needed to keep a bubble growing. The quick succession of Internet companies, now more visible than before, created the Internet "story," the vision that would become the religion of the New Economy until the end of the millennium.

"The consensus was inescapable," said Michael Moritz, whose venture capital firm Sequoia Capital was an intial funder of Yahoo!, "There was not a pell-mell [rush] to invest in Yahoo [among venture capital firms]. Eighteen months later it was all crazy. Front page articles, TV, CNBC. It doesn't take many appearances on *60 Minutes* to create a feeding frenzy."[5]

Bubbles need a story, almost a mythology, of the future that investors put their faith in. Faith is necessary, because with so much uncertainty surrounding new technologies, history and reality seem like poor guides.

One of the more important proselytizers for the Internet vision was George Gilder. His book *Microcosm,* written in 1989 during the computer revolution, would foresee many of the implications of the Internet. "The central event of the twentieth century is the overthrow of matter," the book begins. "In technology, economics, and the politics of nations, wealth in the form of physical resources is steadily declining in value and significance. . . . The overthrow of matter will reach beyond technology and impel the overthrow of matter in business organization."[6]

Investors and people of all walks of life saw indications of this vision everywhere. Gilder wasn't the only one to imagine this future and develop a mythology, but he was among the most quoted. It was so captivating an idea that many very smart and savvy people fell victim to its spell to the point of delusion and detachment from reality. The problem, however, is not that the potential vision is completely wrong. The problem lies primarily in investors' expectations of how quickly the vision will become reality and how to profit from it. The problem with grand visions is that they are not specific. They become so compelling, but do not provide much detail to distinguish what is utopian and what is executable. It is along the rocky road toward the future that we stumble and lurch through bubbles and busts. But eventually after great riches and loses, the economy as a whole gets there.

Bubbles cannot thrive without some grand vision to motivate investors and business people. Biotech bubbles that seem to occur periodically are fueled by wondrous cures for horrific diseases like cancer, AIDS, heart disease, Alzheimer's. Regarding the biotech bubble of the early 1990s, Pitch Johnson, a noted venture capitalist, was quoted as saying, "Those stocks got the public thinking magical cures and wonderful drugs were just sitting out there in the future. That led to a bubble in which companies could go public on high hopes."[7]

The bubble in China is running on the vision of nearly a billion customers and the emergence of the second biggest economy in the world. The personal computer bubble thrived on the "information revolution." The "onics" companies of the 1960s were fueled by enthusiasm for anything related to computers and high technology that seemed to offer great, but uncertain, opportunities to improve businesses.

Radio, railroads, the telephone—they also embodied a romantic vision of a new world. The early entrepreneurs wanted to change the world and had grand schemes about how to do this. Those who were lucky enough to participate in the early years knew that the excitement was not just about money; it was about being at the vanguard of creating a new and better world, of overturning the nature of business and economics and replacing it with something smoother, cleaner, faster, and more equitable.

Josiah Wedgewood was a central visionary during the canal mania of the second half of the 1700s. In 1767, the Duke of Bridgewater's canal connected the coal mines northwest of Manchester to textile factories in the southwest. This first canal was 30 miles long. In the next 20 years, more than a thousand miles of canal would be built transforming the capacity of business for decades by reducing the cost and time to transport goods. Before canals, all goods traveled along slow roads, at best in horse-drawn carriages. Boats moving along water was a comparably smooth, fast, and cheap ride. The driving force was shipment of coal, iron, and other minerals. The cost savings of shipments due to canals and turnpikes has been estimated to be some 50 percent.[8] The Duke's canal alone was considered to have lead to lower coal prices overall during the 1760s. The savings derived from canals connecting Liverpool and Manchester or Birmingham were estimated to cut costs per ton by 80 percent. Perhaps more important, this new network also widened market access for suppliers and buyers.

It wasn't until the 1790s, after this initial wave of building, that canals shifted from growing popular enthusiasm into full-fledged frenzy. The first wave of canals connected the prime routes of key businesses, towns, cities, and markets, leaving secondary canals for to the followers. The prime routes generated a return on invested capital of 50 percent. The public was left with a return of just 5 percent for the secondary routes, which turned out to be more expensive and take longer to build.[9]

The canals required high upfront costs to pay for the construction, but maintenance was comparatively negligible akin to today's telecommunications networks. Part of the initial costs consisted of purchasing land around them.

Wedgewood's initial interest lay in pottery, but he was among the first to see the vision of how canals could lower costs for shipping his goods. His interests were also broader. He was part of a visionary new group of entrepreneurs who were reorganizing production around factories, drawing on significant design and process innovations. Many were members of the Derby Philosophical Society. They all saw themselves as revolutionizing business, and realized canals were part of that revolution. Wedgewood became a significant investor in canal construction. In a letter to his partner he said, "Many of my experiments turn out to my wishes and convince me more and more of the extreme capability of our manufacture for further improvement. It is at present (comparatively) in a rude uncultivated state, and may easily be polished and brought to much greater perfection. Such a revolution, I believe, is at hand, and you must assist in and profit from it."[10]

Like the Internet visionaries, the Derby Philosophical Society saw themselves at the forefront of dramatic economic change. The vision captured the wider imagination and fed investor enthusiasm.

By 1824 more than 60 canal companies were created, raising more than £12 million, equivalent to about $20 billion in 2003—a massive sum for an economy that was far smaller than the United States is today.

On a more day-to-day level the Internet vision translated into a view of how businesses and people would interact. All types of transactions, business or otherwise, could be more easily and more effectively executed over the Internet. "[With] Amazon there is potentially a new economy here where people don't need to go to stores," remembered Habib Kairuz, "they had a huge number of SKUs [products], you could compare prices. This was an opening of people's eyes. It was really new. It could uproot established industries. You can put retailers out of business and put them online."[11] People saw the Internet as a replacement for most of the old big companies. It would transform human activity. "Everything that can be digital, will be," was the mantra, and in the eyes of enthusiastic investors "everything" literally meant nearly everything.

If transactions where done over the Internet, then there would be no need for physical storefronts or other assets that can add costs to acquire and maintain. With the costs of those physical structures avoided, the Internet retailers could simultaneously charge less money to customers and enjoy larger profits for themselves, went the logic. Big firms were destined to be overrun by these new models in the hands of young entrepreneurs. Content of all kinds could be digitized and sent directly to viewers instead of on the radio, television, or CDs. Every aspect of human behavior seemed implicated and offered potential for this new type of business.

Many felt that the arrival of the Internet would unleash "creative destruction." The term was coined by Joseph Schumpeter, an important economist of the early twentieth century, to describe one of the core drivers of a capitalist economy and its ability to innovate. He once wrote that the growth of the economy is a "process of industrial mutation that incessantly revolutionizes the old economic structure from within, incessantly destroying the old one, incessantly creating a new one. This process of creative destruction is the essential fact about capitalism."[12] This idea was very exciting for Internet entrepreneurs. Investors and corporations of various kinds used it, somewhat mistakenly, as a way to argue that Internet start-ups would overturn all established corporations. The Internet story also relied on the belief that this technology would create a New Economy. Traditional business models no longer applied to the Internet economy, so investors and entrepreneurs needed new ways of evaluating business success.

The most sweeping bubbles promised the ultimate nirvana, in which "The business cycle was dead"—as was claimed during the Internet bubble, the railway mania of the 1840s, the 1960s, 1920s, and other bubble periods. Each of these periods promised to create a "new economy" or a "new era" of endless growth. Downturns, recessions, and depressions would be erased. Once the foundations for the stories, the myths, and the data that dazzle investors emerged, the bubble could move into full swing: The New Era has arrived.

CONNECTING THE DOTS IN A BLIZZARD OF DATA

When you look at your reflection in a crystal ball or soap bubble, the image of your face looking back at you is warped: your nose, which is closest to the surface of the bubble, looks huge and bulbous. Your ears appear miles away, barely visible. A similar warped perception of reality occurs for people living in investment bubbles—things that are right in front of you dominate and appear vastly more relevant than objects just a few inches away.

The information available to investors regarding business opportunities at any time is limited. Whether venture capitalists, people in large companies considering acquisitions, or stock investors—none of these individuals have all the necessary information at their finger-tips or even within reach. As much as analysts are swimming in data, the real information is hard to identify. The limited information we have to evaluate the quality of investments—the risks, the potential rewards, the real costs required—always leaves the most important questions up to perception and judgment. During bubbles, even the limited information available becomes warped, making it harder to separate real information from noise, to distinguish the data that create insight from the data that are illusory. The consequences of these limitations are worse during bubbles than during normal business conditions because a larger number of investment decisions are based on more deeply flawed information.

Robert Shiller, a noted economist who studies investor psychology, remarked aptly, "The kinds of opinions for which herd behavior is prominent are not matters of plain fact (which way is north), but subtle matters, for which many pieces of information are relevant and for which limitations of time and natural intelligence prevent each individual from individually discovering all relevant information."[13]

Every day during the 1990s, tremendous amounts of straightforward data were available and pointed to the possibility that the Internet vision was within reach, attainable, and increasingly real. Investors of all types, from those considering starting new companies to big businesses considering new initiatives, to stock pickers of all types, tried to sift through the blizzard of information. While the uncertainty was tremendous, it wasn't hard to connect the dots and paint an incredible story that promised to transform the world and create great wealth for those involved. For many analysts, it was hard to find information to indicate that the speed of the Internet revolution was not a tremendous opportunity.

The stock market produces a lot of data—stock prices of individual companies, sectors, value stocks, growth stocks, trading volume, earnings, p/e ratios, p/b ratios, dividends yields, and many more data points that investors like to use in their tea-leaf readings of the future. Moreover, the information the market produces is broadcast through various media outlets to a wide audience, thus carrying a lot of weight in people's minds.

When considering investments in companies, stock investors generally don't have access to the details of internal board meetings or Power Point presentations that define market opportunities and competitive threats. Generally, they must rely on data generated by the stock market and related press stories as the easiest way to gain a view on business investment potential.

As far back as the 1790s, when Wall Street first emerged, the information it produced and its speed were central issues. The first brokerage houses were set up as close as possible to each other so that messengers could rush from one to the other on foot with stock quotes. As the industry expanded and trading needed to be done between New York and

Philadelphia, traders used telescopes and flags perched on hills and buildings to send signals. In 1844, the telegraph made communication easier and faster across longer distances. In 1867, the stock ticker distilled information into the stream of figures we are familiar with today. In 1878, the New York Stock Exchange got its first telephone. Progressively, radio, fax machines, and computers increased both the speed and the reach of investment information. CNNfn and CNBC broke through Wall Street's shell, and for the first time, made stock investment information available to the general public in real time, all the time. The Internet also enabled the public to conduct stock research on its own. With relative ease, anyone could pick through annual reports, research analyst reports, and detailed stock trading information and make more independent investment decisions.

Deciphering the information available to determine the real value of investments, especially those in frontier technologies, is a challenge. Psychologists and economists have found that people tend to use quick rules of thumb called heuristics to help evaluate investment decisions. The word is actually derived from the Greek word *Eureka* to express the joy of finding a solution. However, economists and psychologists who study heuristics use the term to describe ways that these short-hand techniques systematically distort effective analysis.

Psychologists and economists have found that information that is most easily recalled and available carries more weight in our judgments. They call this the *availability heuristic*. During the boom, data regarding Internet companies were not given equal weight or time in their presentation. Like the appearance of your face in a soap bubble, some data appeared deceptively huge and much more relevant than others. The most easily available information were the announcements blasted from every media outlet that said the Internet was big and real. The most obvious information available was the news about the IPOs of start-ups and the seemingly unending bull market pushing prices to record highs. Over the course of the 1990s, IPOs became marketing events to help young start-ups stand out from the more than seven thousand common stocks available for purchase. With apparent increasing regularity, the prices of these IPOs rose significantly after they started selling on the open market. Those who bought these stocks early made a lot of money fast. In

1999, 117 IPOs doubled in value on their first day of public trading. This compares with 39 IPOs that doubled the first day over the previous 24 years combined. In 2000, 77 more IPOs doubled on their first day. In 1999, the *average* first day return of IPOs was 60 percent compared to just 10 percent in the years 1986 to 1994.[14] Eventually, the bust would end the opportunities of these quick riches: During 2001, no IPOs doubled on the first day.[15]

The most important IPO was Netscape, because it identified the promise of the Internet as a money-making machine. But the booming IPOs kept coming, day after day, solidifying the statistical evidence for many years.

For example, on April 2, 1996, Lycos, a portal like Yahoo!, went public with an opening price of $16 and closed at $51.5, reaching a total market value of $700 million. Ten days later, Yahoo! went public, opening at $13, and closing at $33, reaching a market capitalization of $848 million. In related industries, like telecommunications, where Internet traffic was expected to rapidly increase the demand for network capacity, fiber optic cable companies like Cienna opened at $23 and closed at $45.18 on February 7, 1997, with a market value of a whopping $4 billion. On August 8, 1998 Geocities, which enabled individuals to set up their own website, went public at $17 and rose to $37.3, achieving a market value of $1.1 billion, in spite of having no real prospects for profits. On February 11, WebMD opened at $8 and reached $31.4 by the end of the day, for a market value of $2.2 billion, despite the absence of any revenues.

"IPOs are so high profile now that they're hard to ignore," Kenan Pollack, money editor at Hoover's Online said at the time. "People are reading about guys becoming billionaires overnight. How can you ignore that?" By the end of 1999, 18 new issues had returned more than 1,000 percent.[16] According to one survey of venture capitalists still in business in 2004, some 40 percent also said that rising Internet related stock prices overall was a very or extremely important factor in their decision to invest in specific companies. Thus, many venture capitalists were reading a stock market bubble as an appropriate signal to determine which start-ups to invest in. [Site: Survey by author. See: www.skylight-insight.com/frenzy]

"I had so much confirming information," said Paul Johnson, who was a popular telecommunications analyst for Robertson Stephens at the time. In fact, the wealth of information he perceived prevented and delayed his ability to see the bubble bursting; "it truly took me 6 months [after the bubble burst] to realize that I was wrong."[17]

Backing up the IPO story were also the now infamous analysts' reports some of which gave the appearance of being based on detailed analysis of why the stocks were worth the prices the market was paying for them. At the time, they were among the most authoritative voices for the general public. (Wall Street insiders knew two related things that escaped the public's notice. First, never trust a "sell side" analyst who is trying to sell you stocks. Second, there is an inherent conflict of interest in many banks.)

The reports added fuel to the fire in the echo chamber of media enthusiasm. According to data from Zacks Investment Research about analysts' recommendations on some six thousand companies, only 1 percent of recommendations were "sells" in late 1999 while 69.5 percent were "buys" and 29.9 percent were "holds." Ten years earlier the percentage of sells was far higher at 9.1 percent[18]—although still not what one might expect.

Comments by leading analysts of the day such as Mary Meeker and Henry Blodget could move the markets. Mary Meeker was dubbed "Queen of the Net." She was well aware of her impact and found the role difficult to manage, "Clearly this kind of market power is unique and daunting, especially for such an illiquid yet popular group of stocks," she said in an internal memo that became public after investigations into conflicts of interest. "It forces me to be especially thoughtful about picking my times to comment about stocks and the market (when I speak, inevitably a media event occurs)."[19]

As bullish as the analysts were, they almost uniformly *under*estimated *revenues*. According to one study by several Berkeley economists, 90 percent of the consensus forecasts for revenues were below the real results. On average, analysts forecasted revenues to be about 11 percent less than what they turned out to be.[20]

As a result, analysts were constantly having to revise their revenue forecasts upwards. They were regularly surprised that the growth was larger than they thought it would be. The regularity of these upward revisions were also broadcast throughout the market, reinforcing the idea that surprises were on the upside not downside- crashes were not high on the list of concerns. That does not mean that analysts got the fundamental value of these businesses correct, since other factors, such as costs and competitive pressures were often ignored.

"It snowballs. You see the stock market going up every day and even smart people begin to think, 'it went up the last 30 days in a row, its got to go up tomorrow it's just one more day." It doesn't happen to be true," said one investor.

A *Business Week* survey showed that 52 percent of individual investors in 1999 expected the stock market to go up, a dramatic increase in enthusiasm from 37 percent the previous year. In 2000, at the peak of the market just before everything would slide, only 11 percent of those surveyed said the market was very overpriced, and only 18 percent thought tech stocks were very overpriced.[21] One year later, in March 2001, the S&P would instead drop from 1527.46 to 1139.83, just 75 percent of its peak value. The NASDAQ would drop to just 41 percent of its peak value.

Indeed, for many investors, the mere fact that stock prices are trending up or down may be more information than they think they are able to get elsewhere. Some economists call this an *information cascade*. According to this idea, people make decisions based on what they observe others doing because they assume that everyone else may know more than they. So they buy stocks trending up, thinking, "All these people must know *something*."

For years, numerous academics who believed that the stock market followed fundamental values and rational behavior had succeeded in winning the intellectual battle against those who said it was based more on psychology. Increasingly, investors seemed to view stock prices as rational reflections of the value of businesses. Could all of these academics be wrong?

A key feature of bubbles is that hysteria becomes credible. The patients start running the asylum, compelling everyone to act a little crazily. While skeptics complain during bubbles, it is only after everything bursts that enough investors realize that they had been chasing unrealistic returns all along. The prices that are unsustainably high are fueled by an unsustainable view of reality.

An interesting source for insight into how people process competing information and become convinced by a specific storyline is the psychological literature on jury deliberations. Criminal trials are forums in which competing information is presented in the best light in order to win over public opinion—not unlike the stock market of bulls and bears, optimists and pessimists, buyers and sellers. Research has shown that presenting arguments in certain ways systematically convinces more people. As it turns out, the kind of information reinforcing the Internet story is similar to the kind of information that has proven to sway jury verdicts.

Thomas Mauet, the most influential figure in trial technique research, advises lawyers to use storytelling as strategy: "Good stories organize, humanize, dramatize. They have plot, characters, emotion. The story uses sensory language, present tense, and pacing. The story is woven in a way such that the audience believes they or their loved ones could have been part of it."[22]

Simple and direct language with vivid testimony persuades jurors more than complex language. For example, the story that the robber "took about ten minutes to pick up a box of Kleenex, a six pack of Coors, and a Mars bar" is more vivid than "the robber came into the store and grabbed some items before approaching the clerk."

Storylines with visual presentations, according to this research, are also much more compelling than those that are presented in a purely oral manner. The confidence of an eyewitness turns out to be the most powerful predictor of a guilty verdict.[23] If the marketplace operates in the court of public opinion about stock values, who could be surprised that Internet mania would catch on and cautionary views would be ignored?

The Internet enthusiasts had the best advocates on its side—credible, confident people showing endless graphs of stock prices going up and great stories of newly minted millionaires or billionaires on the grand frontier of a new economy. With the Internet enthusiasts exalted by the press, they certainly projected pure confidence.

Bubbles make real people very rich, thus giving the events a human and personal dimension that make it more memorable than just the stock price of a specific company.

In 1999, Barron's reported that 77 entrepreneurs became worth more than $100 million through IPOs, 7 of them billionaires. Among the richest, at least on paper, was Jay Walker, founder of Priceline.com, an online company that enabled consumers to bid for airline tickets, hotels,

and other items. He was worth $6.7 billion in mid-1999. Pierre Omid-
yar, founder of eBay, was worth $5.5 billion.[24] Mark Cuban, founder of
Broadcast.com, was worth $1.2 billion. What a compelling story! All of
these tales blended into a delicious cocktail of events and personalities
perfect for running and rerunning media stories in the financial press
that were broadcast everywhere possible.

The story "Mark Cuban sold Broadcast.com to Yahoo! making him a
billionaire and he bought the Dallas Mavericks" is much more compelling than, "these stocks do not follow fundamental values."

Bubbles create these typecast charismatic characters that sway investors' decisions and judgments. Steve Wozniak, Steve Jobs, Bill Gates,
and others held the most prominent positions in the 1980s. The early
days of radio featured the early tinkerers Giglielmo Marconi, Prof. Reginald Fessenden, and Lee De Forest. The railroad mania was dominated
by "the railway king" George Hudson. The go-go years of the 1960s
hailed investment manager, 37-year-old Gerald Tsai, founder and president of the Manhattan Fund, which launched in February of 1966 with
initial assets of $250 million.

THE SKEPTICS ARE SHUNNED

The skeptics who argued that Internet stocks were overvalued, in contrast, came off as dour old guys who could merely say, "The stocks are
overvalued because they no longer reflect fundamentals." This was
hardly a compelling argument that could compete in the public eye with
the attention-grabbing stories supporting the Internet stocks.

"Wall Street was writing up over and over—these guys get it and these
guys don't," said one high-level management consultant working with
large technology companies. "Look how dumb these guys are. Everyone
on the 'get it' side was lionized by the press. Endlessly the press was writing about why the old use of P/E was stupid and why cash flow didn't
matter and why the traditional measures of real business should be sus-
pended—across all sectors of the economy."[25]

A key factor that enabled the enthusiasm to continue unchecked was
the systematic diminution of skeptics. Year after year, the ability of anyone to effectively convey and provide compelling cautionary information

became less and less. Gradually but comprehensively, skeptics lost the attention of the media, they lost influence in their organizations, they lost money, they lost clients, and they lost stature. Although not completely silenced, they were gradually belittled, deprecated, and eventually effaced. The viewpoints of skeptics during this period did receive some coverage, particularly in more sophisticated periodicals like *Barron's*. However, their commentary was largely drowned out by the sheer noise of enthusiastic reporting. Bubbles inflate on the enthusiasm of the optimists, but what prevents them from crashing early is the shunning of the skeptics.

"The people who were the voice of reason and tried to bring some kind of historical perspective were viewed as antiques or just 'not with it.' The line was, you don't realize this is a new world order or a new economy," remembered Bob Kagle of Benchmark Capital.[26]

The phrase "You don't get it" humbled many seasoned executives into fearing that all of their accomplishments and experience in business suddenly became a liability rather than an asset. It was the young, wired generation that was now taking over and they knew how the game was played. Interestingly, this is a common theme in bubbles—the young generation overturns the old.

In a historical account of the go-go era of the 1960s, for example, David Dreman recounted, "Those who did not go along were pushed aside. A young gunslinger at the height of the go-go euphoria of 1967–1968 was interviewed on TV about his aggressive investment strategies. When the name of Benjamin Graham, whose measured approach emphasizing full evaluation of risks and conservative pricing formulas, came up, the money manager said 'the trouble with old Ben is that he just doesn't understand this market.'"[27]

The market was split between the "go-go" and "squaresville." In the 9 months to March 31, 1966, the Standard & Poors index of high grade common stocks declined 7 percent compared to 51 percent gain for "low priced stocks." Similarly, the 25 best performing mutual funds were "aggressive funds" and gained 36–80 percent annually by 1966. That compared to conservative funds that made just 6 percent.

Steve Dow of Sevin Rosen Funds remembered painfully the four words, "you don't get it," that instantly seemed to discredit skeptics during the Internet bubble, "Bankers—VCs, entrepreneurs. They said it often enough—it became the truth. They had enough success that we said, shit maybe they're right."[28]

Furthermore, the information and data necessary to illustrate the case of skeptics was far more complex and more nuanced than the obvious fact that Internet stock prices were skyrocketing and investors were getting rich. For the average person, determining the business fundamentals is all but impossible. For sophisticated analysts there are accounting procedures that failed to take hold and indeed, as it turned out, were intentionally manipulated. But believing the skeptics increasingly required people to discard a lot of the observable data.

Perhaps most important, even if one didn't believe the findings of these enthusiastic analysts, one often found oneself on the losing end of an investment, or missing significant business opportunities—whether in the public market, or as a venture capitalist, or when planning business investments.

"You suddenly don't believe your own misgivings when it is proven correct that *this time it is different*," Tony Sun, Managing General Partner of Venrock, remembered. "You don't need to generate profits and you can make a lot of money without profits and it's proven over and over again. Companies go public and the stock jumps ten times and it doesn't even matter what the earnings are and you are reinforced by that. Its hard to stand the ground on this onslaught."[29]

According to a survey of venture capitalists still in business in 2004, over 50 percent of venture capitalists switched their opinion from being skeptical in the business opportunities of internet and telecommunications companies to becoming believers during this period. Among these "switchers," the most commonly sited reason (43 percent) said that they switched because so many start-ups seemed to be succeeding at the time, eventually they had to rethink their beliefs. [Site: Survey by author. See: www.skylight-insight.com/frenzy.]

Bill Hambrecht, of Hambrecht & Quist, saw the diminution of skeptics as more than just systemic; he saw it as market-driven. "You don't get paid for negative research," he said, "As a matter of fact you get a lot of ill will from the guy because, basically, institutions want you to tout the stocks that they own. So, you know it's hard to put that kind of stuff out and be listened to and get paid for it. The incentives are there to be positive. And even when you are negative—what you tend to do is move to things that you can be positive on. That went on in the eighties as well."[30]

No amount of historical credibility seemed to enable skeptical views to break through the cacophony of enthusiasm. Even the most exalted investor, Warren Buffett, was thought to have lost his touch when he decided to stay away from investing in Internet stocks. Ken Barbalato COO of Swiss American Securities, a member of Credit Suisse Group, remembers, "Warren Buffett was discounted—he still had value—but if you looked at his investments during this time he lost considerable amounts of money. So, Warren Buffett can say what ever he wants to say but sour grapes, right, Warren? That's how you could look at it. He's an old guy, he's not getting it. Look at the value of his portfolio. It's down X, it should be up."[31]

The skyrocketing prices during bubbles *seem* to prove the skeptics wrong. The irony is that, in the end, the higher prices get and the more the skeptics are shunned, the more correct they become.

DURATION

Another related factor that can force so many smart and seasoned people to believe dumb things is that the signals pointing to the incredible opportunity *last for a long time.* It is hard to say exactly when the Internet bubble started, even in hindsight, but it certainly lasted years. Over time, the most cynical observers were forced to question their basic beliefs because new Internet companies continued to be created, big companies continued to make substantial investments, and the stock market valuations continued to reach new heights.

"It went on for so long," remembered Geoff Yang founder of Redpoint Ventures, "even if you said to yourself, 'I'm not going to do it, I'm not going to do it, I'm going to be rational'—another year goes by, and I'm wrong again. It's a question of, if you're right in the long run, it doesn't necessarily mean that you are right in every point and time. There were so many reinforcing conditions for it that sometimes if you try to keep a really disciplined approach and you are missing all of these, you kind of wonder if you are being prudent or if you are being foolish. Eventually, you have to look in the mirror and ask, 'does everything I know and all the logic that is keeping me out investing, is everything I know wrong?' It is natural to go through this kind of self-questioning."[32]

Self-doubt emerged even among the most experienced venture capitalists. "Are we that smart or that stupid?" Steve Dow fretted during much of the period. "People seemed to make gobs of money on things we didn't understand. When a boomlet occurs, some win some lose, but it corrects in time for people to return to ways they did before. The Internet bubble went on long enough that expectations changed. People thought maybe it really will change. There was a constant discussion within our firm—how can it *last?* We'd do the math, look at the market cap of these firms. We had a lot of angst—are we really missing it?"[33]

Indeed, after several years of rising prices and confirmable business activity, the thought that occurs to any semi-reflective person is: *When you think that everyone else around you is crazy, that is a reliable warning sign that it might be you who needs the psychological help.*

As Peter Sisson, founder of Wineshopper.com, said, "You can almost see the gradual suspension of judgment as something runs for a long time. It is very easy to recognize this in hindsight, but you have to remember this thing ran for 4 or 5 years and you saw everyone around you getting fabulously wealthy."[34]

John Bogle, founder of Vanguard mutual funds, was a skeptic, but he admitted that for any rational person, "you've got to have doubts."[35]

Furthermore, the longer bubbles last, the more younger people enter the market who don't have experience with anything other than a bubble. "If you started this business in 1992, your entire experience is up, up, and away," commented Barbalato. "This is it. This is the way it works. Investments grow at these rates, not what I read in the history books. And that is your experience and you just react to your experience."[36]

Indeed, the experience of the investment industry was shallow. According to one study, more than half of the more than active 200,000 brokers, financial planners, and advisors began their careers in the decade of the 1990s.[37]

Venture capital funds also saw an influx of young staff that diminished the experience level of the entire industry. According to a survey of the 20 top venture groups, 40 percent of investment professionals in 2002 entered the industry sometime between 1999 and 2002.[38]

As a result, as bubbles continue for years, and the average experience of investors declines, fewer and fewer decisions are balanced by a sense of history.

THE MEDIA

The media reports made the positive information about IPOs, rising stock prices and the Internet economy stand out more than the contrary cautionary views. During that period, acolytes of the new economy could find reinforcement in numerous emerging magazines: *Redherring, Fast Company, Business 2.0, Wired, Industry Standard.*

"I am astonished," said Gene DeRose, former CEO of Jupiter Research and a former journalist himself, "at how the media, who should have been the objective critical foil to the potential unreality bought into it more than anyone—which reinforced the hype that drove the financial markets."[39] The data created by Jupiter projecting the incredible growth of the Internet was among the most quoted by the media. "The media would take our great reports and press releases and run with the headlines," he said. Jupiter's position in the market place was elevated tremendously. "We played that game. It was good for us and then it was bad for us," DeRose added. With so much positive press attention they road the wave of enthusiasm. Their client base grew. They spoke on prestigious panels about the future of business and the economy. But they also helped feed the frenzy. "It was one of those, 'you play with the devil.' We definitely could have managed our own message better. We allowed ourselves to be, what appeared to be, willing engines of the hype."[40]

With technology so new, few journalists understood what was going on. Financial reporters would call organizations like Jupiter to find out. DeRose said, "We would get called and they wanted a quote from us or a data point, and we would usually also stay on the phone basically giving the whole story to the journalist who couldn't figure out what was going on."[41]

There is always a complex relationship between media as a source of neutral information and as an advertising vehicle that can bias information. Readers buy media for information, but profits are made from advertising. The editorial decisions made every day navigate that fine balance. During the bubble that balance was harder than ever to maintain—and certainly in some cases there was little effort to manage that balance effectively.

"Somehow you start believing things have changed," said Barbalato, "The old rules don't apply and so you apply new rules and eventually you start believing them because how could you not believe them? *Business*

Week is talking about it, *Fortune* is talking about it, *Wall Street Journal* is talking about it. It's the establishment that is saying this. This isn't someone selling health juice out of some wagon in the wild west."[42]

The role the media plays in filtering stock information has been examined by some economists recently. One study, by economists Brad Barber and Terrance Odean, showed that individual investors tend to buy more stocks on days when those stocks attract attention—such as when stocks are in the news, trading volume is high, or there are extreme price moves.[43] Barber and Odean found that when stocks were in the news, investors at large discount brokerages bought more than twice as many stocks then they sold. The same held true for stocks with high trading volume and extreme price moves. There is something about grabbing investor's attention, good or bad, up or down, that makes them want to *buy*—not sell.

Bubble stocks certainly generate a lot of news. Other stocks don't attract that much media attention, except perhaps to demonstrate how poorly they are performing compared to the high-fliers. As a result, given Barber and Odean's findings, the media echo-chamber works to perpetuate the buying cycle.

The research from two other economists found that when Maria Bartiromo mentioned a stock during *Midday Call* on CNBC, the trading volume of that stock jumped five times shortly thereafter.[44]

The proliferation of media is common during bubbles. In fact, magazine proliferation might be an interesting early warning sign that a bubble is in full swing. A raft of magazines and newspapers arrived hailing the PC bubble, railways, radio, and many others. Media outlets serve the demands of their audience and if the audience is swept up with frenzy, then they are only happy to oblige.

REAL INFORMATION IS SCARCE

New technologies present a special challenge to valuing investment opportunities because by definition, these start-up companies are new and tend to be defining new industries that have not been considered before. This inherent limit of rational analysis is a central feature of bubbles. Railways, radios, autos, personal computers, biotech, the Internet—all of these created remarkable opportunities that were fairly unknowable and unpredictable during the manias of their day.

For sophisticated business analysts, the best methods available under normal circumstances attempt to calculate cash flow or profits expected in the future, based in part on what has been reported in the past. Future profits are projected based on past performance. The figures are adjusted for the time horizon and the riskiness of this venture compared to alternative investment opportunities. During normal periods and for mature predictable businesses that have a familiar track record, this process works fairly well. However, for many companies, even during normal periods, the basic data points rely significantly on perceptions, judgments, and guesses. (Good analysts would say educated guesses.) For new industries and new companies with no track record, no history, no benchmarks, and nothing that shows patterns of behavior, the basic measurements for future cash flows, time horizons, and risks are pure guesswork. There is little education available to make educated guesses. For the best analysts, using this methodology provides guideposts for what might seem like excessive valuations that defy any conceivable logic.

Another common way to value companies is to look at companies that are in similar sectors, industries, or business segments and use those as benchmarks to value the potential of the company an investor is considering. During a bubble, this very commonly used method is questionable because many companies are overvalued, including the relevant benchmarks. As a result, the baseline is misleading.

There is an honest intellectual dilemma in valuing companies that have no history of their own. Indeed, traditional valuation methodologies rely heavily on historical performance of companies and their industry to determine valuations for the future. After the bubble, many stock analysts were viewed as suspect—and some were embroiled in accusations that they were manipulating the markets by providing biased research in favor of their clients. But the presence of fraud, which appears often during bubbles, does not discount the realistic problems that an honest analyst faces. If your job is to value these new companies and you wanted to be honest about it, it is not clear what the best method would be.

Ken Barbalato commented, "I related it to what happened when the radio industry started or the railroad—speculation on some newfangled something. You can't value it because it is not making money, but you got this sense that it has some value so you come up with some way to put a value on it because investors need some way."[45]

Mary Meeker told the *New York Times* that she started using non-financial metrics in 1993 when she was analyzing Intuit and AOL. At the time, she thought that they were a legitimate way to determine performance potential. "The value of the business is its future cash flows . . . the challenge is figuring out what those future cash flows are," she told the *Times.* "If a company wins in its marketplace, if the market is attractive enough and big enough, and if we can find the company that is going to be a leader, the challenge is to find out how customers can be monetized."[46]

As an example of how she used this approach for an Internet company, she said, "On homestore.com, our point of view is that many people will look for homes online and homestore will be in a leading position. We're willing to make a bet that they will be able to monetize those users."[47]

Interestingly, this logic may work to provide some gauge of whether a company's stock could be a good investment in the *short run.* Unfortunately, that is very different from determining whether the prevailing price in the public market was under- or overvalued.

Several economists studied the new Internet metrics such as "page views" and "unique users" to see if they actually correlated with the observed stock prices on fifty-six firms leading up to July 15, 1999. What they found confirmed that the market prices were operating under Internet rules, for a period of time. As it turned out, fundamentals like net income and book value were *negatively* correlated with stock price. Meaning, when the fundamentals improved, the stock price *declined.* Changes in these fundamentals explained only about 3 percent of the changes in stock price—so using these metrics alone would not have helped buying Internet stocks. However, when adding page-views into the analysis, the analysis improves. Changes in net income and page views explained 34 percent of the changes in stock price—a far better result.[48] This does not mean that these metrics could predict the fundamental value of the firm, but it does mean that they were good reflections how the stock market was setting prices for a period of time—albeit one inflated by bubblemania. It is a sign that investors collectively accepted these new metrics as appropriate for valuing stocks.

According to a survey of venture capitalists still in business in 2004, many venture capitalists cited lack of information as a key challenge to disciplined due diligence. Over half said that the fact that there were "too many unknowns given that everything was so new" was a very or extremely important factor that made disciplined due diligence difficult. About 40 percent said that the fact that "there were many new metrics for evaluating businesses that seemed to get validation by the public markets" was a very or extremely important factor. [Site: Survey by author. See: www.skylight-insight.com/frenzy.]

During the bubble of the 1920s, newfangled metrics also emerged; however, today those metrics are now considered fundamental analysis. The traditional method back then was to price stocks at ten times current earnings and anticipated dividend yields to be higher than bond yields. The discounting of projected profits that today is the basis of most stock analysis was then considered deeply flawed. Benjamin Graham, who began his career during the Roaring Twenties and whose investment thinking is still widely read, criticized this practice after the 1929 collapse, saying, "the concept of future prospects, and particularly of continued growth in the future, invites the application of formulas out of higher mathematics to establish the present value of the favored issue. But the combination of precise formulas with highly imprecise assumptions can be used to establish, or rather to justify, practically any value one wishes, however high, for a really outstanding issue."[49]

Online information also makes data about stocks much more available to individual investors than in the past. One might expect that this could improve the ability of investors to make better informed choices. However, that does not appear necessarily to be the case. Data is not the same as information or knowledge. More data can lead to improved information or it can increase the level of noise. Some researchers have even found that information overload can actually undermine people's predictive abilities.[50]

"Too much" data can also lead people to be overconfident in their decisions because they believe they are better informed than they actually are. Economists who study this phenomenon, like Terrance Odean, call this the *illusion of knowledge.*

Venture capitalists have additional information beyond the public echo chamber. The serious venture firms that achieved substantial track records have seats on the boards of large technology companies they helped create. From this vantage point they gain significant insight into where the new technologies fit into existing operational or business needs.

They also have significant access to top-tier management that can be installed in start-ups they fund and have a substantial amount of control over the start-up once the investment is made. Despite these privileged positions, most VCs are no less susceptible to the momentum of the markets. (Indeed, they thrive on momentum, if not fuel it.) The information created by public market stock prices tells them what ventures might become hot IPOs and thus might provide a quick return. There is also information brought by the start-ups who come knocking on their door.

"We always think we are on to something if we see three companies in a space," said Tim Draper of Draper, Fisher, Jurveston, one of the first investors in Hotmail.com. If Draper observed 30 start-ups trying to do the same thing, then he would realize that the market is already becoming saturated. But "If we see three, then we go, mmm, which one is best?" he said.[51]

TRUSTING THE EXPERTS AND RISK SCHISM

Periods of rapid innovation force decision-makers to confront far more uncertainty than usual. Business managers and investors must make investment decisions about things they know little about. During typical periods, decisions can be informed by experience, historical patterns of business practices, research reports by trade associations, and so on. The sources of knowledge and insight about the auto industry, for example, are deep and broad. When everything is new and the world appears to be changing, the foundation for so many sensible decisions made in the past appears to evaporate. There are no benchmarks, no historical patterns, no specific industry business experience that can provide guidance, because it is all so new—or at least, so it appears.

During bubble years, with so much confusion and so little experience, a handful of people and institutions become the pivotal sources of information, insight, knowledge, and ultimately, *trust*. They become designated as the experts or gurus. Big decisions rely more than normal on the few trusted sources to provide insight.

Drawing on expert opinion is typically a smart thing to do. However, special problems emerge during technology bubbles. One problem is that the number of people available to consult as experts is small since only a handful of people can point to hands-on experience. As a result, a disproportionate weight is given to their comments—disproportionate, at least, compared to their true insight and disproportionate to the ripple effects that their statements and actions have in the marketplace.

Given that these new technologies typically evolve quite quickly, "expertise" is a highly malleable term, and few people could really claim to understand the Internet at almost any point during the 1990s because there just wasn't enough time to gain relevant experience among a broad enough group of people. But that didn't matter. Investors needed to find someone to provide trusted information, and there certainly was no shortage of people who claimed to have it. As a result, what emerged was a kind of trust pyramid, in which a large number of business managers and investors were trusting a small number of people to have critical insight into this new technology.

Dave Dorman, now CEO of AT&T, remembers that across the board in big firms, "everyone went out and got their Internet guru. There was among old economy CEOs who were juxtaposed to new economy companies a deficit of understanding. They looked around the room saying, no one knows more about this than I do. I've got to have people who understand this new business. Smart people [who] were thirsting to learn glommed on to people who seemed like they knew what they were talking about."[52]

Venture capitalists were among those who were part of this trust pyramid—some inadvertently while others took advantage of their newfound clout. "Everybody is looking for an expert and an answer," said Don Valentine founder of Sequoia Capital and one of the elder statesmen of venture capital. "We've always been caught in the chain of being polled on position on certain kinds of things. People are asking the question from a context in which they can't understand the right answer, even if they get the right answer."[53]

According to one investor, "There is no question that a lot of people made investment decisions based on who else was investing, which, you know, in normal times can be pretty sensible. In go-go times it might not tell you anything."

"The outside technology experts frequently had the upper hand because they could talk in a language that no one understood," said Jim

Lessersohn, vice president for finance and corporate development at the New York Times Company. "Therefore nobody could challenge them because no one even knew what questions to ask, and if they did no one would understand the answers anyway. The whole world seemed to be saying that this new technology would change everything."[54]

The *New York Times* itself was doing well during the booming 1990s from dramatically increasing advertising. But an investment bank warned the company that its business would suffer unless it made some substantial changes. The pressure on the *Times* and almost every traditional company to *do something* was intense. Internal discussions about whether and what to do were not simple, because the *Times* is a 150-year-old news organization that is very protective of its brand and corporate discipline. But so many business decisions seemed more confusing and harder to evaluate clearly than in the past because so few people understood what the Internet was, much less how it would impact the *Times* business.

"There were several of us who said we don't see the ultimate payoff," Lessersohn explained. "Those of us who were used to doing acquisition analysis over 10, 20, 40 years wanted to at least see a scenario where we could see where the payoff would ultimately come. There was tremendous pressure from investment bankers saying, a lot of people smarter than you have been dealing with this, they are convinced it's there. If you hesitate you'll be lost. . . . It became a dynamic where you'd have the financial experts and tech experts both saying the world has changed."[55]

With so little information available, the *New York Times,* like so many businesses, was put into a position in which it was pressured to trust others to provide expert opinions. "I don't understand this stuff . . . but *these* guys must know," was a common refrain within many businesses.

SS+K was a consulting firm who at the time was providing integrated media, marketing, and advertising services to the growing dot.com client base. Like so many businesses trying to do the best they could during the explosive opportunities bubbles create, SS+K became caught in the trust pyramid. It was a successful boutique among the many firms gearing themselves to serve the immense demands of dot.coms. SS+K won UrbanFetch as a client, which for a brief period became an exciting Internet company that provided online delivery of items within one hour for the high-end consumers on the run. SS+K also won a business-to-business client that proposed to transform the entire supply chain and seemed to have support from Andersen Consulting and other heavyweights. Both were big wins for the small, fast-growing consulting firm and provided a large percentage of its revenue.

Without the sophisticated ability to evaluate business plans itself, they relied on the signals from others. "Firms like ours, including ours, never look at business plans. Never,"[56] said Rob Shepardson a partner of SS+K. "One day people would say to us, 'oh, UrbanFetch's business model is flawed' and the next day someone else would say, 'oh, this the greatest thing.' What do we know? We don't have any standing to figure that stuff out."

Lenny Stern, another partner at the firm, echoed, "We didn't have time to breathe. We were moving fast. We didn't know. Smarter people than us were saying this was the way the world was. So you just sort of got caught up in it. The environment was such that what was a specious questionable approach was a given—and who were we to question that when Mary Meeker and everyone else was saying go do this? So we were just like, ride that horse."[57]

Shepardson reflected on the period, echoing the dynamics that rippled across so many firms. The Internet entrepreneurs "were always trying to make you feel like you missed the meeting, you missed that graduate school class where they knew that this idea was going to be successful. We would do a little due diligence and do some calls and you sort of base it on the reputation of the VCs. Of course at that time, every VC seemed to have a couple winning horses in the race."[58]

Neither the business-to-business firm or UrbanFetch survived the first wave of Internet blow ups. As a result of these losses and other declines, SS+K had to lay off more than 20 percent of its staff. Consulting firms across the country eager to serve the exploding, exciting demand faced similar decisions and suffered similar fates.

For some participants the trust pyramid was apparent, and the effort to create the essential image of trust was deliberate. "It's all theater," said Mark Walsh, founder of VerticalNet, an early business-to-business start-up. "Like good theater it has all the elements of putting on a show for the audience. First it recruits the audience, then it puts on a show, then it gets the audience excited, then frightened, then excited gain." His memory of the discussion with his lead bank the night before VerticalNet went public to discuss the opening price was vivid: "When they brought us in into a beautiful oak paneled room, the lights are quiet, the senior guy at the bank, he brings in the chairman, the largest outside investors. They sit us down, little packets in front of you with the logo. It was drenched in credibility. Their main analyst comes in—we've done a lot of analysis, we're very excited about our relationship, we're excited about the initial public offering," Walsh said. "It was beautiful. Seamless."[59]

Tom Perkins, the founder of Kleiner, Perkins, Caufield, one of the best-known and most established venture capital firms, watched the actions of his own firm ripple through the system. The start-ups they invested in were given a golden seal of approval from the best-of-the-best and others would trust their investment decision as almost proof that the company would succeed: "If Kleiner Perkins does it its got to be good,"[60] he noted.

Key figures always play leading guru roles during bubblesthat have an exaggerated influence on everyone else. Bubbles lend themselves to these kinds of trust pyramids because of that complex mix of opportunity and uncertainty. Gerald Tsai was a guru during the go-go era of the 1960s, for example. At Fidelity Funds he gained a reputation for picking winners. One observer remarked, "if anyone hears you say, 'Tsai is buying' you'll have a crowd around you in no time"—the trust pyramid was fully formed. George Hudson, the "the railway king" had the same effect during the railway mania in England in the 1840s.

A disturbing example that reveals the origins of the trust pyramid in human beings generally lies in a classic psychological study by Stanley Milgram, *Obedience to Authority*.[61] For the study, he fabricated a situation in which the experimenter told a subject to push a button that would administer electric shocks to someone who could not be seen. The putative victim would fake screaming in pain each time the subject pushed the button. The results were striking, and they were filmed. The subjects continued to push the button and shock the person behind the screen even as the screams became increasingly intense, and even though the dials on the console indicated that the electric currents were dangerous or even lethal. The subjects often showed deep concern about what they might be doing to other human beings, but with persistent urging from the experimenter and the explicit statement that all was fine, the subjects continued the victim's "electrocutions." Milgram noted that the subjects believed the experimenter to be a medical expert who knew more than they did—they trusted him. The subjects accepted the authority of the apparently knowledgeable expert even though it contradicted the subjects' own experience and the evidence of pain inflicted on another person.

Tying investment evaluations to another person's actions, no matter how expert, has proven very dangerous unless one knows a lot about what lies behind that decision—especially how the person approaches *risk*.

For example, venture capitalists, a commonly cited source of insight, have a very specialized approach to their investments that differs from the approach of stock investors, or large companies considering an acquisition, or even consulting firms considering a commitment to Internet clients. When venture capitalists invest in a company, most are absolutely convinced that it is going to succeed. Most venture capitalists do not speculate on the companies they put money into. At the same time, VCs also know they can be wrong. In fact, history has taught them that they are wrong far more often then they are right. But several key aspects of the venture approach to investing protect them from these lopsided odds. First, the start-ups that do well make massive amounts of money that far outweigh the ones that fail and go out of business. Second, they can manage the risk of their investment because they put relatively little money in up front. They use that money as leverage to gain a strong role in the early management of the business in an effort to reduce the risk. Finally, given their close working relationship with the firm, they can avoid further losses by pulling out early if it looks like the start-up will fail. Their investment decision has a very particular structure learned and honed through time and experience as venture capitalists.

The big problems arise when onlookers use venture capitalist investment choices as an indicator that the company is "good"—*generically*. Chances are that these onlookers do not have the same capacity to manage the risks of start-ups—they are neither as diversified nor do they have the same control of the company. As a result, observers are unwittingly drawing the wrong conclusions—they do not recognize that their risk profile is different from venture capitalists.

"They look at what we do in a vacuum and draw the wrong conclusion," remarked Valentine.

Corporate acquisitions also seemed to provide generalized stamps of approval. When a large company made an acquisition or launched a new initiative based to some degree on the insight of outside experts, other watchful investors took this investment decision as further proof of the viability of the venture and the Internet more generally.

Large companies "become part of the gasoline on the fire syndrome," said Tom Perkins. "When you get big corporations buying things, you get people saying, 'it must be real, look, they are buying this thing, they must know.' And to a certain extent they do know."[62]

Cisco, for example, was buying companies at huge valuations. Many critics later said that Cisco helped push up the prices of many telecommunications start-ups because they seemed to validate extraordinary valuations. "If Cisco says it's worth this much, then it's got to be good," was a common logic and response to the acquisitions. While it was likely that Cisco did pay too much for some poor companies, the onlookers typically did not realize that they were misinterpreting these signals. Many companies are worth more to Cisco than to anyone else. Cisco has an extremely powerful and effective sales force and brand that can sell out to the marketplace better than most firms. Cisco can extract more profit from newly acquired firms than most other companies; as a result, it is willing to pay more for them. It's not that Cisco's acquisition price reveals an inherent value of those firms, it reveals the value of that firm if it is embedded in Cisco's operations. Equally important, Cisco usually paid for those companies with its own inflated stock, thus mitigating the effects of the bubble market.

Onlookers who used Cisco's behavior as a signal for fundamental market valuation of a firm, and *trusted* it, because "it must know," failed to see these layers. As a result, this led to the misinterpretation of the value of comparable firms and thus poor investment decisions.

DECLINE OF DISCIPLINE SOWS THE SEEDS OF DESTRUCTION

As much as information and analysis can be warped during bubbles, they also typically run on so much enthusiasm that perceived investment opportunities contradict basic logic and 2 plus 2 equals 16 becomes acceptable thinking. Despite the difficulty of separating information from noise, many people do not try very hard or simply do not bother at all.

Henry Blodget said bluntly in a report three months before the market began its collapse, "Valuation is often not a helpful tool in determining when to sell hyper-growth stocks."

Bad analysis can justify any stock valuation, and bubbles tend to attract bad analysis. On the one hand, the bad analysis and new metrics helped inflate the stock prices by creating flawed rationales for their valuations that nevertheless convinced many investors. On the other hand, to some degree, those new metrics emerged to explain the stock prices observed in the market. The analysis and the prices reinforced each other in an unholy cycle: Bad analysis inflated stock prices, and higher stock prices motivated bad analysis to explain them.

"Values were created out of thin air based on hype and on projections rather than on past records," said Alan Patricof, an early investor in Apple Computers and Office Depot. "It was multiples of sales that were the measures by which companies were being financed. Companies were bought and sold and merged on these metrics."[63]

The idea was that these new companies were competing in a frenzied land grab to capture significant market share. They needed to build fast to get there first. Once there, they would be big enough and have enough customers to start generating real profits. Focusing on profits too early would penalize them inappropriately for the high spending required for fast growth. The logic was that profits would come once they positioned themselves successfully as the market leader.

"There are fundamental principles that VCs must follow and these tend to be common sense," said Tony Sun. "However, during the boom, many rules were broken and the rationalization is that the new economy dictates new rules. For example, many of the dot.com companies had business plans that made no sense. The more revenues they generated, the more money they lost. However, this was explained by the 'land grab' theory and no one wanted to address the business model as long as the stock market was willing to accord such companies lofty valuations."[64]

For example, Alladvantage paid people to surf the web. Members downloaded a "ViewBar" program that beamed ads onto the bottom of their computer screen while they surfed the web. They received 50 cents for every hour logged. More importantly, and more damaging to the company's finances, if members referred a friend, they received 10 cents for each hour that person surfed. The users didn't have to click on any ads or buy anything. They just had to allow Alladvantage to beam them advertising at the bottom of the screen.

By the end of the first quarter of 2000, Alladvantage had two million members. The refer-a-friend strategy encouraged some 125,000 members to refer 20 or more friends *each*. Alladvantage employed 587 people with offices in London, Paris, Tokyo, and Sydney as well as several locations in the United States. It sounded promising—at least by Internet metrics.

Except that their fee structure meant that they paid out $40 million to members leading to a loss of $66 million for that quarter alone. Total loses for the year reached $102 million.

The revenue, and ultimately profit, was supposed to come from highly targeted advertising based on data collected about users' surfing habits. But the demand for that data was not nearly as high as the company's leaders fantasized. Between March 1999 and 2000, Alladvantage collected only $14.4 million in revenues.

With economics like this, Alladvantage quickly burned through its $135 million invested by several VCs. When the IPO window closed in March 2000, so did the company's potential new source of cash and the willingness of VC to go along with the game. By February 1, 2001, Alladvantage shut down.

"Once the greed glands started pumping, there were a lot of disciplines that fell by the wayside," observed Bob Kagle of Benchmark Capital, an early investor in eBay. "The discipline of being very methodical in the process of company building went away . . . people slowly lose touch with reality and the measures that in a more rational period are important to determine success like profitability, revenues and things like that fall away to other convenient measures that people can hang things on to—eyeballs, page views. That can give people some false sense of security that there is some sort of rational basis to their behavior—but those are not grounded in firm economic principals. A lot of long-term, tried-and-true disciplines that are constructive in company building process just go out of vogue."[65]

Bubbles don't operate on truth. This kind of analysis created information that justified high valuations for investment in untested companies. The information, moreover, was being developed and reported by the most established organizations in the business. Across the board, the biggest banks were producing glowing reports, the most respected media touted them to the public, the venture funds were talking up a storm. If you can't believe these experts, whom can you believe?

One of the most noted examples of a stock valuation that made no sense was the IPO of Palm on March 2, 2000. Palm's parent company, 3Com, sold 5 percent of Palm's shares, retaining ownership of 95 percent of the company for itself. But defying basic logic, the value of Palm become worth more than the value of 3Com. On the first day of trading, Palm closed at $95 a share and 3Com closed at $82. Even three months after the IPO, this substantial gap remained. The Palm example has some exceptional features in the sense that short sellers often enter the market during such price discrepancies and drive down the price. But short sellers could not find anyone to lend them shares of Palm. As a result, it wasn't possible to take advantage of this price difference for arbitrage trading purposes.[66]

By February 2000, the Internet sector equaled 6 percent of the market capitalization of all U.S. public companies and 20 percent of all publicly traded equity volume.[67] In 1999, Internet companies had a total market value of over $1 trillion, while accumulating *losses* of $9 billion for the same year. Even if you accepted the new metric mania and allowed for the possibility that today's profits could be sacrificed for tomorrow's growth, these firms had revenues of just $30 billion leading to a price to sales ratio of 33 compared to the broad-based historic norm of roughly 1.[68]

Mark Walsh was CEO of VerticalNet, one of the first stellar business-to-business performers. He was very early in thinking about the Internet not as consumer media or commerce but as a vehicle to serve businesses and improve purchasing between companies. When he was shopping around the business plan to go public, he described VerticalNet as an Internet-based trade publisher. His pitch to investors was that every type of media had been impacted to some extent by the tsunami of the Internet, except trade publishing. "There was this 'aha' moment in every meeting," he said. "You would see it every time. They would sit back in their chair and go, 'makes sense' and most of these meetings really had a kind of 'makes sense' kind of yardstick. The majority concluded to give me a piece of this action."[69] "Makes sense" became the only standard for so many start-ups pitching themselves to venture funds or to the public market. Toward the end, even that flimsiest of standards could be ignored.

Mark Walsh was not a 20-something start-up guy. He was a former executive at AOL and at GE. VerticalNet's presentations had lots of spreadsheets with sound analysis showing a reasonable growth rate as the company was consolidating online trade publications. Despite that, "the romance took over," he said. "Our story was fresh and new. No matter what the spreadsheets say, if you're fresh and new or first, no matter what the industry, there is a certain panache that comes with that."

Internet Capital Group (ICG), another high-flying stock, appeared toward the end of the bubble. Its plan was to become a holding company of business-to-business companies—a GE for the new economy. At the peak, an ICG stock was trading at $212, representing a market value of $56 billion—more than the combined value of the "old economy" companies Alcoa, Caterpillar, and Eastman Kodak *combined*. ICG went out of business when the bubble burst.

The market-driven metrics, however, fed on themselves. The decline of analytical discipline was cumulative as the market seemed to confirm its own worst thinking.

"It's a slippery slope, intellectually," explained an investment banker directly involved with some of the most prominent Internet IPOs, "once you kind of say, 'I don't have any fundamentals to decline this piece of business. I can't say it's too early, I can't say it doesn't have revenues, I can't say the management team is not intact, I can't say it's not profitable.' Pretty soon, you've thrown every rational argument out the window. The only thing left is, well, is this a good piece of business and will they be around in 3 to 5 years and potentially a leader in the space? If your team says yes, and they think the stock will go up, that pretty much became the only basis to judge whether to take companies public."[70]

Discipline declines quickly among many investors when market signals are not telling investors who use these valuation techniques that they are wrong. Even worse, the market prices for stocks sometimes surpass even the most exaggerated claims.

The venture capital industry, "lost its discipline by being co-opted into believing that new business models could succeed," said Tony Sun. "Some of these new business models clearly had no economic principles but [were] based on momentum and impression. The trouble is that you get co-opted easily when the market continued to reinforce the idea that your erroneous assumptions can turn into profitable investments."[71]

"It's the fog of war," said Barbalato, "You're just in there going to work every day. You get up in the morning, you pack your bag, you go to work, you do your job, you go home. You don't sit back and pick your teeth and analyze every little thing. You just don't have enough information."[72]

The decline of discipline that occurs during all bubbles means that companies that never should have been created got funded, and many entered the public market sowing the seeds of its own destruction. The enthusiasm of the day makes endless opportunities look probable rather than possible and everything else look easy.

Reflecting on one poor business venture during the Internet bubble, Michael Moritz, a partner at Sequoia Capital and lead investor of Google, bemoaned the sentiment of the time: "The promise of the un-introduced service is infinite. In part you delude yourself. All the risks were spelled out in incredible and graphic detail in all the documents. I think there was enough encouraging stuff happening that people felt the income statements and balance sheets would eventually catch up with the promise."[73]

Alan Patricof remembers one investment he considered and was glad he stayed away. Kozmo.com proposed 1-hour online delivery of things like ice cream, videos, and so forth. It was valued very highly. The CEO was just 29 years old. "There was a lot of interest," Patricof remembered, "I tried it out. Ordered three videos. They messed up the order a few times. I started thinking, each delivery, back and forth, the labor, the bill processing, for 3 videos. They didn't charge for delivery. This is like Chinese food take out. No Chinese delivery company is worth $200 million."[74]

It wasn't just venture capitalists or overexcited stock investors who let discipline fall by the wayside. Big businesses also suffered from bubble-thinking. "By 1997, everyone started getting excited about it. And we, like everyone else, got more excited. A certain amount of irrational enthusiasm crept into the business and by 1998–99 everyone was irrationally enthusiastic," remembers Strauss Zelnick, former CEO of Bertelsmann Music Group.[75]

He opposed Bertelsmann's plan to provide Napster a $100 million loan *after* the bubble burst. Napster was a file-sharing service that enabled music lovers to trade their favorite songs for free. The courts shut it down for copyright infringement. Despite this, Bertelsmann wanted to keep it alive, use its brand, and convert it into a legitimate service.

After some analysis, Zelnick and others, couldn't see a path that would ever get Napster to be a viable pay service after being free for so many years. "There was a lot of 'you don't just get it.'" In response to Zelnick's analysis, "They just ignored it and rejected it out of hand. They just said, 'no, you're wrong, this is going to work. Because *we believe*.' I think Bertelsmann did it bigger and more foolishly than most, but a lot of other people made the same mistake too."[76]

Zelnick added, "The disagreement we had was a disagreement between magical thinking and analytical thinking."

Discipline declines precipitously during bubbles, and as a direct result, the seeds of its own destruction are laid. With each investment that creates or fuels an unsustainable business, the market becomes weaker and weaker, less and less viable over the long term, and thus destined to collapse. Each of these bubble start-ups is like a time bomb, ticking away investors' money, counting down the time to explode and destroy the party that so many investors are enjoying.

The mania for personal computers, automobiles, radio, and railways all attracted poorly thought-through companies if not outright shams. Investors asked few questions and required little analysis.

During the radio mania, it appears that De Forest was well aware that his business, Wireless Telegraph Company of America, would benefit from and perhaps require overexcited markets. He wrote in his diaries, "Soon, we believe, the suckers will begin to bite. Fine fishing weather, now that the oil-fields have played out. 'Wireless' is the bait to use at present. May we stock our string before the wind veers and the sucker shoals are swept out to sea."[77]

Like so many Internet companies, De Forest began to generate startling sales figures by charging unsustainable low prices. He was attempting to gain market share, funded by the capital markets, not by customers. For example, in a competition for a contract with the U.S. Navy, he offered prices 80 percent lower than Fassenden's NESCO and won the contract.

Just as during the Internet bubble, illegitimate shell companies were formed just to be marketed to the public because they seemed to buy anything related to radio, but that had no real underlying business rationale. The American Wireless Telephone and Telegraph Company, for example, was formed primarily to sell stock to the public.[78] After investors witnessed Marconi's first demonstration of the opportunity, this shell company was able to tap frenzied followers and raise $5 million, or about $345 million in 2002.

A sales document promoting De Forest's company reflects where investors' mindset was, "There is not enough stock to go around. You have the opportunity. Will you grasp it 'at the flood tide' and ride on the shore of plenty, high and dry above the adversities which often beset old age, to land of our dreams, where the wealth is unbounded and every wish gratified. . . . Or will you hesitate and doubt. . . . Think ! It is time for you to decide! Think well! Buy! Do it now!"[79]

SIMPLISTIC COMPARISONS

The most pervasive graph circulating around the desks of start-ups, venture funds, investment banks, and large corporations was the Internet adoption curve—a fabulously beautiful hockey-stick-shaped line, rapidly sloping up to the heavens. The bottom-line message of the graph to many was that consumers seemed to be signing up for some kind of Internet access at an incredible pace—faster than in any previous technology. This was proof, in the eyes of many, of how transformative the Internet could become and provided some indication of the speed of shifting consumer behavior.

Habib Kairuz, managing partner of Rho Capital, remembered, "The rate of growth of Internet adoption made it convincing . . . so much faster than any other medium, the slide that everyone was showing was how long it took for cable to get to 60 percent penetration, how long it took for TV to get to 60 percent, and Internet was so much faster. And the application for the Internet was not just media, here you have media, you have commerce, you have business communication, you were looking EDI only serving 10 percent of corporations and this could open it up to everyone else. Whenever you talk about figures like trillion dollar markets, people get very excited. No one questioned those big numbers."

If all these people were online, then the customer base for various services and content was large and growing fast. However, for so many firms this line was used as a signal not just for Internet adoption but also adoption of their own businesses. There was an assumption that if the Internet grew this fast, they should too. Business plans were written and funded on this basis.

Several psychological studies show that when faced with uncertainty, people tend to assume that past events will indicate what will occur in the future. People exaggerate the degree to which one event is a good representation of another event. Psychologists call this a *representative heuristic.*

This is similar to the mental slip that occurred when investors forcasted that all start-up efforts would follow the same growth path in the future as the Internet adoption did in the past. People overestimate how much past events will represent future events.

In an excellent history of early radio, Susan Douglas captured a central driver of investor enthusiasm this way, "All the eager dreamer had to do was recognize what giants Western Union, Bell Telephone and General Electric had become to calculate where wireless might be in the future and what fortunes might accrue to those who had had the foresight to invest early."[80] Bubbles lead investors to repeatedly project parallels in between the infant companies and the established mega-players to delude themselves that they are on the inside track of a great opportunity. The same dynamic drove some of the highest valued Internet companies: Internet Capital Group imagined itself to become the GE of the Internet, and Yahoo the Disney of the Internet, and Webvan the Wal-Mart of the Internet.

EASIER TO IMAGINE THAN TO EXECUTE

Technologists often dreamed up wonderful uses for new software that they developed, and built companies based on the simple idea—"this is so great. Of course people will use it. They'll all switch tomorrow." Scott Bertetti worked at Wingspan, one of the early online banking efforts. "We're trying to launch a bank from nothing in 6 months. We're going to get a big chunk in year one. We thought [Internet banking] was so much easier, and there was so much value, why wouldn't you do it?"[81]

But many consumers didn't take up the service that seemed so obvious to the young entrepreneurs. Bertetti explained their mistake at Wingspan this way, "You come up with an idea and get really enamored with it. You lock yourself in a room and look at it logically and you say, you know what, this is a no-brainer—people are going to love this."[82] But in reality it doesn't work that way. Psychologists have found that this kind of logic is a systematic flaw in the way we approach decision-making. They call this *simulation* heuristic. According to this notion, judgments are biased toward information that can be readily imagined or mentally simulated. It was a syndrome that made many start-up investments seem far more plausible than they really were. It is a malady that afflicts any new technology investment decision because it is always far easier and more compelling to imagine how a new technology will perform amazing feats than to run a business that executes the technology successfully day in and day out.

This problem was made worse by the fact that those who were forecasting these great changes in human behavior were innovative technologists, not average consumers. As a result, what seemed like obvious forecasts of speedy adoption turned out to be very poor understanding of real market consumer dynamics.

One consultant described the gap in thinking this way, "they thought it would be so easy to become a billion dollar company. It was this logic as if they were saying, 'If you can get everyone in China to give you a dollar, well you would have a billion dollar company.' But that is really hard to do. But everyone seemed to have this view, like, its just one dollar, it couldn't be that hard."

DISTINGUISH VALUE FROM PROFIT

"The venture community was making a lot of money on these deals, so take it seriously," was the prevailing attitude remembered by an investment banker directly involved with some of the most prominent Internet IPOs from one of the leading bulge-bracket investment banks. "You can touch and feel this technology and people started to realize this was having an impact. There was something real and huge happening here."[83]

Despite this sense that the Internet was beginning a revolution, that is different from knowing how to derive real business-driven profits. One of the lasting failures among investors was separating the idea of value from potential profit. Many Internet opportunities produced tremendous value, but there was no way to make money. Just think about e-mail. It is now ubiquitous and has transformed the way human beings communicate. Yet it is nearly impossible to make significant profits from e-mail services. Typically, e-mail is now offered for free—not much profit there. Increasingly, e-mail service providers are trying to attach other subscription services such as extra storage so users can send, receive, and save larger e-mail files. But the value is in e-mail. Instant messaging is similar.

One of the most important reasons for this gap between value and profit is that it was easy to start an Internet business. There were no barriers to entry. It is easy to start an e-mail service company, for example, and many did because they thought e-mail would be "huge" and imagined this meant that there must be tremendous profits. But if there is no barrier to entry and no competitive advantage it is very hard to make a profit. With so many companies competing for the same customers, they compete by dropping their price. Since each additional e-mail customer doesn't really cost the business anything, companies don't really have to make money on each customer to make up the costs of serving them. As a result, businesses dropped their prices to zero.

For people with little experience in business or economics, there is something counter-intuitive about a product or service that contributes so much value, like e-mail, but does not generate profit. "Surely someone will want to pay for this" is the obvious logic. Indeed, customers would pay for something valuable and would pay for e-mail. What many young entrepreneurs didn't realize or forgot was that the world is not static. Other businesses enter the market to generate similar value in an effort to capture those profits. So while customers might pay for e-mail, they would not if a competitor were offering it for less or even nothing.

Turning value into profit in a competitive environment is far harder to do than many people realize. Profit doesn't really come from the amount of value businesses create. Profit comes from generating more value than the competition or providing the same value at lower cost.

In the heat of bubble markets, even investors who know better forgot or ignored the many ways to distinguish value from profit. The focus instead became a gut sense that an investment was going to be very valuable. "*This is going to be huge!*" was a common valuation standard.

Internet Capital Group offered a grand idea for making money. It was an Internet holding company making VC investments, except that it would be focused on business-to-business, the next wave and "big thing" for the Internet. "Everyone just said, this makes so much sense," recalled a senior management executive who was there. "We raised $1.2 billion in January 2000—people just leapt, they took that leap of faith, and boy, did they jump. They didn't realize that they were not going to land on their two feet. The next think you know all of these big companies were scared to death."[84]

Mark Walsh's investors also fell into the trap of not seeing the difference between value and profit. The logic of his audience would run something like this, he said: "This Internet is a big thing, business-to-business, never heard of it before, but businesses do buy a lot from each other, and if the b2b [business-to-business] market is anything at all like how the Internet is affecting the consumer marketplace like Amazon for books or E-Trade for stocks and transactions, this is going to be huge. So even if these guys are .001% of something that is huge, they are going to have great revenue growth."[85]

Bubbles seem to create this gap in thinking because the opportunities do seem so significant. Referring to this slip in thinking during the biotech bubble of the early 1990s, Roger McName, who ran the T. Rowe Price Science and Technology Fund at the time, said aptly, "The biotech industry will save a lot of lives. But it is not clear that it will treat the investors as well as the patients."[86]

"There was, ultimately, an inherent contradiction in the Internet hyperbole of 1999–2000," commented Hal Varian, an economist and now dean of the Berkeley Business School. "The Internet was supposed to remove all barriers to entry, encourage competition and create a frictionless market with unlimited access to free content. But at the same time, it was supposed to offer hugely profitable investment opportunities. You do not have to have a PhD in economics to see that both arguments are rarely true at the same time."[87]

CONFIRMATION BIAS

People tend to trust and agree with arguments and information that reinforce their existing beliefs. Or, more succinctly, people believe what they want to believe. In fact, studies show that people actively seek out information that confirms what they want to believe and avoid information that might challenge those beliefs.

During the bubble, prospectuses fully articulated the risks of their business. Wall Street analysts have been much criticized for fooling investors into buying shares of stocks they knew were inflated. However, the public market continuously ignored strong and surprisingly frank warnings. Henry Blodget was one of the most criticized analysts for having deceived the public—he was caught with e-mails illustrating that he didn't believe his own stock advice. However, in 1998 he said, "valuations are arbitrary. You are really just buying a vision of the future."[88] In 1999 he remarked that the market was "willing to fund any Internet business at any price."[89]

Even if readers were ignoring the fine print, headlines in major magazines and newspapers periodically worried about the bubble. In June 1998, a *Fortune* headline read, "Have Net Investors Lost Their Minds?"[90] In December 1998, a *Wall Street Journal* article warned, "There's No Mania Like Internet Mania—Historically, This May Take the Cake."[91] And *Time* magazine in January 1999 took a slightly different spin with a headline, "Internet Mania" and the tagline, "The biggest bubble in 350 years will inevitably burst. Here's how you can profit—if you dare."[92]

While they were typically given less exposure, it is remarkable how few people heeded these warnings.

Mary Meeker was also accused of misleading investors. But she provided some prescient warnings that many chose to ignore. In an interview with *Barron's* in December 1999, she warned of the coming mini-bubble of business-to-business exchanges: "the business-to-business companies that we have seen to date don't all have business models. And it is very easy to set up an exchange, or in theory set up an exchange to sell widgets . . . many of those models will probably be aggressively accepted by the public markets because they are in the right space. Yet many will not have shown that their models work in the year 2000."[93]

OVERCONFIDENCE

Another problem that occurs frequently during normal economic periods but becomes exacerbated during bubbles is that people who make a lot of money become overconfident. They mistakenly believe that if they made a lot of money, it must be because they are remarkably smart or talented rather than just lucky. Even worse, with the trust pyramid at work, other people are also treating them as smart or talented rather than lucky.

Bill Hambrecht said, "The typical opinion is yeah we know things are heated up—but I'm careful and I know we are with the right guys. Yeah, there will be a shake out, but because I'm smarter than the rest of the guys, then I have the best money managers, then I will be in much better shape."[94]

Several economic studies of how investors trade support the idea that increasing returns leads to increased trading volume, suggesting that investors believe they are smart and can pick winners.

Strauss Zelnick remembers seeing overconfidence plague management decisions: "There would be people who would say, 'Because I'm rich I must be smart.' There is an element of, 'I don't want to believe that what I achieve in the last year is entirely related to luck, therefore, it must be related to my brain.'"[95]

Overconfidence can be very damaging to investment decisions because it can lead investors to have too much faith in poor investment decisions. If they bet right in the past, they believe they will be right in the future—and that's when mistakes are made. A striking warning of how drastically mistaken confidence can be: two days before the stock market crash of 1928, the *New York Times* lamented, "traders who would formerly have taken the precaution of reducing their commitments just in case a reaction should set in, now feel confidence that they can ride out any storm which may develop. But more particularly, the repeated demonstrations which the market has given of its ability to "come back" with renewed strength after a sharp reaction has engendered a spirit of indifference to all the old-time warnings. As to whether the attitude may not sometime itself become a danger-signal, Wall Street is not agreed."[96] Overconfidence leads investors to believe that they can make better bets than everyone else. According to a survey of venture capitalists still in operation in 2004, three-quarters thought that they were investing during a bubble, but over half thought that their "investments were among the best and thus would come out as the winners and remain good investments."

SOMETIMES MAGICAL THINGS HAPPEN

Magical thinking persuaded many smart people to toss analytical discipline aside and to spend lots of money on poorly conceived ideas. However, during this period, magical things did seem to happen and served as hopeful models for others. This fact poses one of the deepest challenges to managing bubbles effectively. With so much new untested technology, no one really knows what will work in unexpected ways and what will fail.

"This is also a period that birthed companies and other businesses that hadn't existed before, that no one thought were possible," pointed out Michael Moritz.

Think about Yahoo!, which started as a hobby of two grad students making lists of their favorite websites. A great business? Now it's part of the S&P 500 Index. "We financed Yahoo! right off the campus, two guys who didn't have three minutes' worth of business experience," said Don Valentine. whose VC Sequoia Capital were early investors in Yahoo! "They were Ph.D. students and they were bored. And they created by accident a hobby that became a business. There was no real management there. There was no proven business model there. All of that had to be created." Valentine noted that they could have easily become one of the dot.com disasters all too common of the era, but "Fortunately, they had a good idea and integrity as people."[97]

In hindsight, we can point to crazy dot.coms like Alladvantage and say that they never should have existed, that VCs were fooled by the mania. But it is not clear that many crazy dot.coms are obviously different from Yahoo! or eBay or Amazon. New technologies and the bubbles that emerge out of them create uncertainty that make it hard to determine the difference between a lack of discipline and a new world. Yahoo! and Alladvantage point to the difference between a company that became an S&P 500 leader and a company that never should have existed, in *hindsight*.

"It is very hard to understand whether somebody's business is going to be 1x or 10x in size," Chip Morris commented. Morris was portfolio manager of the T. Rowe Price Science & Technology Fund. Under his direction, assets in the fund related institutional accounts grew from less than $200 million to over $24 billion, making it the largest science & technology fund in the world.

It is a challenge not just to decipher the future of seemingly magical Internet companies, but also serious hardware firms. Consider Cisco. As one of the more successful technology companies, producing real machinery at the core of the Internet, it is not some flighty new concept about how people will interact in the digital age. And yet during the early years of Cisco, it was far from clear that it would become such an important market leader. "I remember when Cisco went public the market for multi-protocol routers was thought to be quite small," Morris said. "Then things evolved, where at first it was only used to go from the corporation outside. Then all of a sudden people started using routers to segment their networks inside. That was enormous. They had a slow quarter or two in 1995 and then boom the Internet took off and all of a sudden the amount of traffic that had to leave and come in from outside sources just mushroomed. So, I don't think when people were selling Cisco at 12 times earnings anyone had any clue how big the Internet was going to be. I am not really sure that there was enough information out there. It just sort of worked out that way."[98]

INFORMATION MANIPULATION

Information is naturally limited and warped during bubble markets. However, on top of this natural handicap, there are also intentional efforts to manipulate the available information, further distorting investors' ability to see reality clearly. Fraud and information manipulation are common features of bubbles throughout history.

In the aftermath of the Internet bubble, New York Attorney General Eliot Spitzer went on a crusade to expose this practice. He found that during the bubble a number of improper activities distorted information available, further hyped the enthusiasm, and provided a select group of insiders more access to the profits.

Investment banks competed aggressively to become the lead underwriters that took start-ups public in "bake-offs." As part of the decision to sign up with one bank or another, start-ups sought research coverage of their stocks in the belief that the coverage would improve their credibility and generate higher IPO prices. Morgan Stanley used its extremely high profile analysts as marketing tools to win this banking business. More importantly, Spitzer found, "Morgan Stanley at times implicitly suggested that analysts would provide favorable research coverage, pending completion of due diligence, by noting analysts' past favorable coverage and/or emphasizing its enthusiastic support for the issuer."

In one example, the management of Loudcloud told Morgan Stanley in 1999 that receiving research coverage was a key factor in deciding whom to choose for taking the company public. The head of worldwide investment banking at Morgan Stanley told Loudcloud in an e-mail that Morgan had "developed a successful model which combines the best of technology and telecom research at Morgan Stanley to properly position Loudcloud in the capital markets; specifically, enthusiastic sponsorship." Loudcloud selected Morgan Stanley, which generated about $4.7 million in banking fees.

In a memo to top managers, a senior analyst said, "it's best to match me (plus someone on my team) with one of our traditional analysts to win IPO mandates. . . . it is not unusual for Internet companies that are not directly in my coverage universe to demand my research participation in order for us to garner acceptable deal terms—TMP worldwide, Covad, RealNames, Akamai, and Inktomi come to mind as especially prickly situations."

Compensation and performance ratings of analysts were found to be explicitly tied to how well analysts contributed to investment banking.

The attorney general, however, did not find concrete and explicit examples in which this conflict of interest at Morgan Stanley led directly to analysts making stock recommendations that they did not believe in order to satisfy investment banking needs.

He did find that in 2000 and 2001, four senior analysts maintained "Outperform" ratings on 13 stocks, indicating that they would do very well, even while the stocks declined by over 74 percent. Chemdex, for example, was rated an Outperform for almost 9 months while the price collapsed 96.2 percent. FreeMarkets was maintained as an Outperform for almost 2 years while its stock plummeted 74.3 percent. And Verisign was also kept as an Outperform even though the stock dropped 83.3 percent. Whether the cause of this was laziness, poor analysis, a direct result of conflicts of interest, or pure marketing frenzy, the end result was that Morgan Stanley was producing information that hyped the growth potential of stocks even as their value was collapsing.

To settle the charges, Morgan Stanley agreed to separate its research arm from its investment banking with separate reporting lines, pay a fine of $50 million, and contribute $75 million to an independent research fund.[99]

Henry Blodget and other analysts at Merril Lynch were more directly accused of fraudulently producing information about stocks that he did not believe. The Martin Act prohibits and makes illegal any fraud, misrepresentation, description, concealment, promise or representation that is beyond any reasonable expectation. E-mails regarding Goto.com illustrate the gap between public statements and more private thoughts. When, on January 2001, Merrill Lynch initiated coverage of Goto.com, an institutional investor e-mailed Blodget asking, "What's so interesting about GOTO except banking fees?" Blodget replied, "Nothing."

Another company, Infospace, was rated as a one by Merrill Lynch (which meant according to its scoring system that the stock was expected to grow by 20 percent or more). However, despite this top rating at the time, an analyst commented on July 13, 2000, "this stock is a powder keg, given how aggressive we were on it earlier this year and given the 'bad smell' comments that so many institutions are bringing up."

In October of the same year Goto.com was still ranked one, and an analyst called it a "piece of junk." Infospace stock price peaked on March 2, 2000, at $261. But Merrill maintained a one rating even as the stock slid steadily, reaching just $13.69 on December 10, 2000, a 95 percent drop. During this period, Merrill was also working on a deal to sell Go2Net to Infospace which was finalized on October 26, 2000. A little over a month later, on December 11, Merrill lowered its rating to "accumulate." On December 20, 2000, Merrill issued a bulletin indicating that the InfoSpace vice president had filed a lawsuit against the CEO, alleging multiple securities violations and racketeering. Despite this announcement, the accumulate rating was maintained.

Another company, Internet Capital Group, was ranked two (implying expected 10–20 percent growth) by Merrill while an analyst said on October 6, 2000, "No hopeful news to relate . . . we don't see things that will turn this around near term. The company needs to restructure its operations and raise additional cash, and until it does that, there is nothing positive to say."

Excite@home was also rated two while an analyst commented at the time that it was "such a piece of crap."

The analysis Merrill was providing to the markets was not just wrong; the company was not just hyping stocks as good investments even as the companies were collapsing; it appears that Merrill didn't believe what it was saying. Its information was deliberately misleading.

Other banks as well as individual bankers also faced fines for violating standard practices.

Individual companies also engaged in fraud and malpractice in the heat of the bubble. Perhaps the most significant was WorldCom. WorldCom was a telecommunications company that fueled the sentiment that the Internet would drive staggering demand for network traffic. It quickly became the darling of Wall Street for demonstrating incredible performance and was rewarded with huge valuations. As it turned out, much of that performance was based on fraudulent accounting.

In 2001 and 2002, for example, the company reported $3.8 billion as an investment. This allowed them to spread this huge sum over years. However, this money was in fact used for normal operating expenses, which should have been paid for on the books up front as a one-time hit. By spreading the costs in small amounts over years rather than one large amount in a single year, its profits appeared far better than they actually were. Thus, instead of making a $1.3 billion profit in 2001 as they reported, WorldCom was deeply in the red. Seeing only the remarkable reported profit, Wall Street rewarded it with staggering market valuations at the expense of competitors like AT&T.

Indeed, the entire telecommunications industry was being compared to this fraudulent benchmark. Wall Street was pressuring management across the industry to develop strategies to respond to a mirage. These pressures were unrelenting and intense and contributed to some very poor investment decisions.

Bubbles naturally warp information. Part of the reason is that there is always some group that benefits so much from the inflated investments that it purposely distorts information in its favor.

The ways bubbles distort information and perceptions are multi-layered and reinforcing. In general, information about investments of any kind is limited and relies significantly on judgment. But during bubbles, when so much more uncertainty exists, special problems emerge. Exciting bubble stories about great new inventions and fabulous wealth emerge and dominate less compelling but more rational views of the world. Successful investors and entrepreneurs are hailed as visionaries. The enthusiasm produces real data about investment successes that make the hysteria increasingly credible. The longer bubbles last, the harder it is to remain skeptical in the face of a litany of data and captivating stories. Analytical discipline declines just when it is most needed.

Gurus of various kinds emerge to provide "insight" into the unknowable and investors follow their lead because they don't know what else to do. A trust pyramid develops as a disproportionate number of investment decisions are informed by a small group of people—disproportionate that is to the true information they, the gurus, provide.

Information also becomes purposely manipulated by people who have immense financial interest in maintaining and exploiting the bubble for as long as possible.

All of these factors that tug on our cognitive capacity are further exacerbated by powerful emotional forces that distort perceptions. Peer pressure compels people to share the enthusiastic views. The attraction of greed and the sex appeal of these new investment opportunities are hard to resist.

For all these limitations in our individual ability to evaluate investment opportunities in bubble environments, there are many more distortions that occur as people interact in a competitive environment.

COMPETITIVE CASCADE

Even if you're on the right track, you'll get run over if you just sit there.

—Will Rogers

AS MUCH AS THE INFORMATION AVAILABLE AND OUR PERCEPTIONS of investment opportunities become warped during bubbles, there are also strong market-based competitive incentives and pressures that distort *actions*—making it extremely hard to resist the momentum, no matter what view an investor has about the prospects. For many investors, the prospect of making huge amounts of money is an incentive so great that the information and analysis just do not matter.

SEX APPEAL AND GREED

Thirty years before the Internet bubble, during the go-go era of the 1960s, rumors and tips circulated the market pushing some of the more innovative issues higher. They focused on anything related to color TV, for example. Many people worried about the newcomers who were too young to remember the crash of 1962. The boom destroyed the discipline necessary for good stock picking; "they're chasing the fast buck, and their attitude is, 'don't confuse me with the facts,'" said one broker.[1]

"I wouldn't invest in anything unless I thought it could potentially become a bubble . . . unless the idea was sexy enough—and that is not a trivial word," said Tom Perkins. "Everything we have done at Kleiner Perkins has had to have that excitement, that sexy aspect to it, or we would not have touched it in the first place. We're interested in unreasonable returns, we're not talking about making 10 percent on an investment, we're talking about making 10 times on an investment. Whatever you are going to invest in, it has to have the potential to be great: *wow, it's new, everybody is going to need these things, it's going to open up whole new industries, blah blah blah blah.* Fortunately, sometimes all that is true. So when you find this sexy, new frontier, and it's a mixture of technology and markets and new ideas, it's exciting, you can't put numbers on it."[2]

Sex appeal creates a powerful magnetic allure of the new new thing. The people and businesses involved in the Internet became visionaries, leaders, cool, and rich. Money is a fantastic motivator. Bubbles create fabulous channels for more and more people to satisfy greedy impulses. Sex appeal goes beyond just money however, it also confers status.

The emotional drive leads people to work harder than they ever imagined possible. In addition to the greedy impulse to become rich, much of the excitement was driven by many thinking that he or she were part of the vanguard of the new economy, contributing to a transformation of the world far beyond him or herself. That was all very exciting.

"This was the life of the party," remembers Paul Johnson, a leading telecommunications analyst for Robertson Stephens. "This was living. Not to be there—you were not living."[3]

"We felt like we were going to change the world," said Dan Estabrook, head of marketing for Covad, "People were living on this vision and this hope. We were a $10 billion company at one point."[4]

"It was consensual insanity," said Mark Walsh. "Everyone was so blotto from the potential of corporate growth that we said goofy shit. So then it happened, then we had the interviews on CNN, CNBC. The excitement, looking back, it was a great feeling. You had a lot of young people who felt that they were now part of something that was just so much bigger than them."[5]

Ken Barbalato pointed out that greed is a powerful elixir, "I suspect a lot of people wanted to believe it because it was making a lot of people a lot of money."[6]

COMPETITIVE CASCADE

Sex appeal and greed are obviously very powerful forces and play driving roles during bubbles. Less obvious than these incentives are the pressures compelling certain kinds of investment decisions. While many investors are enthralled participants in the frenzy, many others find themselves gradually slipping away from familiar rational investments toward more speculative endeavors. The incentives and pressures on investors to comply are intense.

A key feature of bubbles is that they create self-propagating cycles of bad investment decision-making. Bubbles create investment traps that for many seem inescapable. The system builds over time. Winners attract followers. The most innovative and adventurous initiatives break out first and take leading roles experimenting, using, and investing in new technologies. The inflated valuations they receive mean that even moderate successes, if not outright failures, appear extremely profitable to many investors. The leaders become bellwethers that all others aspire to become. They seem to demonstrate that huge profits are possible, if not easy, and set in place certain models for how to get there.

The competition to outperform everyone else leads to powerful pressures to play the game. The result is a competitive cascade of bad investment decisions rippling through the entire marketplace—steamrolling more disciplined and measured approaches. In the face of protracted pressures, some investors become *converted*—they start believing the hype. Others simply *capitulate,* they start joining the crowd because they can't afford not to play. As a result of these bad investments, amid the frenzy, the seeds of its own destruction are laid. Bad companies are formed, too many good companies emerge for the market size, thus progressively weakening the long-term viability and sustainability of the market.

The most notable during the Internet bubble was Netscape, Yahoo!, and Amazon. Many more followed these leaders. Large companies faced competitive attack from start-ups building on the Internet vision. Financial Services faced Charles Schwab and Wingspan, the travel industry faced Travelocity, the music industry faced Napster, Barnes & Noble faced Amazon.com, and the list continues.

The system affects each of the key investors from those financing start-ups, to managing stock portfolios, to large companies considering acquisitions or building initiatives.

FINANCING START-UPS

It is a basic tenet of economics that large profits attract new entrants into the market who try to capture those profits from competitors. For venture capitalists, this tenet leads to 2 results. First, it leads to the creation of too many new venture funds. Second, it leads to funds starting far too many companies that they think have the potential to generate tremendous returns. Followers rush in to "get a piece of the action." The competitive cascade forces overinvestment—too many VCs, putting too much money into too many start-ups to be sustainable.

In 1993, there were 352 venture firms. That almost doubled to 761 by 2001, according to the National Venture Capital Association. The number of individuals who were driven to join these firms also grew accordingly. In 1993, there were 3,420 venture principals in the industry. By 2001, the population more than doubled to 8,891.

The newcomers often lacked experience. "The riff-raff were able to come in," said Michael Mortiz about some of the new venture funds, "funded by people who were desperate to get in. We had a group who came in with checks and handed over the check and said, 'send us the paper work sometime.'"[7]

Don Valentine called such investors "tourists," meaning they were just there for the ride, not to build lasting companies. They wanted to get rich as fast with as little effort as possible. But they also have widespread effects in the market because they create momentum. According to one survey of venture capitalists still in operation in 2004, nearly 30 percent started between 1999 and 2000.

COPY CATS

The massive uncertainty that existed around these new start-ups meant that it was hard to know where the profit potential really lay. In the end, many venture capitalists just watched where other VCs were investing, assumed that signaled the next hit category of start-up and made similar investments. The competition among venture capitalists created the generic need to have the latest brand of Internet incarnation because it was perceived as the "next thing." There is a joke about venture capitalists that paints a vivid picture of the ethos: What do you get when you breed a sheep with a lemming? You get a VC.

"Everyone wants to have a company in a market segment that has proven successful. People are saying, I need one of these," said Tony Sun. Despite the mimicry, he said, "everybody believes that their investment is the right one."[8]

The incentive was to make a lot of money, but few really knew where that would come from. The response was to follow the herd that might know more than you. "One will explode and you don't want to be left out," remembered Steve Dow, general partner of Sevin Rosen Funds. "Better to move fast than smart."[9]

Over time, venture capitalists created too many companies to fight over a reasonable market. "Everybody was sort of multiplying these 'plays,' and each segment was saturated with competition at the very earliest stages of development. Which made the underlying economics even more challenging," Bob Kagle said.[10] The market just isn't mature or large enough to support all of the businesses. While there are legitimate market opportunities for a number of these companies, it just not big enough for all of them. The result is that many, if not most, did not make it. Despite the fact that many VCs knew they were creating too many companies for the market to sustain, it was the only way they knew how to participate in the frenzy.

"People need to put money to work," commented Bob Kagle. "The easiest way is to do a me-too deal. You don't have to be creative or inventive at all. You just need to go out and find a couple of people and copy somebody."[11]

Selling to consumers, (B2C) was perceived as extremely profitable for a period of time sparked by the vision of Amazon. The fantasy was that such a virtual company had no costs associated with the storefront and so could both charge less money and make higher profit margins. Within this sector, copycat firms started selling everything they could think of in strikingly narrow segments.

Among the companies selling pet supplies online, for example, there were allpets.com, petopia, Pets.com, PETsMart, Petsore.com, and Waggin Tails Pet Essentials. All of these firms attracted over $1.6 billion in venture funding. According to a report by market-research firms NPD Group Inc. and Media Metrix, 75 percent of pet owners who went online were aware of Web pet stores in 2000. However, only 27 percent viewed their websites at them and a mere 14 percent made an actual purchase.[12] There were far too many online pet companies given this environment. But that did not stop many venture capitalists from trying.

Selling Toys online also became very popular, spawning eToys, Toys-mart.com, Toytime.com, Redrocket, SmartKinds.com, and Internet extensions of existing retailers: KBKids.com, Toysrus.com, and Amazon.com. They largely failed, but not before reaching astronomical valuations. One of these, eToys, reached a market capitalization of over $10 billion but eventually sold its assets to KB Toys, for less than $54 million. Toysmart, Toytime.com, Redrocket, and SmartKinds.com all went out of business by the end of 2000.

Remember Alladvantage, the start-up that paid members to surf the Web? The idea of using the Internet for targeted advertising was so enticing, despite the lack of track record, that even these shaky economics didn't stop many copycat firms from popping up. By one count, there were some 40 companies trying similar things, including Spedia, Click-Rebates, Jotter, Radiofreecash, and AdSavers.com

The central importance of this is not so much that the Internet bubbles created too many pet supply or toy companies, but that bubbles in general always create too many companies in the hot category—and sometimes the hot category can be defined very narrowly. When selling *pet supplies* becomes hot, it's a sign that the market is oversupplying for some pretty narrow segments of a new technology. In the end, the number of copy-cats entering the market result in unsustainable over-saturation and insures that the bubble will burst.

In some respects, the Internet bubble was not one big bubble, but a collection of many bubbles arriving in waves of the new hot category. Venture capitalists all hope to make the best bet within these categories. "During the bubble it became all about *momentum play*," sighed Bob Kagle of Benchmark Capital, an early funder of eBay. "Did you have your deal in this sector, did you have your eCommerce deal, your infrastructure deal?"

The surge of copycats during the radio mania occurred after World War I when soldiers who operated the radios during the war returned home with a keen interest to remain very involved in the technology. They began to turn radio, which had been used for one-to-one communications, into a broadcast medium. Frank Conrad, an employee at Westinghouse, was broadcasting music on the side. Noticing the enthusiastic interest, Westinghouse created KDKA in November of 1920 as a formally established broadcaster. In 1913, there were just 322 licensed amateurs in the market experimenting with radio. Just 3 years later there were 10,279. Between 1915 and 1916 alone, 8,489 were granted licenses. After the war, in 1920, the annual grants grew to 10,809.

The canal mania copycats picked up by 1824 when more than sixty canal companies were created, raising more than £12 million, equivalent to about $20 billion in 2003—a massive sum for an economy that was far smaller than the United States is today. Shares in canal companies were bought as subscriptions and many were significantly oversubscribed. There was too much money, chasing too few deals, creating widespread price inflation.

The auto craze was creating its own copycats when in 1895 the U.S. Patent Office was flooded with over 500 applications for patents connected to the automobile.

The biotech stocks of the late 1980s and early 1990s also followed the same pattern. "Biotech stocks are fashionable right now." Roger McNamee said at the time. "Amgen is really a unique company, but the valuations for the biotech group implies that there will be about 25 other companies that are virtual Amgens. Are they losing money? That is an understatement. These companies are little more than research labs."[13] According to McNamee, the rate at which biotech stocks were going IPO "has been staggering, at a rate of about one a day."

DISTORTION OF RISK

Once the leaders and followers establish a notable presence among venture deals, the competitive pressure to participate becomes nearly inescapable. The pressure is extremely powerful, regardless of one's view of how rational or viable the investment climate really is. With each passing month as more and more start-ups go public at tremendous valuations, it becomes harder and harder for venture capitalists to resist the market enthusiasm. It becomes more and more enticing to play the game. Increasingly, even the most skeptical cannot afford to sit out the frenzy and watch the stock price of other companies rise, or watch their competitors steal deals.

The pressure is atmospheric, social, financial, and for some a matter of competitive survival. The pressure, in the end, shifts everyone's approach to *risk*. Most investment decisions are based on rates of return. The competitive pressure to at least meet the potential growth rates available elsewhere in the marketplace is unavoidable, even if those rates are based on bubbles. For many, the risks of not making significant investments in the mania become larger than the risks of joining the crowd—*even if those investments fail.* Put another way, there is safety in being wrong with the herd. Who can blame you? You did what everyone else was doing. When a competitive cascade is in full swing, bucking the frenzy can be deadly. It is the force of the competitive cascade that makes bubbles inevitable. For so many investors, there is just no escape. It is one thing for a group of enthusiasts to get caught up in the moment and for another group of speculators to take advantage of their excitement. But for a bubble to reach scale, for it to get big enough long enough, many people need to jump in. People who should know better need to participate. It's the competitive cascade that brings in the masses regardless of their orientation to the new opportunities.

"You were penalized for not being caught up in it," said the managing director of a late stage fund.[14]

Bubbles thrive on this distortion of risk. They shift the evaluation of risk away from analysis of the specific economics of an investment opportunity. Bubble risk includes perceived costs and rewards of following the enthusiasm and momentum.

For venture capitalists, the pressures also came from limited partners who have entrusted the VCs to make great investments in start-ups and create extraordinary returns on their money. Even the most experienced and sophisticated venture capitalists feel this pressure. The limited partners flooded the venture funds with money; the VCs in turn needed to spend it somehow. According to a survey of limited partners, 20 percent said that they encouraged or pressured VC funds to invest in start ups, and nearly half said they invested in VC that had little track record.

"It is a truism, you have to invest to make money," said Perkins. "You raised the fund and then how do you go to your limited partners and say, '*Well, gee, you know, we just didn't invest because the prices were too high,*' when everyone else was getting drunk at the bar."[15]

During bubble periods the possibility of making extraordinary returns becomes disconnected from the viability of the companies that are being funded because the market fails in its ability to distinguish sufficiently between market leaders, profit chasers, and illegitimate firms. Desperation to *get in* mixed with wild imagination also leads to companies that should never enter the market. A sub-market of illegitimate companies emerges and further distorts the already saturated landscape.

These illegitimate start-ups act like time bombs in the market, waiting to explode, triggering the end of the bubble.

Don Valentine has seen this pattern repeated over the bubbles he knows well. Like Tom Perkins, he is among the elite elder statesmen who have seen it all and were still shocked by the scale of the Internet. Don Valentine founded Sequoia Capital in 1972 and was one of the original investors in Apple Computer, Atari, Oracle, and Electronic Arts. He was a founder of National Semiconductor and a senior sales and marketing executive with Fairchild Semiconductor.

"Let's look at the 90s or, more specifically, 1995," he said, "when the Internet gold rush began in earnest." The power of the Internet changed the business landscape. First movers, armed with reasonable business plans, passion and commitment, were able to attract VC financing. Problems began when a half-dozen copy cats sprung up in every category. First they got the money, then they tried to piece together a business plan, believing that e-commerce could overcome a lack of business sense . . . the funny thing is that we should have seen it coming. Valentine saw the same dynamic in past bubbles. "In the last 30 years, other new technologies that brought similar waves of mania include microprocessors, PCs, disk drives and biotech. . . . The 70s list of venture-backed successes included Apple Computer, Inc., Intel Corp, and Oracle Corp. In the 80s, Sun Microsystems Inc, and Cisco Systems. . . ."[16]

Because the market cannot distinguish legitimate from illegitimate firms, the stock prices of all types of companies soars. In some cases, a large company will buy start-ups, further confirming for observers the profit potential and proving value in the distorted information. This in turn attracts new start-ups to the market.

"At the time, in the late 90s, we knew that we were getting 19 pieces of horse-manure for every one pony but it was really hard to figure out which one was the pony," remembered a frustrated Morris. "You couldn't know how profitable one company would be compared to another, since business models were largely indeterminable."[17]

Bubbles regularly generate companies that have no merit. Hundreds of radio companies emerged in the radio mania, many of them scams. The railway mania created numerous companies that were little more than accounting shells. The PC/software boom coined the term "vaporware" for software companies that created little more than what the press release promises of what they might do in the future.

As the Internet bubble progressed, almost anything could get venture money. "You're looking at firms who just have no filter and are writing checks for just everything that walks in the door," remembered Geoff Yang, founding partner of Redpoint Ventures and investor in Excite, Juniper, Ask Jeeves, and TiVo.[18]

With so much demand, and so much money to be made, venture capitalists would be stupid not to provide supply. Once Internet companies entered the public market through an IPO, their valuations confounded any rational analysis. As a result, however, the normal reasons to turn down an investment disappeared. "Companies go public and the stock jumps ten times and it doesn't even matter what the earnings are and you are reinforced by that," said Tony Sun. "You don't need to generate profits and you can make a lot of money without profits and it's proven over and over again . . ."[19]

The choice for many seemed to be: do you want to have a chance at earning billions on a speculative venture deal or let someone else have it, because in the bubble environment those deals got funded by someone. "The statements were made that if we didn't finance it, someone else would and if we're in this business we have to be in this business and that my thinking was out of date," said Alan Patricof. "In the end, the answer was we had had to go along with the current valuation metrics. We couldn't avoid investing in these companies, because other people were doing those deals on this basis and for 2 or 3 years they were right and I was wrong . . . until the music stopped."[20]

The missed opportunities were a notable driver for many investors to become increasingly less cautious or skeptical. "You would pass on deals," remembers one late-stage venture fund manager, "and the valuations you thought were too high would go public three to six months later at a valuation that was a multiple of what you would have paid."[21]

"I would say, 'I missed the boat,'" Sun said, "That made me want to jump in the boat next time. It is hard to stand the ground on this kind of onslaught."[22] About 43 percent of VCs still in operation in 2004 said they shifted from being skeptical in internet companies to believing that they could be viable business because so many seemed to be succeeding.

In the beginning, one venture capitalist passed on numerous deals because they just didn't seem to add up. Etoys was particularly memorable for him: "We just couldn't get comfortable with the margin structure, with the amount of inventory you had to hold on to. It ended up going public and trading at an enormous valuation. We just completely screwed up. Verisign was another one. We just thought it was too expensive, but then it ended up to be worth a mint."[23]

When eToys went public in May 1999, it opened at $20 per share and leapt to $76.56, reaching a market value of nearly $8 billion on the first day. The infant company that was losing money became valued at 35 percent higher than the value of Toys 'R' Us. eToys reached a peak five months later at $10.3 billion—two and half times the value of Toys 'R' Us.

If this VC had invested in eToys and if he had been able to effectively time the disbursement of his investment to limited partners, he could have made a tremendous amount of money. Time, however, is key here and in practically any investment made during bubbles. By February 5, 2001, after the bubble burst, eToys stock was trading at just $0.28 per share. NASDAQ forced eToys to delist from the exchange because it was not able to sustain a price of more than $1 for 30 consecutive days. The company closed its websites in March 2001 and filed for bankruptcy.[24]

Idealab, an incubator that invests and nurtures start-ups, was able to benefit from this timing. It invested $100,000 in eToys in June 1997. Late in 1999, they sold over 3.8 million shares when the stock price hovered in the stratosphere of $45.50 to $69.58 per share. On that sale alone they earned a profit of $193 million.[25]

Verisign would have provided longer term value. At the close of its first day of trading, on January 29, 1998, the company was valued at $514 million. Five years later in 2003, it proved a lasting success and was worth more than $4 billion.

The two examples offer telling accounts of the 2 ways investors try to make money during bubbles. Verisign proved to be a long-term success story. A VC or stock investor could have made an investment during the bubble and still come out ahead after the bust. eToys also offered the chance to generate incredible returns for investors, but only if they were able to time it right—that is, to see the decline coming and liquidate their holdings quickly enough.

Because of this distortion of risk, bubbles briefly reward investors for starting businesses that are unsustainable. As a result, they lay the seeds of their own destruction.

VALUATIONS

The pressure to play warped decisions not only on which companies to fund, but also how much investors were expected to invest in the start-up for a given share of the equity. As the market progressed, the prices of those venture investments rose dramatically.

Many venture capitalists felt that they had to go along in this inflationary environment. Despite the lofty venture prices, the returns in the public market still seemed to make them, for a period of time, worthwhile. The logic of turning down a deal based on rational pricing analysis quickly eroded. "I think it is very easy to sit there and say this does-n't make sense, we're going through a pricing bubble right now. These valuations don't make any sense for companies that are not doing any revenue," Yang said. "Then someone says, yeah, but they are all getting done and that is the market price and if you are going to play, if you are going to be in the market you have to be in the market."[26]

One managing director of a venture fund saw some of his own venture investments surpass his own judgments of fair values: "We were getting exit multiples or IPO multiples of huge numbers. So when you are doing your justifications for your valuations, it was easy to justify high prices because you could say, 'but this thing can go public in 6 to 12 months and the public price will be a billion dollars and so paying $300 million today made sense.'"[27] About 40 percent of venture capitalists surveyed in 2004 said that inflated prices could still generate high returns given the frenzied IPO and acquisition market.

Resistance to investing even in illegitimate start-ups had high costs, while joining the frenzy had high rewards. Ironically, the problem was that despite the incredible lack of discipline, despite the fact that it lead to many illegitimate companies getting funded, this approach was *working*. Many funds that invested in illegitimate start-ups were generating huge returns through the IPO market or corporate acquisitions, adding pressure to everyone else to shift his or her posture and join the game. "Here are guys just knocking the cover off the ball," Yang said. "We asked ourselves why are we making it so difficult on ourselves. Maybe the world has changed and we are not changing with it."[28]

Bad investments can make a lot of money during bubbles. This is possible because bubble markets value enthusiasm and momentum rather than the underlying business opportunities. That is what makes investing in them irresistible to investors in a competitive market, and that is what is so distorting to efficient markets.

As money flowed into venture funds they also felt more equipped to write bigger checks. As infant companies successfully went IPO, a comfort zone was created for investment banks to take increasingly younger and wild companies public.

Bubbles lead to 3 critical financing mistakes for venture capitalists. They lead to creating copycats that saturate the market, creating poor business concepts that act as time bombs in the market, and they encourage overpaying for all businesses—even those that have legitimate prospects.

Alan Patricof, founder of APAX ventures, was skeptical at every step throughout the Internet bubble. He started in the venture business back when he founded Patricof & Co. ventures in 1969, which has been an investor in reasonable successes, such as Apple Computer, America Online, and Office Depot. But he was deeply torn about how to position himself during the period. During the bubble he challenged the younger staff to think more thoroughly about the investments, but he didn't kill the deals. "As the managing partner I would have demoralized everyone in the firm," he reflected, "So, do you demoralize everyone in the firm or do you let yourself be demoralized and accept the change in valuation metrics."[29]

Thus, bubbles not only warp the information available, the perceptions, and *analysis,* as discussed before; they also create competitive environments that compel investors to *act* accordingly. They create a competitive cascade the imposes remarkable pressures to play.

The stock market fueled much of this momentum and skewed many of the prices of start-ups. They created fabulous "exit strategies" for venture capitalists to earn massive returns on their investments far faster than normally and for companies that would quickly die.

THE STOCK MARKET

FUELING START-UPS WITH GASOLINE FROM THE PUBLIC MARKET

The public markets had an insatiable demand for taking Internet companies public. This made any venture deal seem like a winner. "Investment bankers go out into the orchards and shake the trees—by that I mean—they deal with the venture capitalists," said Tom Perkins. "The stuff that is ripe and ready falls to the ground rather quickly. Afterwards they are still shaking the trees and trying to finding something to sell to the public, and guess what, they will always find *something*."[30]

Furthermore, the public market can channel vast amounts of money that dwarf the venture capital funding capacity, into unprepared start-ups and leading to damaging business practices. The stock markets do not usually accept infant companies. But they do during bubbles. They did during the railways, the high-tech "onics" companies of the 1960s, biotech, and PC bubbles. The extraordinary stock valuations of start-ups are not just the most visible sign of a bubble market. They also fuel the bubble by creating incentives and pressures for new start-ups to be formed and bought.

During the Internet bubble, investment banks faced the decision of sticking to their traditional approach of taking established companies public or shifting that approach to take advantage of the seemingly incredible opportunities of infant start-ups.

"We had a capital market that was saying, we are willing to pay on a relative basis for revenue growth and we think the business models will flesh themselves out, as long as you are showing decent revenue growth," remembered an investment banker directly involved with some of the most prominent Internet IPOs. "It was a very different market psychology and a different way of looking at companies. Which is, as we all now know is an incorrect way to look at it. Nonetheless as investment bankers, we are a conduit to the market. So you listen to the themes out there that investors are willing to pay for and how they are willing to evaluate equity stories and then you advise companies, yes you can or cannot tap the markets."[31]

Yahoo! was taken public by Goldman Sachs very early in the cycle. But it was not an easy or obvious decision for Goldman to pitch the business of taking Yahoo! public, said an investment banker there at the time. Yahoo! could barely have been any younger, untested, or experimental. Goldman Sachs typically followed more traditional IPO pipelines in which the new company might not be a leader in its industry but would at least have 8 to 12 quarters of real revenue.

In this environment, however, the risks to investment banks of not playing the game and taking these companies public, despite their untested history, loomed large. The decision within Goldman Sachs to pitch Yahoo! was debated. Morgan Stanley had taken Netscape public, and Excite and Lycos were preparing to do the same. At that time, in 1996, the IPO market for these companies was not so insatiable as it would be in 1999. But there were strong signals that the markets would be very responsive. Furthermore, Goldman thought that it was also probably the beginning of something very big. Not being there at the beginning could be very costly. A key competitive question for Goldman was, "Do we miss out on building an investment banking franchise because we passed on this business, because we didn't even pitch Yahoo!? The markets were receptive to issues like them so you needed to take advantage of it or lose out."[32]

When Yahoo! went public, Steve Harmon, an investment analyst at Mecklermedia Corporation, captured the sentiment that would plague investors for many years to come: "Everyone is hoping for another Netscape."[33]

As it became increasingly established that the public markets wanted as many Internet companies as they could get, the competition among banks became fierce, and eventually there were accusations of fraud and kickbacks of various kinds in the efforts to win business. Bubbles breed fierce competition. Along the way, ethics is one of the many casualties.

The banks and fund managers drawn in by the high returns followed the same copycat patterns as the venture capital firms. The incentives to take the next hot category public was significant. One investment banker noted, "If the whole mortgage/lending area is going to be big, then we sort of need to have eLoan as a cornerstone franchise client. Otherwise there might be five others that come along. Need to have a CBS Marketwatch because it was the content space and it was important to have that play. If the stocks go up, everyone is happy."[34]

Bringing such infant companies into the public market had dramatic effects on anyone managing a portfolio of stocks.

PORTFOLIO MANAGERS

Investment funds managers also faced the same pattern of competitive incentives and pressures. Ken Barbalato explained the pressure concretely: "Say I'm an asset manager. I've been managing assets for over 30 years. And the growth rate of these assets is X, and so a prospective client comes in the door and says I'd like you to invest my money. My neighbor is getting a 30 percent rate of growth. Well, you say, that's abnormal. They say, they've been getting that for the last 2 or 3 years. I'll take my business elsewhere. So as an asset manager, you have a choice.

Your existing clients are now challenging you. You have potential new clients that are looking for outsized rates of return. How do you position yourself? At the end of the day these people are still feeding their families."[35]

David Shulman was one of the first skeptics to fall. In December 1996, Alan Greenspan, wondered aloud about possible "irrational exuberance" in the market and Shulman agreed. The rest of the market, however, did not. "It was a lot easier to hang in there when I had company," noted Shulman, then an investment strategist at Solomon Brothers. "After I became the last one, I started to think a lot more about how I was measuring the market and trying to figure out if things really had changed."[36] The sales team at Solomon had gotten frustrated with his bearishness. By 1998 he left his post, noting, "I was bearish from December 1996 on and that was wrong."[37]

The human dimension of the marketplace is pivotal. "This is a business that is transaction oriented and there's enormous pressure to be optimistic and bullish," remarked a strategist for CIBC Oppenheim Corp at the time. "We're all looking for reinforcement."[38]

As far back as December 1995, the *Wall Street Journal* noted that "no real cautionary voices remain." In the same article, Byron Wein, market strategist at Morgan Stanley, worried that "as the last of the skeptics fall away, the environment grows more treacherous."

The environment created three results for stock funds. There was a massive growth in the number of tech and growth funds. The inflow of money was shifting away from poorly performing value funds into tech and growth funds, and new money entered the market chasing the highest returns in the most spectacular companies. In order to maintain their clients, fund managers increasingly had to shift their portfolio toward the tech stocks that were generating high returns.

Foster Friess, the manager of the Brandywine Fund was considered one of the best growth fund investor in the United States. From the fund's inception in 1985 to September 1997, Brandywine returned 20.4 percent annually. After the 1997 Asian economic crisis and the continuing rise of overvalued tech stocks, Friese became nervous and sold all of his shares in technology and moved two-thirds of the $9.5 billion Brandywine Fund into cash.

"Individual and institutional investors were chasing momentum and Internet stocks with no earnings," Friess said, "We require a company to demonstrate three years of earnings history before coming onto our radar screen. That steered us clear of Internet start-ups."

Avoiding the hot stocks cost him clients. He added. "We had a lot of redemptions by impatient investors."[39] Thus, not only is cautionary *information* less available to the marketplace during bubble enthusiasm, as described before, but cautionary *actions* are punished by the competitive cascade.

Chip Morris was the portfolio manage of T. Rowe Price Science & Technology Fund and at its peak of $24 billion became the largest tech fund in the world. But even he felt the pressures acutely. "Given the stocks momentum, there were a lot of pressures to play," he said. One of the most important pressures on every portfolio manager, even those that were large and successful, was that they were all being compared to each other on a monthly basis in a bubble environment. The competitive benchmark that all managers were measured against included the funds that were most aggressively involved in the momentum of the frenzy. "There were 250 other tech funds and they were all loaded to the gills," Morris said. "Even though I was running a relatively conservative portfolio and I was up 100 percent in 1999. I got nasty letters asking what happened because my benchmark was 120 percent."

It was a dangerous game and many investors knew that they were playing with fire, that they were going to pay a high price when the market came crashing down. Some embraced the thrill and thought they could time the market. Others felt like they had no choice.

According to one portfolio manager, it was the pure Internet funds like Munder Net Net that emerged late in the bubble that played a critical role in fueling the competitive cascade. "All the newbies were going to run flat out as if it was a sprint every day. So, I needed as much juice as possible because I needed to beat 75 other funds. We knew that was going on. It tended to tilt the competitive universe more aggressive," the manager said. "If you stray too far from a peer group that is increasingly becoming aggressive you are going to put yourself in a box. Do you really want to be 200th out of 200 funds?"[40]

Even value funds that traditionally looked for cheap stocks, stocks with low price-to-book ratios—began shifting their focus.

"Money managers who were real value oriented guys who really took a stand against it lost a lot of assets," remarked Bill Hambrecht.[41]

Finally, some firms that refused to bend simply shut down. From 1980 to mid-1998, Tiger Management focused on value stocks and returned an astounding rate of 31.7 percent per year after fees, a track record that places the company in the Halls of Honor with Warren Buffett and Peter Lynch.

Then, starting mid-1999, Tiger proceeded to lose half of the gains it had built up over the previous 18 years. During this time it stuck by its philosophy and old-economy stocks such as General Motors and US Airways and shunned the Internet.

In April 2000, Tiger gave up and announced that it would liquidate and give back their investors' $4.5 billion. "There is no point in subjecting our investors to risk in a market which I frankly do not understand," wrote Julian Robertson, who managed the fund at the time. "What's more," he went on, "there is no quick end in sight . . . of the bear market in value stocks."[42] Ironically, shortly after this announcement, tech stocks started their slide, and his value approach would have served his investors well.

On the way out, he remarked, "I think it's going to be one of the greatest collapses of all time in this stuff," he said, referring to Internet stocks. "I've never been so convinced of the value approach, but it has been very frustrating lately. This isn't the environment for investors like ourselves."[43]

Comstock Partners' Charles Minter had been bearish from the beginning of the 1990s. But by 1997, the pressure on him was intense to change course and join the market enthusiasm. The only alternative, as he put it to the *Wall Street Journal,* was to "hide under the covers and cry and go out of business. But we feel we owe it to our customers."[44]

Bubbles create enormous pressures on every business in its path. The financial markets and the businesses designed to serve them channel the money according to demand. For many investment funds that meant creating sector funds to serve the fomenting demand for hi-tech and dot.com stocks.

Even John Bogle, founder of Vanguard, was not immune to the competitive cascade. Vanguard is one the most respected mutual funds for charging low fees to its shareholders and providing excellent financial education. Bogle himself cut his teeth during the go-go years of the 1960s and remembers well the wreckage left when that party ended. But despite this experience in similar dynamic bubbles of the past, he felt the pressure of the marketplace. "I decided we had to be more aggressive and bring out sector funds because Fidelity had these funds," said Bogle. Sector funds focusing on high-tech, Internet, and even specific subgroups within the Internet, such as portals, media, business-to-business, business-to-consumer all emerged. Fidelity was at the forefront of these offerings. Vanguard created a fund that largely mirrored technology stocks. "It was dumb," Bogle continued. "I had seen in my study of the [mutual fund] industry that back in the 1950s this industry had all these sector funds then as a dominant part of the business. After the war you bought group securities steel shares. Steel was the big thing then and all the money went into steel. Of course, as soon as that happened steel did poorly. I saw it again in the go-go era [of the 1960s]. I saw it in 1985." All of this experience did not prevent Bogle from starting his own tech fund during the Internet bubble, "I wanted to compete with Fidelity and get money in here that was going in there."[45]

The pressure for returns and herding of the investment managers went beyond playing the tech market as a whole. The environment created the need to hold specific individual stocks. Erik Gustafson was a co-manager of a Stein Roe Young investor fund with assets of about $1 billion. He had avoided buying AOL because he thought the price was wildly high. By November 1998, however, he couldn't resist any longer and bought 300,000 shares. By his account, "To own a company like AOL, you had to throw out traditional measures of valuing companies. We had to say we have to own what we think is the dominant franchise in the Internet. It was a space that as a money manager you simply have to be in."[46]

Jeremy Grantham, a value investor of Grantham, Mayo, Van Otterloo & Co., told Forbes, "There is no mercy shown to people who don't buy Yahoo! and AOL. But that has nothing to do with the prudence of the investment. That's just the craziness of benchmarking returns."[47]

These pressures follow a standard pattern during bubbles. For those like Bill Hambrecht, who was around during the bubble of the 1980s, seeing them again during the Internet bubble was ironically familiar. "I think what was feeding the 90s market was *look what you missed in the 1980s.* A performance driven market is just that, performance driven. There is tremendous herd instinct in this thing. Pressure to perform relative to your peer group is enormous pressure."[48]

Mary Meeker also first cut her teeth as an analyst during the PC boom. As early as February 1996, she drew the same parallel and provided an early forewarning to Internet investors. The *Morgan Stanley Internet Report* she produced became essential reading for many and in it she noted, "Any public investor who's lived through the development of the PC business knows what rough-and-tumble, volatile investing is all about, knows the thrill of buying Microsoft shares in the IPO and holding on . . . a single investment that allowed one to make a lot of poor investments and still come out way ahead."[49]

The pressure to follow the herd appears to be especially acute for younger mutual fund portfolio managers. According to a study by economist Judith Chevalier, younger managers are more likely to be fired than older managers if they deviate from consensus views. It is no surprise, then, with such a strong incentive, that the study also found that younger managers tended to follow the herd more than older managers did.[50] When the consensus views become bubble views this incentive structure is dangerous.

The hot stocks of the go-go years in the 1960s were color televisions, airlines, parts of the electronics industry, and "*stocks with a story.*" Not to forget the classics: Polaroid, Syntex, and Xerox. Xerox, for example, closed in 1964 at 68 5/8 and reached a high in 1965 of 215 and by May of 1996 a high of 262. Polaroid closed in 1964 at 45 7/8, reaching 1965 highs of 130. National video was just 8 1/2 at the end of 1965 and reached 91 7/8 in 1965.

The market split between winners and losers, creating the pressure to play. The New *York Times* noted, "one result of the brilliant performance of the aggressive funds has been pressure on portfolio managers of hitherto conservative institutions . . . to make a better show of it. The quest for quick and steeper gains has been leading them into more speculative buying, and this in turn has contributed to the volatility of the stock market."[51]

Richard Baily of the Massachusetts Investors Funds noted that despite the poor fundamentals in 1969, "there are a lot of people with a lot of cash who are more afraid of being left behind by an up market than being hurt further in a market decline. And this nervous money will stick pretty close to the market."[52]

The search for the next big Netscape, was, in 1969 the next Xerox. "We are looking for growth stocks that haven't been exploited—the Xeroxes of two years from now," said Eldon Mayer Jr., vice president of Hartwell Management Co. He saw the exploited stocks as "concept stocks."[53]

As late as 1970, the market still appeared to be looking for an upswing. Michael David ran a portfolio of small closed-end funds that focused on shorting the market. He observed, "institutional salesmen still call with the same 1967–68 concept stocks each time the market seems to stop going down . . . the buying impulse is there."[54]

During the PC bubble, every investor hoped for the next Apple; during the biotech bubble every investor hoped for the next Genentech. The pattern of hope is similar.

The competitive cascade for portfolio managers is similar to the dynamic that affected venture capitalists. First, a few big opportunities generate tremendous returns. Second, these attract "newbies" or "tourists" into the market in an attempt to replicate those returns. For a period of time, they are successful, thus creating a frenzied momentum to invest in those companies. The momentum players start riding and fueling the wave. For portfolio managers this also includes the emergence of sector funds. Finally, and most damaging to the long term sustainability of the market, the serious investors increasingly get sucked in as the competitive pressures force them to capitulate or become converted to the new ways of thinking. These 3 stages are overly schematic. Reality is a little messier. But is a useful framework to see how a competitive cascade ripples through investment decision makers.

THE FOOLS RUSH IN

Many analysts and economists believe that most of the stock investments during bubbles are based on the greater-fools theory or follows a ponzi scheme model. According to this idea, savvy investors speculate on stock prices rising because people who are greater fools than they are willing to buy the shares at increasingly high prices. For savvy investors, as long as there is someone dumber than they willing to buy their stock at a higher price, they can make money.

Individual investors or "retail investors" can often become more easily enamored with stocks that they know nothing about. As a result, they become the suckers in a gambling game where the odds are stacked against them. Numerous people reported that they went online, saw a dot.com they liked, and bought it, with no knowledge or insight into the meaning of price they were paying for that stock. They did not know what the market value of the firm was, they did not know who the competitors were or what were the driving forces of the business. They were buying on gut enthusiasm for some cool-sounding company, or seeing the stock price go up and up. They did not understand how to evaluate this information and make an effective investment decision. They saw prices go up, they had friends next door getting rich, and they wanted to participate in easy money-making.

"It was pure greed," said one investor. "I bought Amazon, Yahoo! all these stocks. They were going up so fast. I made a ton of money and then lost almost all of it."

There is some information demonstrating that uneducated investors, particularly day traders, accounted for a notable share of trades during the market peaks of individual stocks. There is also anecdotal evidence that during the bubbles of the 1920s and 1960s, the market became accessible to a large group of new and perhaps naïve investors. The number of households investing directly in stock grew by over 30 percent between 1995 and 1998.[55] The precise effect of their investment activity is hard to quantify, but their role is felt by many in the market.

One of the areas in which naïve individual investors are suspected of playing a very strong role is the rapid run-up in IPO prices. An investment banker remembered, "You just weren't used to seeing all of these retail investors coming in out of nowhere." The retail investors created special confusion for setting IPO prices. Traditionally, when bankers set a stock price for a new company entering the public market, they create a "shadow book of demand" that is basically gleaned from shopping the stock around with some exploratory prices and meeting with investors and gauging demand in the market place informally. But retail investors posed unexpected challenges to this approach because they were not part of the typical circuit bankers visited: "How do you gauge the shadow book of demand of investors in Omaha that you never met or heard of?" worried an investment banker involved in some of the most important IPOs of the day.[56]

This created powerful incentives to push stocks into the market simply because naïve investors were willing to buy them. In the end, retail investors suffered dramatically in a game where the odds were dramatically stacked against them. Between 1996 and 2000 some 170 Internet companies were taken public by the top 8 underwriters. In total, these start-ups were selling for nearly 70 percent more than institutional investors paid when they committed before the IPO. However, the same stocks were down nearly 25 percent from what most retail investors were paying for them after they went IPO.[57]

Individual investors can get into the market through several avenues. Many individuals involved in the stock market are not active traders or decision makers. Rather, they are indirectly invested through their retire plans whose funds are handled by portfolio managers. These managers are the key decision makers in picking individual stocks to own. Some retirement plans offer a small number of options where individuals choose to be more or less aggressive, such as a growth fund, a S&P Index fund, or a bond fund. But in these cases too, the real stock-picking decisions are done by portfolio managers.

Individuals who are directly involved in the market buy stocks through brokerages or through specialized funds of various kinds. The Internet opened the doors to far more people by enabling direct online trading. Online trading was estimated to account for 37 percent of all retail trading volume in equities and options for 1998[58] and 40 percent in the first quarter of 2000.[59]

Day trading, a subset of online trading, consists of the most active and speculative traders. By one estimate there were just 5,000 day traders in the late 1990s, but according to another study, 20 percent of new orders into NASDAQ stocks came from firms catering to day traders.[60] Online day traders were estimated to account for about 14 percent of the stock market's daily trading volume and about two to three times that for many internet trading.[61]

Finally, initial evidence also suggests that all the extra trading that individual investors do ends up hurting them. Despite their sense of having great knowledge from all the information at their finger-tips, they don't end up making good investment decisions. As a result, according to one study, active traders using one discount brokerage earned returns 6 percent lower than the market each year between 1991 and 1996.[62]

Retail investors however do not just affect their own buying decisions, they can affect the entire market place as other momentum investors try to anticipate their behavior, how they will affect stock prices and then act accordingly. According to Morris, "The institutions started playing the retail investors off on themselves," he said. "It meant that—do I really want to buy this stock that I think is worth 6, going public at 20, yes I do because I believe the retail book will open this at 50. Then all the fundamental guys said, there is money on the table, let's do this."[63]

While naïve investors likely played a role, bubbles are far too large and multilayered to provide a sufficient explanation. Moreover, some of the savviest investors remained invested in Internet stocks even as the bubble was bursting. Many venture capitalists, who perhaps knew the most about what lurked within these Internet start-ups, did not sell their shares during the fall either.

John Bogle rejected the notion flatly. "The investor did not create 496 new economy funds. The investor did not advertise in *Money Magazine* in March of 2000."[64]

CORPORATE INVESTMENTS

Many large companies, no matter how big, old, or savvy, were not immune. The involvement of corporations may have been one of the most important signals to the public and private markets confirming the hype of the Internet. Many of the other investment decisions could easily have been based purely on speculation. However, large business cannot speculate on its existence. Their investment money spent on poorly performing initiatives undermines profits and strategic position. While asset traders can get in and out and VCs can often liquidate via IPO or acquisitions, corporations must live with the legacy of their investment decisions.

During investment bubbles, the stock prices of businesses detach from what is occurring in those businesses and become driven more by enthusiasm or pessimism. However, business are very concerned with their stock price, and when the stock prices of competitors are rising because they are perceived as embracing the "new thing," and yours are falling because "you don't get it," there is a strong incentive to chase rising stock prices—even bubble prices not based on real business operations. In this environment, financial markets increasingly dictate the terms for growth strategies, forcing business to figure out how to support inflated stock price expectations.

"Senior management was saying what are you going to do about this Internet thing," recalled one venture capitalist, "and that pressure was pushed down where they had to do something and you as a senior manager had to answer to your CEO, that you had a response."[65]

The pressure from Wall Street to launch, very publicly, an Internet initiative was widespread among incumbent companies. Those who complied were rewarded, at least initially. According to one study, incumbent firms that announced an Internet initiative received a 14 percent cumulative abnormal returns after a 10-day period (meaning 14 percent above the market average for firms with similar risk).[66] Another study showed that existing firms that simply added dot.com to their name saw their stock jump. Between June 1998 and July 1999, the study found that approximately 95 companies changed their name by adding dot.com. About a quarter of these companies changed their focus from old economy to Internet-related business. The core business of 10 companies that added dot.com to their name was totally unrelated to the Internet.

Despite this, all of the name changes resulted in a significant price jump. The name changes produced cumulative abnormal returns of about 74 percent for the ten days surrounding the announcement, and the effect appears to last.[67]

For example, K-Tel International Inc., long known for bad commercials selling music on late-night television, was a small company. The company's stock was about $7 a share, and on some days its shares didn't even change hands.

But after the company announced that it would be selling music online, its stock soared to $41.625. K-Tel's market capitalization went from about $30 million to $170 million in a week. The stock's trading activity was an astonishing 14.2 million shares, or more than three times the number of shares outstanding.[68]

In other cases, all that was needed to placate the market hunger was repackaging existing work as a separate new economy effort, spinning off the division, or creating a tracking stock. One telecommunications consultant explained the logic among many technology corporations: "I'm not serving my shareholders well if I don't structure this initiative publicly in a way that I can get these incredible multiples attached to something that I'm doing anyway. So everyone creates an ISP [Internet Service Provider]—everyone does a wireless—to try to give visibility . . . you were almost derelict to shareholders if you didn't do that because, heck, you don't know and, heck, give them the opportunity to make the money."[69]

Unfortunately, for many businesses the pressure often went far deeper than simple press releases, repackaging, and spin-offs of existing efforts. Challenges were made to the core business of many companies. Numerous companies were afraid of being "Amazoned"—meaning that they would be entirely replaced by a virtual version of their company, a faster, more nimble company, unencumbered by physical structures and stodgy old management that "didn't get it."

FIGHT FOR SURVIVAL

Some companies, most notably Barnes and Noble, faced a direct attack by Amazon on their core business. For other companies the competitive dynamic was less clear, but the risks of inaction were perceived by many to be extraordinarily high. "At the time, in 1997, Amazon had higher market cap than Barnes and Noble with significantly less sales and was growing very fast," remembered Habib Kairuz, managing partner at Rho Capital and a lead investor in iVillage, among others. "And this is the argument that we were all making. We're going to put you out of business. And they understood that. They were worried. Every big grocery was involved in some online venture. Pharmacies had their own ventures. They could not afford to not play the game."[70]

Numerous industries were impacted by the rapid arrival of the Internet. Some moved faster than others. Some leaped immediately, while others sat in denial for a number of years. By 1999 and 2000, the roster of companies that made the Internet a central piece of their public strategy reached GE, Ford Motors, Time Warner, and numerous others.

Technology bubbles challenge the existing order of the marketplace. Knowing how to best respond in this distorted environment is very complex. Entire industries across the economy were impacted. Perhaps one of the most remarkable features of the Internet bubble, and a testament to its sheer size compared to previous bubbles was the degree to which large corporations participated.

The media industry perceived itself as perhaps the most vulnerable. Regardless of what niche they had in the industry, most companies eventually became concerned by the possibility that the Internet could undermine their profits. Images, video, music, and text can all become digitized and delivered cheaply over the Internet. Many also saw a huge opportunity to become leaders in this newly forming industry.

Disney spent a large amount of money during the period. It bought Infoseek, a search engine like Yahoo!, as late as November 1999. It launched Go.com, which had losses over $1 billion in fiscal year 1999 after $991 million of losses the previous year. Disney also built EPSN.com and ABCNews.com. To explain Disney's strategy, Eisner said in 2000, "I don't know where all of this is going to end. I know only one thing: We are going to be there technologically."[71]

Edmund Sanctis was senior vice-president and general manager of NBC Digital Productions and deeply involved in many of the company's interactive initiatives including its partnership with Microsoft to launch the new cable channel and website MSNBC. He noted, "The urgency was accentuated by the competitive landscape. Fox, Disney—you had this view on the competition, they would have an announcement and you would feel like you have to react. You looked at Yahoo! building Yahoo! Finance into the leading finance presence online and we're here with CNBC thinking well, hell, what are we going to do? How do we make them come to CNBC online? People were working at hyperspeed because there was so much money to be made. There was a gold rush mentality—I got to get my stake. I need to get it, or someone else will take it from me."[72]

The music industry was perhaps most at risk by online services such as CDNow.com and MP3.com. Eventually the industry's worst nightmare arrived in the form of Napster, enabling consumers to share millions of songs over the Internet *free*. Start-ups were bought at incredible valuations by music companies afraid for their core business and who saw a potential great new market. Bertlesmann bought CDNow for $117 million. Vivendi in turn paid $372 million for MP3.com. Both failed.

Strauss Zelnick, the CEO of BMG (the music division of Bertlesman) was no stranger to the promise of interactive media and start-up culture, having run Crystal Dynamics, a gaming company in 1993. He was an enthusiast of the Internet. He had drunk the "Kool-Aid," he said. But he also had a no-nonsense approach to business. Despite this, he said, during the bubble the pressures were hard to resist. Regarding one of his investments, he said, "At one point the CEO came into my office and said in order to make this big we need to be offering this service *for free* to increase customers. I said, 'How are we going to make money?' He said, 'Well, we're going to upsell them premium services. Once they are customers.'"

Zelnick wanted to see an analysis of how this would really lead to a growth in customers that would generate profits. But the reply was, "Now the most important thing is to grab land. And if we don't grab it someone else will. And Wall Street is paying for a land grab and we need to do it because Wall Street is telling us to do it and if we don't do it, someone else will do it."

This didn't sit comfortably with Zelnick, but in the end he complied. "I'm a very rational guy, and I thought that was kind of nonsense, but I did it. I did it because eventually, if everyone else is doing it, it is very difficult to maintain your discipline."[73]

Thomas Middlehoff was brought in to head Bertelsmann in part to be the New Economy guru. His mission was to change the course of the 150-year-old company and bring it into the digital age. It was quite an undertaking, especially when the dimensions of the digital age were so unclear. Middlehoff was far more enthusiastic than Zelnick was. "At one point Middlehoff came to me and said 'You're not spending enough money on digital music,'" Zelnick remembered. "'You need to spend $1 billion.' I was spending under $50 million. I didn't have a good use for the other $950. I couldn't do it. He thought we had to be more aggressive."[74]

Perhaps one of the most dramatic examples was the merger between Time Warner and AOL. It was an extraordinary feat. At the time, many heralded the move as a brilliant combination of the best of the old and new economies, while others saw it as the disaster it turned out to be. But the driving motive for Time Warner appeared to be competitive pressures and fear of being left behind in the New Economy. The market, Gerry Levin thought, was not valuing Time Warner fairly amid its frenzy for digital companies, saying in an internal memo, "We all feel a degree of frustration at the failure of the market to value our company in a way that approximates its superior worth."[75]

According to one source reported in *Stealing Time*, a book about the merger of AOL and Time Warner, "Board members felt an enormous amount of pressure. The feeling was Time Warner was lacking a strategy in the digital world."[76]

For Steve Case, founder of AOL, it represented not a remarkable achievement to embrace the New Economy but a perfectly timed escape from the bubble. Others in AOL thought that merging with Time Warner was *a step down*. They didn't need such an Old Economy behemoth on their backs. But Case reportedly explained in a meeting defending the merger that he thought the Internet and especially rickety dot.coms were already overvalued by hype and were destined to crash. The crash would take AOL with it. As a result, he thought it strategically important to lock in the inflated valuation of AOL through a stock transaction with Time Warner. It was all about "Capital preservation," he said.[77]

Jim Lessersohn noted that the public attention added to the difficulty of making effective investment decisions. "People felt they had to make bets and were very visibly making bets," he said. The results were that the perception of risk became distorted. "There is safety in numbers. So if you're doing what everyone else is doing and you're wrong, it's a lot easier to explain than if you are doing something different and you're wrong. If you put in too much too early—everyone loses faith and then it is impossible to gear up when you have to. If you put in too little too late then you've failed before you start. Putting the right amount in at the right time is very much an art—not a science."[78]

The telecommunications industry faced a wide array of challenges during the second half of the 1990s. Only some of this challenge was related to the Internet bubble. The Telecommunications Act of 1996 further deregulated the industry after the 1984 act broke up the AT&T monopoly. The resulting competition on top of the already hyperactive mania generated by the Internet was intense. One of the biggest investment decisions connected to the Internet bubble was the building out of fiber-optic cables and the upgrading of cable systems to handle what was projected to be enormous demands for data, music, and video over the network. Similarly, wireless networks were established to serve the emerging cell phone customer base and create the ability to deliver the Internet everywhere.

The old sources of revenue were also potentially in jeopardy. For example, faxes, once 50 percent of international phone revenue, were largely replaced by e-mail attachments.[79] The sheer size of the telecommunications industry and the amount of money needed to build large-scale network infrastructure meant that the "telecom bubble" dwarfed the "dot.com bubble" although both were related to the anticipated Internet future.

A race was on to serve those new customers, handle that new traffic, and seize the revenue opportunities. Numerous start-ups emerged to build out capacity—in the end, far too many start-ups and far too much capacity. But many companies quickly went IPO at tremendous valuations and became formidable financial players. Incumbents also built capacity and upgraded their systems to serve the anticipated demand driven by Internet portals, commerce, and video streaming. "AT&T was spending $8 billion a year during the bubble. It was building new fiber, new IP networks, hosting centers and lots of local fiber rings, driven by new business opportunity around internet and local services," said Dave Dorman, the current CEO of AT&T. [80]

But as it turns out, the data this spending was based on was Internet hype. "The great variable—our forecasts," lamented Michael Armstrong, the CEO of AT&T during this time, "both in the industry and at AT&T in '98, '99, and 2000 were always wrong. [The forecasts] were always much more bullish than how reality turned out to be."[81] The result was massive overspending by corporations and far too many start-ups, which created a glut in the network that will remain for many years.

In addition to miscalculating the demand for the Internet, however, the competitive environment also created an imperative to make large investments in speculative endeavors. "We didn't have a choice," Armstrong noted, "because we had a $35 billion business with 30 percent margin in which we were the brand of choice in both the consumer and business market. So, our flexibility in deciding what to do was limited. We couldn't just wait. What would happen if we waited? All of the new guys would take our business from us."

A top-level telecommunications consultant explained the industry this way: "The new technologies are real, those are not made up. The technological opportunities created the ability to move information so cheaply, it's very difficult to keep up. What you would have liked to have done, if you could, is you would like to say, let's not push this quite so fast, let's slow this down, let's slow the rate of product generation. Competitive market cannot do that, because if you're not going to put your router out, someone else damn sure [is] going to put theirs out there. So, you basically run as fast as the technological performance trajectory enables it in a competitive economy and before you know it you over achieve it relative to demand."

This dilemma was part of the competitive dynamic in the marketplace at the time, across the board. In some cases, according to one consultant, there was growing awareness that the bubble was creating too much capacity in the nation's network, which would eventually go bust and leave a massive oversupply. "In private some people would say, we've run the numbers and this looks like an accident waiting to happen and they'd say, 'I'm running into an oversupply situation.' If you are leading a big company, unfortunately you're in the game and you have to play. I think the perception incumbents was, Jesus, this doesn't make a lot of sense but it persisted long enough that people genuinely begun to fear it may not make sense but my company will be taken over while we're working this out."

―――――――――――――

The banking industry was also significantly impacted. With the growth of ATM usage already established, moving banking online seemed like a natural expansion. Similarly, brokerage services could be replaced by on-line stock trading. Whether it was the teller in a consumer bank or a broker on the phone, these intermediaries between the customers and the business were suddenly perceived as unnecessary business expenses. Those jobs, it was thought, could be much more efficiently done online, which would provide faster and better service for customers. Those jobs would be disintermediated—removed from the process. This seemed to open a tremendous opportunity for start-ups to capture customers and offer them various banking services. For existing banks, the threat and opportunity appeared enormous.

Maziar Dalaeli of DeutscheBank said bankers were "Frightened by being put out of business by a couple of geeks in a garage, [and could] steal billions of revenues. A few companies were becoming threats. It was the pattern of every single investment bank. They were spending $100 million because of the threats and they wanted to see what was going on. Goldman, Morgan Stanley, poured huge amounts into silly stories, but that was the pattern of behavior. MyCFO and Jim Clark were seen as a big threat. We all had Amazon in mind. Barnes and Noble could be out of business, Yahoo! could buy Disney."[82]

Tim Mullany, of JP Morgan's Venture arm, Lab Morgan, remarked, "JP Morgan missed the Schwab boat. We were worried that Schwab could buy us. And eTrade, ameritrade were eroding our brokerage margins."

Jack Welch for years considered the Internet a mere "popcorn stand" that wasn't worth his attention as the head of a multi-billion dollar company. But by January 1999, he turned around, launching a companywide initiative called DYB ("Destroy Your Business"). The idea was to destroy your own business with innovation before an Internet start-up did it for you. The process was focused on determining where the Internet could cut costs, improve customer service and productivity in every business unit before a start-up could take advantage of this opportunity. Part of the exercise involved imagining how an Internet start-up could compete and erode GE's customer base and develop an effective response before the scenario played itself out in reality. Describing the imperative, Welch commented at the time, "we've got to break this company to do this—there's no discussion, we've just got to break it."[83]

By December 2000, Welch told *Newsweek* that GE was buying $6 billion in materials that year through online auctions and saving $1.2 billion using the Internet to increase efficiency. The company also had $13 billion in online sales.[84]

In addition to large strategic spending, another common investment was the "hedge" or "insurance policy" investment. Strategic investments were spent defending the perception that a corporation's core business might be under direct attack. Insurance policy investments were put into more uncertain and speculative endeavors. In the whirlwind of change, no one knew what would be a threat and what would be a passing fad.

AT&T's investment of $1 billion in Net2Phone was an insurance policy, according to Michael Armstrong, CEO at the time. The possibility loomed for Armstrong and others that portals might to take over the world, including handling voice phone calls. Net2Phone offered an early technology to be able to do this and had contracts with the most important portals, Yahoo, AOL, and MSN, to handle voice calls through their websites. AT&T was concerned that the Internet could become the network of choice for handling phone calls and the company needed to be able to benefit if that happened. "We did it because we weren't sure. Our thinking was, if it takes off it will be with AT&T. If it doesn't take off, then we may lose on our investment but we had protected our business." In the end, Net2Phone went out of business in part because the speed at which consumers shifted their calling to the Internet was far slower than anticipated by some.

During the radio mania, indeed, Wall Street also penalized the incumbent cable companies in anticipation of being overturned by wireless. The *New York Times* reported on December 22, 1901, "The fall in securities of cable companies, which commenced with the success of Marconi's experiments in having signals transmitted across the ocean by his wireless system of telegrapy has been continuous throughout the week." Anglo-American dropped 7 points between December 14 and December 22. This Wall Street pressure continued with similar commentary as cable companies dismissed the technology. Indeed, Wall Street seems to repeatedly, but falsely, anticipate the imminent demise of incumbent companies. At the time, few guessed that radio would become its own broadcasting system rather than undercutting voice calls from cable companies.

DISTORTED COMPETITIVE ENVIRONMENT

Large businesses are used to operating according to familiar principals. But many technology bubbles force existing companies to respond. In the 1980s, IBM had to respond to the arrival of Apple Computer. At the beginning of the twentieth century, AT&T tried to respond to the arrival of radio, thinking that it could compete with telephone service by delivering two-way communications. Canal companies tried to respond to the arrival of railroads. However, companies trying to assess their newfound competition from start-ups face some unusual market distortions as a result of bubbles. Their newfound competition does not operate in normal competitive environments.

Start-ups during the Internet bubble, for example, were largely funded by venture money and benefited from bubble valuations if they were public. This freed them from operating like normal competitive enterprises and enabled them to be purely expansionary organizations regardless of the economics. Such an artificially supported competitor can pose serious damage to large companies. "A competing business does not have to be profitable to do damage," remembered Jim Lessersohn, "Even if their business models didn't make any sense, the dot.coms had all this money to throw at the market."[85]

In order to compete in this bubble market, many large companies ended up taking on initiatives that they would not have otherwise and tried to execute them too fast in order to keep up. Some might call this an improved competitive environment that forced sluggish behemoths from their comfortable posture. While partially true, the result was also that many companies ended up spending too much too fast, thus expanding the bubble. Ideally, an intense competitive environment forces all companies to become more innovative, effective, and efficient. Bubble competition, however, also forces companies to invest in foolish endeavors.

Dave Dorman put it this way: "The market hysteria, the euphoria, distorts management thinking. It causes rational people to do riskier things than they would and it is usually because they don't understand. They can't extrapolate, can't see through the clouds—and the price of being wrong either way is dramatic."[86]

Another distortion in the competitive market was that the risks associated with venture funded start-ups and large companies are asymmetric. The risks of failure for a large company and its managers are far larger than for start-ups. "If you were a 24-year-old dot.com entrepreneur, and you were not the first mover, you could fail and all you lost was whatever money was put in, which was probably someone else's money anyway," pointed out Lessersohn. "If you're working at a newspaper company that is a hundred and fifty years old, you don't want to be featured in the last chapter of the company's history. In this case, the penalty for being wrong if it works seems much greater than the penalty for being wrong if it doesn't work."[87]

Tim Mullany of Lab Morgan expressed the attitude of many young entrepreneurs and newly minted MBAs during the day: "Who cares if the bubble bursts—if this blows up I can do something else. You could blame the market."

A positive effective of this can be that start-ups can take more risks that make them more innovative. A negative effect can be that it compels everyone to spend recklessly.

The competitive cascade shifts the way businesses and investors of various kinds understand risk and opportunity. There are powerful incentives to jump in and reap great rewards, and there are also powerful pressures forcing everyone to play in the mania. The perceived risks of investing become warped because many investors are no longer focused on the analytical merits of a specific deal. The risks of investment decisions become loaded with factors related to the distorted competitive environment of the bubble. Since this distortion occurs systematically across many investment decisions, across notable segments of the economy, the entire competitive marketplace becomes warped.

Another advantage public start-ups possessed was paper-power. That is, inflated prices of their stock that they could be used as currency.

Sketchy business plans, could become substantial competitors in the industry by using their inflated stock price to acquire real assets. Perhaps the most striking example of this was WorldCom.

COMMON INNOVATION

The continuous search for competitive returns is not the source of the problem. What happens during bubbles, however, is that the normal competition becomes a cascade of investments in very similar opportunities. There emerges a more homogenous view about how to achieve great returns.

In normal business conditions, competition and innovation are fragmented throughout the economy as each company faces its own competitive struggle. In normal business conditions, competition breeds innovation. Efforts at identifying great investment opportunities focus on identifying or creating value where others have not.

During technology bubbles, innovation affects businesses across the board in similar ways. Innovation is less fragmented; it becomes more homogenized because the same technology is sweeping across numerous businesses. Each business can tweak the new technology, but the real innovative benefits occur with real learning after the bubble, not during the mania. While bubble periods feature extreme innovations, many investments are, as we've heard so many times already, merely copycat efforts.

When a new technology that is widely available, like the Internet, is introduced, the benefits of the investments in that technology do not accrue to that firm alone. The benefits go to everyone—or even to the economy as a whole. Those investments do not bestow competitive advantage because everyone has them. In fact, investing in the new technology becomes not an advantage but a requirement for everyone to remain as competitive as everyone else. The entire playing field has been technologically elevated.

Imagine if the baseball commission relaxed its rules preventing batters from using corked bats. The new bats introduced into the game are like new technology. If the Yankees pick up the corked bats and start hitting more home runs, they will not necessarily win more games because the teams they compete against also have these bats. In fact, once the bats are allowed, everyone has to use them or risk losing. Along the way the game is changed. With so many more home runs, baseball scores would start looking like basketball scores. Strategies would shift. The short-stop would diminish in importance while the outfielders would become critical. Some in the audience might feel that the game is more exciting. Others might bemoan the loss of the traditional style of baseball.

The same dynamic occurs when transformative technologies are widely introduced to everyone in the marketplace. This is not to say that tremendously profitable companies cannot emerge out to the wreckage that is left when bubbles burst. eBay, Apple Computer, Ford Motors are all remarkably profitable businesses for a period of time that shaped their industry as they were creating it. But overall, while bubble investments always try to become the "next Apple computer," they are more likely to be investments in copycats, illegitimate investments, or legitimate business opportunities but offered at excessive prices.

SHIFTING AWAY FROM COMPETENCE TO CHASE PROFITS

A fascinating side effect emerged as a result of the competitive cascade. Venture capitalists, start-ups, corporate activity, and the public markets all warped their traditional ways of operating and converged toward the most efficient way to gain access to the fastest profit potential available in the of the frenzy. The stock market began acting more like venture capitalists because it was providing public money to early—if not seed—stage companies. Venture capitalists and entrepreneurs in turn were increasingly acting more like the stock market by shifting from the traditional approach of building long-term companies to building companies that can be quickly flipped into the public market. A number of start-ups became packaged assets with no real underlying business to be marketed to the public. Many firms of various sizes changed their business to gain proximity to the potential riches.

Geoff Yang noted that a lot of venture investors eventually asked the question, "'What is the market interested in buying either through acquisition or through a public offering?' And then people started that company. There were a bunch of reinforcing data points for that behavior. People started thinking about projects that could be quickly acquired or taken public without thinking about how to build a business—build to flip versus build to last."[88]

Increasingly venture capitalists were funding companies for the primary purpose of *marketing* those firms to the public.

The public markets, however, were also increasingly acting like venture capitalists because they were buying companies and bidding up valuations on untested business concepts.

In an internal Morgan Stanley memo, Mary Meeker referred to the public markets as "unprecedented low-quality, venture capital style public market financing volume."[89]

In a separate memo she explained that Morgan Stanley needed to manage this market carefully. "It is critical for us to identify companies at early stages of development . . . in this unusual period of Internet 'public venture capital' the decisions to determine which companies to support are very difficult . . . we need to continue to improve our decision making process/judgment."[90]

An investment banker commented on the strange shift in the public markets: "I was in essence a late-stage venture guy. If the markets are that overheated and receptive to accepting growth companies before they are really seasoned, then the public is saying they are willing to take that kind of risk. As a banker your job is to essentially tell a company whether that window exists for you."[91]

Companies of various sorts also distorted their business practices and strayed, and in some cases strayed very far, from their core competency. One of the most remarkable examples of this was Vivendi. Jean Marie Messier joined Générale des Eaux as chairman and CEO in 1996 and renamed it Vivendi. He set a course for the company to become "the world's preferred creator and provider of personalized information, entertainment, and services to consumers anywhere, at any time, and across all platforms and devices"[92]

However, despite this grand vision to seize the future, the company was rooted since 1853 in water and sewage utility under Napoleon III. Over many years it grew into a conglomerate with far-flung interests in environmental services and a cable channel, but little experience with the roller coaster ride of the high tech frontier and innovation. Remarkably, through the sheer force of desire and lavish spending on acquisitions, Messier was able to build the world's second-largest media group, at least for a period of time.

In December 2000, he spent $34 billion in an all-equity acquisition of Seagram, the Canadian liquor group that owned the entertainment company Universal—which included a film studio, movie and television archives, theme parks, the world's largest music company, and a part of USA Networks. They paid 21 percent more than the Seagram's stock value at the time. They bought MP3.com, a music downloading site, for $372 million and Houghton Mifflin, a U.S. publisher, for $2.2 billion. In late 2001, Vivendi bought the remaining part of USA Networks as well as Sci-Fi and USA channels for $10.3 billion.

Vivendi also owned Canal Plus, a leading European pay-TV company; a number of telephone operators in France and Havas publishing, which was a leading French publisher that Vivendi purchased in 1997.

How this patchwork of acquisitions scattered around Europe and the United States was going to effectively work together much less build toward Messier's vision, much less compete against behemoths like Viacom, AOL Time Warner, and Disney was not at all clear.

Perhaps most strangely, many of these acquisitions were taking place just as the market was beginning its slide. On July 3, 2002, the Vivendi board finally ousted Messier. By late 2003, NBC bought most of the entertainment assets of Vivendi for far less than Vivendi paid just a few years ago. NBC paid just $3.4 billion in cash and assumed $1.7 billion in debt.

The Vivendi story is unusual in its scale and in how late in the bubble some of the biggest deals were done. But the drive to ignore standard business principals and stray far away from core competence in order to chase after the apparent profits generated by the frenzy was fairly common.

Nearly every consulting firm, whether equipped or not, began an Internet practice of some kind in order to serve immense demands of the new industry. Often fees were paid in equity in the hopes of striking it rich through a well-timed IPO.

This dynamic appears to be common. During the PC bubble, companies such as Matel and Timex explored making computers. During the auto craze, car manufacturers included bicycle companies. The frenzy is so alluring during bubbles, that every business wants to participate and will ignore basic business principals to do so.

ENDLESS MONEY AND THE DECLINE OF RISK

The incredible returns of bubble companies attracted a lot of money. The venture capital funds expanded and new venture firms emerged to channel the capital that the existing funds turned away. The public markets also swelled with people putting money into individual stocks, growth funds, and increasingly fast emerging tech funds. This capital found its way into various businesses new and old that were perceived as being on the forefront of the new economy. Connecting young start-ups on the frontiers of new technology to the incredible voltage of public market provides access to vast sums of money. As big as the venture industry has become, it still does not compare to the public market that can channel tens of billions into funds and stocks on a monthly basis.

When venture firms go out to raise money for a new fund, they typically have a cadre of limited partners and others they can call. During the bubble, demand was so high among limited partners who wanted to share in the fabulous returns that most funds had to turn away money rather than actively recruit new investors.

"We've been so successful. It was so easy to raise the money," remembered Tom Perkins. "We raised money in days over the telephone from our existing investors. We have been compounding—for 30 years roughly 40 percent. During the bubble, our more recent partnerships were compounding 100 to 200 percent annually. Those numbers were real. The value wasn't but the numbers were."[93]

VCs were increasingly encouraged to make bigger, bolder investments. The flood of money available created distorted incentives and made many investments seem practically risk-free.

Geoff Yang saw a noticeable shift in venture deals that were being funded. "Normally, venture capitalists guide start-ups by saying, 'Don't try to boil the ocean, start with something small and manageable and in your control in bite-sized pieces.'"[94]

By contrast, Yang saw this as a period of time when "if you tried to boil the ocean, it was—the bigger, the bolder [the] idea—the more interesting it was to investors, to potential management and corporate partners."[95] The shift among investors to maximize boldness as a way to maximize returns was based on real experience—real, at least, in the bubble environment. "It started off with a couple of very intriguing companies that would experience rapid success, and every time you stepped out further and further with something that was a little bit more ambitious and a little bit wilder, it would succeed bigger," Yang said. "The whole phenomenon fed on itself. The success indicator, initially, was massive growth in users and revenues. And then stock price. That kind of kept feeding itself to more and more intangible metrics. As long as you could tell a story about how this could get big, then people would really get interested and towards the end of the mania—it was big just to be big—without ever thinking about should a stock price have some correlation to the discounted value of future cash flows. That kind of went out the window towards the end in favor of—just show me how it gets big. There was a feeling that there was a real land-grab mentality that the investors as well as the companies—if we can be the biggest one and fastest growing, we will figure out a way to monetize that position and revenues and subsequently profits."[96]

Furthermore, venture capitalists have a great luxury in the pipeline of money flows. They enjoy remarkable position regarding risk, at least when there is a seemingly endless supply of capital for future funds. To put this in striking context, Benchmark capital's $3 million investment at the early stages of eBay led to over $4 billion returned in disbursements to its limited partners. Certainly, eBay is an extraordinary case, but that single hit would make up for many flops. Indeed, $4.5 billion would pay for 1,333 flop investments of $3 million. The comparison isn't fair, since VCs do not use those returns for making new investments; they give them back to their limited partners. But this comparison is nevertheless instructive. Single blockbusters pay for all the other very poor investments in start-ups that go out of business. Every individual investment is extraordinarily risky, because start-ups usually fail. Funds as a whole, which consist of many start-ups, *appear* to be far less risky than the public markets relative to their high rate of return, certainly during bubbles.

So far, the venture industry as a whole has not had a single year showing losses. Compared to the public market for stocks, that is extraordinary. Those losses may be fast approaching for the first time and may be large as the Internet bust ripples through their portfolios. Funds that started in the last years of the bubble and invested in the many start-ups that are now out of business or missed out on the IPO window may become the first to show loses. For these funds that started in the waning years of the bubbles, all of their companies may have gone out of business or their stock price dropped to extraordinary lows. This reality of venture risk can drive reckless spending during bubbles when money is so freely available.

It was this risk profile during bubbles that enabled venture funds to invest in start-ups that had slim prospects. Bob Kagle explained the dynamic this way: "Since capital was essentially free it created this environment where people were literally willing to throw caution to the wind in pursuit of some collection of metrics which they could promote to the investment community and give them greater access to capital. There was such demand. Anytime you are taking companies public that were less than 2 years old and don't even have solid revenue models, much less profitability, and you are getting paid 50 times your investment to do that—it would take super-human discipline to say no, thanks. That is more than you could expect from anyone."[97]

Funds can do poorly if there are no home runs, and many of the companies that receive funding go out of business during a bust. But during bubbles the opposite is true. Just about any firm seemed to generate fabulous returns. Savvy fund managers saw the public market valuations of start-ups as excessive and expected a downturn. But even if the valuations dropped by half, they still came out ahead on their initial investments. The big shock to venture funds during the bust was that even their most dour estimates of how far things could drop were not low enough.

"The prices of public stocks were trading up to were too high. The purchase prices by large companies were too high. What we were saying is that we can buy at a deep discount to that so we can make a whole of money. What we didn't appreciate was the fact that these prices could come down by a factor of 5 to 10 rather than a factor of 2," commented a venture capitalist.[98]

When infant companies growing in bubbles are suddenly able to raise huge amounts of money not just from venture capital firms but also on a far bigger scale than the public markets, their methods of operation become warped and self-destructive. During normal periods, it typically takes 4 years or so for a company to reach a level at which it might raise additional cash by issuing shares to the public market. At this point in its development, it is looking to expand its operations in some way and has already gone through several periods of performance that can be analyzed. The management, business model, and market all have some history that can be used and gauged to determine the fair value of the new issues of stock.

Bubbles short-circuit that process, enabling infant companies with no history of performance to draw additional money from the vast resources of the general public. This makes it pretty easy for start-ups to be valued with metrics of enthusiasm rather than realistic future business performance.

Not only does this create froth in the public markets, but it also creates froth within those businesses that become elevated by massive market capitalization and cash. Even worse, many start-ups have easy access to secondary offerings, creating the perceptions that capital will be endlessly available. As a result, their approach to the risks of running their own business becomes warped.

Bill Hambrecht bemoaned the corrosive effect this perception of endless money had on running new businesses: "It was a presumption that if this company has what I think it does technically, they can raise as much money as they need. So people didn't pay any attention to what was on the balance sheet. It was an assumption that the market would continue to give them the money they needed."[99]

As a result of such a seemingly endless supply of money, businesses operating in a bubble are encouraged to create unsustainable strategies and practices. One of the most notable examples of this was Webvan.

Webvan was able to raise $1 billion in venture capital to provide on-line delivery service of groceries. The plan was to build from scratch a national network of warehouses and logistical operations to deliver groceries from online orders. The core business idea of online orders of groceries was unproven. In fact, experimenting with a similar service in the Midwest, Krogers found that the initiative could not become profitable and shut it down.

After the bubble, it seems like insanity that such an unproven idea could have attracted so much money. However, it attracted some of the most sophisticated venture capitalists and business managers. Sequoia Capital and Benchmark were the earliest investors. George Shaheen, former CEO of Anderson Consulting, was recruited to head the start-up.

Benchmark and Sequoia Capital, as early investors, put in only a few million dollars. But excitement was extremely high for the venture and for the stellar team that was assembled. Excitement ran high despite the complete lack of evidence that the business was viable, much less worth the amount invested or capable of demonstrating a notable return. Subsequent investors joined on terms far less favorable and far more risky than those enjoyed by Benchmark and Sequoia. It is hard to imagine how the core business of Webvan, delivering groceries, could ever create high returns on the $1 billion that was invested. Bob Kagle explained the logic used by those who invested on riskier terms this way: "You look at the market cap of Wal-Mart and you say why isn't Webvan the new age Wal-Mart? That can be a very difficult argument to lose in this environment." Kagle added, "People aren't forecasting on the risk in that environment. They are just projecting rosy scenarios, and no one is looking at the thorny scenarios. The notion of a rosy scenario leads you to even further detachment from reality."[100]

The sense of endless capital affected every business decision at Webvan, from buying staplers to choosing warehouse expansions to establishing complex logistics support.

Webvan, as could have been expected, ran into innumerable logistical and operational challenges. The managers learned, further, that the business of delivering groceries is very hard to bring to scale quickly. It needs to grow organically and slowly in order to insure that there are enough customers and deliveries to pay for all those costs. The new CEO who replaced Shaheen, Robert Swan, demonstrated clearly how the warped bubble environment undermined the company's ability to make sound business decisions. "We made the assumption that capital was endless and demand was endless," he said.[101] The firm folded on July 9, 2001.

After the bubble burst, the core idea of Webvan reemerged locally on smaller scales in parts of the country. Now growing organically are Fresh Direct in New York and Simon Delivers in Minneapolis, which serve only a handful of Zip codes. Right now they seem like profitable businesses.

While Webvan represents a single case of these bubble business dynamics on an extraordinary scale, a similar dynamic affected every Internet start-up in almost any decision it made.

"We were a victim of the times," commented Michael Moritz on the environment. "The world was rewarding us for raising $250 million and penalizing [us for] raising $25 million. Plaudits were given to expanding nationwide rather than regionally. Daring to be great overweighed being cautious."[102]

Bubble environments regularly and systematically distort the business incentives for everyone in the market. At the time, a growing number of start-ups were paying for time during the Super Bowl in order to capture customer attention. "If everyone is behaving irrationally by buying Super Bowl ads, then you have to as well," Peter Sisson, founder of Wineshopper.com, said. "It's an unvirtuous circle. Capital was not an issue, there was an endless supply. The only mistake could be not to be equipped to serve customers."[103]

Another example of the destructive effects of so much money was that companies sold goods at unsustainably low prices—or even gave it away for free. The idea was that start-ups would keep prices low to attract customers at a significant loss in the hopes that companies could turn a profit by raising prices once the customers were "locked in." Don Valentine lamented that a "group bought into this concept that if you gave it away to enough people, somehow the business model would work. What made it difficult to realize that it wasn't true was that money was fairly free."[104]

For example, OnSale announced in January 1999 that it would launch a service called "atCost," which would offer a broad selection of computer items at wholesale prices. The company expected to make money from advertising. Buy.com launched a similar effort on a broader array of items from computers to books to music.

Kagle noted that when so much money floods the system, "the need for focus dissipates. You don't really have to make something work in order to get the next traunch of capital. All you have to do is promote and create the perception that there is momentum."[105]

UrbanFetch and Kozmo.com both planned a service of 1-hour delivery of videos, food, and other goods. They hoped that initial sales of cheap products would lead consumers increasingly to buy more expensive products like electronics. To attract customers, delivery was free, tips were not accepted, and for long periods of time, many products were sold at a discount.

These efforts were possible only so long as these start-ups received money from venture capitalist funds because they could not be supported by normal business economics. Both started fairly late in the game. As a result, the slide that began in March 2000 closed for them the possibility of going IPO and getting significant public money to maintain their unsustainable practices. With the IPO window closed, the possibility of future venture rounds also quickly evaporated. Both businesses failed.

"When you are in business at some point the business needs to support its own growth," commented Alan Patricof. "Here the only thing supporting the company was raising additional rounds of capital. You can't sustain any company, I don't care who it is, with continued raising of equity capital because at some point someone wakes up and says the emperor has no clothes on. All I am doing is funding losses."[106]

TIMING AND SPEED

Time and speed are key factors during bubbles. No one knows how long they will last. People involved in bubble markets are compelled to work fast to win the competitive race. During the 1980s, personal computer and software entrepreneurs were run ragged with limited sleep.

The same dynamics occurred during the Internet bubble. There were two powerful concepts that made speed a motivating factor in how investors perceived the potential for success. The most popular concept was "Internet speed." According to this idea, the Internet was making everything faster. In the digital world of bits and bytes moving through phone lines, cable lines, and the air, there was no friction that normally occurs in the physical world. Businesses did not need fixed assets, inventory, or in some cases even people, who slowed down the pace of operations, business growth, and the entire economy. In addition, since it appeared so easy to start an Internet company, it was essential to become the biggest first in order to beat out the competition. The idea was that the Internet was a giant "land grab" in which the most profits would be available to those start-ups who reaching a dominant market share first. Once scale was reached, the real business profits could follow, or so went the bubble logic.

It was known that there was an oversupply of start-ups. The copycat ventures meant that each of the competitors were vying to become one or two of the largest firms in their segment because it was thought that only those would survive and only those would benefit from high valuations in the public market.

"This is a new opportunity, the new players will take it all and now is the time to establish yourself as the number one player because you are not going to have room for 3 bookstores online," remembered Kairuz. "People realized you have limited timeframe to throw Barnes and Noble out of business. You had to capitalize the company very quickly, with a lot of money, to establish a brand, because it is all about branding and bringing traffic to the store, and quickly establish yourself as the number one player. The bankers were not interested in taking the number three player [public]."[107]

Webvan was also a victim of the drive for speed. Webvan's rush to go national instantly was motivated primarily by the fear that Amazon would seize the market before it did.

Value America was a notable example of the Internet speed/land grab myth. Value America was founded by a housewares salesman—the goal was to become Wal-Mart on the Internet, despite the fact that Wal-Mart was going online as well. Value America went public on April 8, 1999, at an opening price of $23, but rose to a high of $74.25. The core idea, in contrast to Wal-Mart's, is that it would carry no inventory—Value America wouldn't hold the things you bought from it. Instead, the company would simply connect consumer orders to manufacturers who would in turn ship directly to consumers. It was a classic example of a virtual company. It was "frictionless" since it never touched physical objects. It attracted top tier investors including Paul Allen and FedEx chairman Fred Smith. But Value America needed to move fast—too fast in the end. In the aftermath, Smith noted, "they got going too fast, they got unfocused."

The founder commented, "In the Internet world no one is willing to invest in a company moving slowly."[108] Reportedly in 1999 Value America spent $69.6 million on advertising alone—second only to E*Trade.

Alan Patricof said, "instead of taking time to nurture and develop and weed out companies, the good and the bad, venture capitalists were just much more aggressive in bringing companies to market that were not ready."[109]

One former VC, Michael Barach, put it more bluntly. "You could invest in a company, take it public and cash out before you proved your business model."[110]

Not everyone thought that access to huge amounts of money would last forever. A second concept related to Internet speed, more accurate but less well-known, was that the bubble was a window of opportunity available only to those who got in and out before it shut.

"One of [the bankers] said memorably in one of our meetings before we decided to go public, he said, 'Everyday that you go to bed without having taken a step getting you closer to becoming a publicly traded company is a wasted day,'" remembers Mark Walsh, founder of VerticalNet, an early high-flying business-to-business start-up. "There is a tunnel, and at some point the tunnel will collapse upon itself. Get in and out of the tunnel as fast as you can because you want to be on the other side of the tunnel because it will not remain forever. The bank said there is a finite number of dollars available for IPO investments and the earlier you ask for it the more you'll get and the tougher you'll make it for the competition when they ask for it. If I get my money and Purchase Pro doesn't, then I'm stronger and they're weaker."[111]

Tom Perkins has a fabulous track record for timing that window: "it's all timing—you've got to be out by the time it dawns on everyone that it was a tulip. You'd better plan on creating value on what you do rather than the hype around what you do. Now that is easy to say and hard to do. There has got to be a foundation under the thing, a product, service, something you can charge for—a real business."[112]

"I would call it making hay while the sun shines," commented Bob Kagle.[113]

Speed was generally accepted as essential. Those who viewed it as important because investors needed to "time the market" were proven correct in theory—although they may have timed it wrongly in practice. Most of those who viewed it as important because it was a land grab were proven fatally wrong.

In the end, the idea of Internet speed would prove to be one of the most destructive myths to investors and businesses alike. As fast as innovations appear, transformations take far longer to imbed themselves within consumer behavior or within every organization, let alone sweep across the economy. As the bubble began to crest, investors slowly realized that technology moves far faster than people. In the end, however, businesses can make money only by serving people not technology.

As we have seen, during bubbles three kinds of bad investments far outweigh the good investments. There are too many copycat investments that saturate the market, there are too many investments in poor business opportunities, and even the legitimate businesses suffer from excessive valuations. Each of these collectively means that more and more money is spent on unsustainable and unprofitable targets, ultimately insuring that the bubble will end in wreckage for most investors.

THREE

FOLLOW THE MONEY

Try not to become a man of success but rather to become a man of value.

—Albert Einstein

CAPITAL SPIRAL AND INFLATION

During bubbles, the distorted perceptions of investment opportunities and competitive pressures affect individual investors, fund managers, financiers of start-ups, and business managers. Collectively, these individuals' decisions and investments ripple through the entire economy. The competitive cascade creates a whirlpool, sucking in money that is chasing the highest available returns. The result is a self-reinforcing capital spiral in which the inflow of money increases the perceived returns, attracting more money, and inflating values further in a vicious cycle.

Bubbles suck capital away from other investment opportunities into an already saturated market. During the Internet bubble, it was much easier to raise money for a crazy dot.com than for a manufacturing plant. It was probably easier to raise money for a personal computer company than a plastics company during the 1980s. "Easier" means not just that there were more financiers available in the public and private market, but that those investments were done on more advantageous terms.

Financing start-ups

Overall, the money flowed through a fairly simple system during the Internet bubble. Limited partners such as pension funds, university endowments, and state investment boards invest money in a range of areas from stocks, bonds, and T-bills. A limited amount is invested in private equity and venture capital funds—typically just under 5 percent. The VCs use this money to make investments in start-ups. During bubble markets, venture firms can earn huge returns as start-ups go IPO or are acquired by other larger companies and they eventually disburse these returns to their limited partners. As the overall market increases in value, the limited partners find themselves, like everyone else, with a lot of money to invest. Even if they kept their 5 percent allocation to private equity, since they have more money, that same percentage channels more dollars. With more money flowing in venture funds, they were compelled to start more businesses in the anticipation that they will be able to produce the same astonishing returns. During this period, limited partners actually increase their allocations for venture deals generating even more inflows to venture funds. "Angel investors" also help dramatically increase the fund size of venture firms. Angels are wealthy individuals, often former entrepreneurs who are still interested in participating in innovation and making money. They can make substantial contributions to venture funds or start-ups.

The first venture capital firm was American Research and Development back in 1946, founded by Karl Compton, President of MIT, Harvard Business School Professor Georges F. Doriot, and a group of local business leaders. The industry as a whole, between 1946 and 1977, typically never exceeded a few hundred million dollars. In 1978, capital gains taxes were lowered, and the limits on how much pension funds could invest in venture firms were lifted. At this time, individuals accounted for 32 percent of the $424 million put into venture funds. Pension funds accounted for less than half as much. By 1984, the industry grew to $4 billion with pension funds accounting for more than half this total. Along with the high sums came deeper organizational infrastructure through limited partnerships. The entire venture industry did not invest more than $10 billion until 1995. In 1998, this grew to $31 billion and peaked

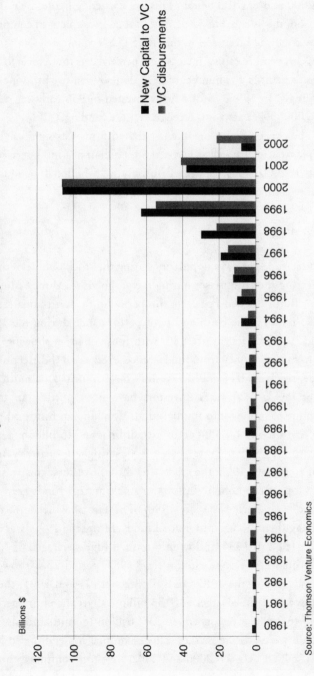

Money Goes In - Money Goes Out

Billions $

■ New Capital to VC
■ VC disbursments

Source: Thomson Venture Economics

in 2000 at over $100 billion. This is a staggering figure. By way of comparison, this is equal to 12 percent of total investment in equipment and software by all businesses in the entire U.S. economy.

With venture capital increasingly perceived as the vehicle to make the greatest returns, the number of deals done by venture firms increased accordingly. In 1995, venture firms invested in 956 early stage start-ups. By 2000, 3,491 start-ups received venture funding.

The concentration on Internet-related firms was significant. For example, venture capitalists invested $8.9 billion just in IT service companies in 2000 alone, compared to only $2.5 billion for industrial and energy companies, less than a third as much.

PUBLIC MARKETS

Mutual funds grew in popularity during the stock bubble of the 1960s, reflecting the enthusiasm during the go-go years. Money entering into stock funds reached a peak for this period in the fourth quarter of 1968 at $4 billion. The crash and poor performance during the 1970s left funds squandering until 1982, with most quarters showing investors withdrawing money from funds. Since 1982, with the exception of the 1987 stock market crash, investors have returned to mutual funds. Over the last 20 years, investors have been putting an increasing amount of money into mutual funds, reaching an historical record in the first quarter of 2000 at an extraordinary $375 billion. This represents $150 billion more than the next highest quarterly inflow of money in mid-1996 and, sadly for those investors, this was also the very top of the bubble. Inflows to stock mutual funds grew to enormous levels during the late 1990s. The rate at which investors were moving their money into mutual funds during the 1990s was amazing. From 1982 to 1995, inflow into mutual funds averaged $37.7 billion each quarter—even excluding the 1987 period that showed withdrawals due to the 1987 crash. Between 1995 and 2001, the average inflow was 4 times larger at $153 billion. Over the entire period from 1995 to 2001, investors added $3.7 trillion to mutual funds.

Sadly, even as the market value of mutual funds dropped by nearly $800 billion between 2000 and 2002, investors continued to add $1.3

WAVES OF FRENZY

Venture Capital Disturbsements as % Total By Indsutry

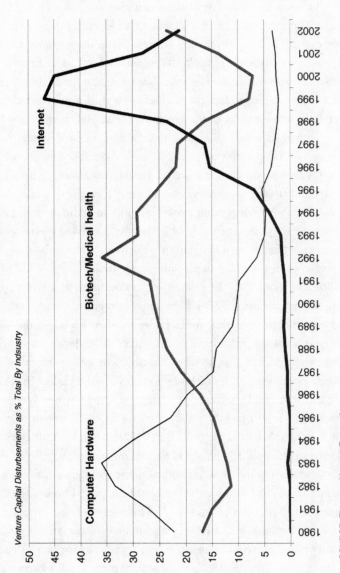

Internet

Biotech/Medical health

Computer Hardware

SOURCE: Thomson Venture Economics

trillion to mutual funds. Those investors, lured by the frenzy at just the wrong time, lost extraordinary amounts of money.

Mutual funds, particularly popular passive index funds, must maintain key allocations in order to replicate the market value they are indexed to. If fund managers think the overall market is overvalued there is not much they can do, so long as individuals keep giving them money to invest. When Yahoo! entered the S&P 500, generally S&P Index funds had to hold Yahoo! no matter how far managers thought it might drop later on. Even actively managed tech funds must invest their money in tech stocks even if the whole market is overvalued. As a result, inflow of money forces the purchase of stock that may already have inflated values, further putting upward pressure on prices. In both the public and private markets, the high returns, however artificial and unsustainable, generate more money and attract new money, which further fuels the system.

Investors were not putting money into just any mutual fund. Increasingly, over the course of the bubble they were steering their money to capture the highest returns found in growth and tech funds and moving their money out of poorly performing value funds.

Prior to July 1998, the inflows into value funds and growth funds were similar, averaging $2.3 billion going into growth funds per month and $2.2 billion into value funds. However, after this point, the inflows diverged. Between July 1998 and the end of 2000, inflows into growth funds averaged $11.2 billion per month compared to monthly *withdrawals* from value funds of $3.1 billion. Toward the peak of the bubble, investors were rapidly increasing the amount of money they were putting into growth funds. In July 1998, investors added $5 billion to growth funds; in October 1999 they added $10 billion, and by April 2000, they added a tremendous $35 billion in that month alone. Sadly for investors, they were putting the most amount of money into growth funds just as the bubble was about to burst. Over the entire period from July 1998 to December 2000, investors added $335 billion into growth funds.

Funds focusing exclusively on technology stocks also became extremely popular, attracting many investors and spurring many managers to set up new funds. In 1997, 10 new technology funds emerged and 8 opened in 1998. But by 2000, an incredible 79 technology funds were created—that is, more than one fund opening every week of that year.

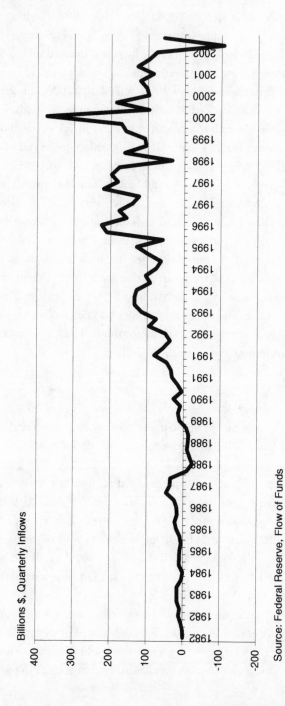

Investors Moving Money Into Mutual Funds

Billions $, Quarterly Inflows

Source: Federal Reserve, Flow of Funds

Between January 1993 and December 1998, monthly inflows into technology stock funds averaged $171 million. However, starting in January 1999, inflows to tech funds increased dramatically to $2 billion for that month alone and rose continuously, peaking at $13 billion in March 2000. Between November 1999 and March 2000, the very top of the bubble investors added $56 billion into tech-stock funds.

Even as the tech stocks started to slide, investors continued to add to their growth funds. From March 2000 through the end of the year, the NASDAQ dropped from a peak on March 10 of 5048.62 to 2052.72, while investors continued to add $122 billion into growth funds and $16 billion into tech stocks. It wasn't until February 2001 that investors began slowing new investments and withdrawing money from growth funds.

The capital spiral is common during bubbles. Those who finance start-ups overfund hot companies and underfund others. Investors become enamored of sector funds that seem to offer them targeted access to the skyrocketing shares while still claiming to be diversified across many shares. The personal computer bubble and biotech bubbles of the 1980s each created their own sector funds. The go-go years of the 1960s created funds focused on the high fliers.

INFLATION

The flood of money and competition for deals generated by the capital spiral leads to inflationary pressures on stocks, portfolios, and venture deals.

Even with corporate mergers and acquisitions activity, large companies faced rapidly rising prices of start-ups they were considering buying. Marty Yudkovitz noted, "We could never catch up—we'd make a bid [but] the price would just go higher. The speed was getting out of hand. . . . Couldn't get a deal closed. We thought a price might be ridiculous at $100 million, then we'd say okay but then it would come back at $200 million."[1]

When national economies face recessions, governments can try to stimulate growth by increasing the amount of money in the system. They do this by lowering interest rates; in the old days they printed money in order to stimulate growth. While the first effect tends to provide resumed

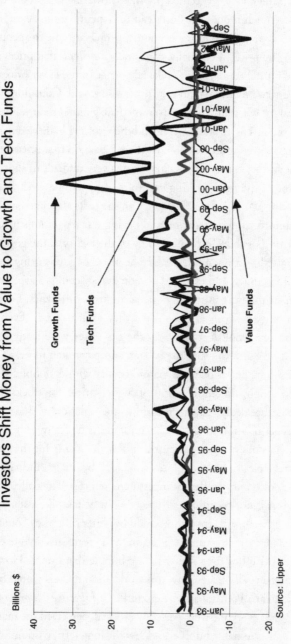

COMPETITIVE CASCADE

Investors Shift Money from Value to Growth and Tech Funds

Billions $

Growth Funds

Tech Funds

Value Funds

40

30

20

10

0

-10

-20

Jan-93
May-93
Sep-93
Jan-94
May-94
Sep-94
Jan-95
May-95
Sep-95
Jan-96
May-96
Sep-96
Jan-97
May-97
Sep-97
Jan-98
May-98
Sep-98
Jan-99
May-99
Sep-99
Jan-00
May-00
Sep-00
Jan-01
May-01
Sep-01
Jan-02
May-92
Sep-02

Source: Lipper

economic stimulus, sometimes a more powerful effect can be rising inflation. If the policy is executed poorly by lowering rates too much or printing too much money, this can lead to hyperinflation. As more and more
money is pumped into the economy, people are able to spend more, thus
driving up prices. Eventually, consumers *anticipate* that prices will increase
in the future. As a result, to take advantage of the lower prices today, they
rush out to buy more than they otherwise would. Consumers basically get
a discount when buying goods immediately rather than waiting until they
need them. The rush of buying and the resulting higher demand drives up
the prices even more, reinforcing the expectation that prices will be higher
in the future. It is a vicious circle that is very difficult to short circuit.

One of the most striking examples of hyperinflation was in Germany
following World War I. After the war, the costs associated with rebuilding
the country after destruction and paying war reparations made payments
nearly impossible. To finance some of these efforts, the government simply started printing money. With the prices of goods rising so fast, people
bought as much as they could as soon as they could to avoid much higher
prices in the near future. By one account from Keynes, Germans would
often buy two beers at once when they went to a bar. Even though the
second one would get warm by the time they were ready to drink it, it
would be worse to wait, buy it later, and pay much more.[2]

A similar inflationary dynamic occurs within bubbles. If it goes on
long enough, the anticipation of higher prices for stocks, acquisitions,
and venture deals will further add to the inflation of these prices.

Hyperinflation in national economies is typically caused by bad government policy. A single agent can bear the blame for the ensuing crisis.
Capital spirals, however, are generated by many individuals putting
money into many different investment vehicles. The collective activity of
investors is not coordinated. They do not behave like a single agent, such
as the government. Investors would be better off if they could collectively
moderate their investment positions and create sustainable profits over a
longer period of time rather than a bubble that bursts. However, efforts
to pull back all of these investment decision makers would be like trying
to herd cats. Political scientists call this a *collective action problem*.

Even if everyone were perfectly rational, perceived the market as being
in an unsustainable bubble, and saw the long term wisdom of collectively

pulling back, it is not in the interest of any single investor to do it alone or to be the first person or even among the first one hundred people to pull back. Those who do would be the first ones to lose out on the short-term sizable returns. Coordinating their activity for their collective self interest is impossible because their individual self-interest cannot be timed appropriately.

Also, government can learn from its mistakes and make a deliberate decision to avoid bad policies in the future. It is far harder for so many disparate actors to learn the same lesson and act accordingly.

In stark contrast to learning that prices can go *too* high, venture capitalists are trained during bubbles that the sky may be the limit given their special position in the risk pipeline. "If they paid 2 to 3 times what they should have paid, they are still making 50 times their money rather than one hundred fifty. So 50 times your money is still a pretty good return," noted Bob Kagle.[3]

Two economists proved this inflation effect on venture capital prices statistically between 1987 and 1995. Paul Gompers and Josh Learner found that the amount of money entering venture funds increased the valuations of new investments they made—even after adjusting for the quality of deals. The authors found the two primary drivers for increase private equity valuations were inflows into funds and rising public markets. A doubling of inflows into venture funds led to a 7 to 21 percent increase in valuation levels, while a doubling of the stock public market led to an increase of 15 to 35 percent. The public and private markets are intertwined through the capital spiral that fuels the system.[4]

In the first half of the 1990s, the average amount of money a venture fund invested in a start up was just $3.85 million. By 2000, the average amount invested by a VC into a start-up was $8.9 million—more than twice as much.

Competition for deals also intensified as the anticipation of increasingly higher IPO potential became apparent. There was so much venture capital chasing so few start-up opportunities—prices were bid up to extraordinary highs. In the stock market, investors were pilling billions of dollars into just a *relatively* small number of shares in Internet companies. In 1998, the typical Internet company sold off just 18 percent of the company when it went IPO. That was 10 percentage points fewer than non-Internet companies.[5]

Commenting on the public markets at the time, Henry Blodget said, "Never have there been so many investors chasing so few quality shares."

Data in this area can be sketchy. However, rough calculations using data from Comstock, indicate that there were less than 10 billion shares outstanding in 1999 among 215 Internet companies that were started by venture capitalists. But in that year alone, investors were piling $37 billion into tech funds and $108 billion into growth funds. Investors added another $52 billion into tech funds in 2000 and $210 billion in growth funds. That is a lot of cash chasing a handful of shares over a short period of time. It is worth noting that while it appears that the inflows into these funds accompanied price increases, the inflows continued at a similar pace even as share prices were declining precipitously from March 2000 onward. This indicates while investors inflows chasing a handful of shares may create inflationary pressures, inflows do not prevent a market collapse.

After the bubble, lawsuits were filed against brokerage firms and companies for artificially inflating IPO prices and giving preferential treatment to favored clients in exchange for fees or for agreements to purchase additional shares of the companies in the open market after the initial offering. On June 26, 2003, three hundred companies involved in selling new shares agreed to pay $1 billion unless a separate $1 billion lawsuit against the underwriters who took these companies public succeeded.[6] The specific IPOs implicated included Global Crossing, Akamai Technologies, Ask Jeeves, Copper Mountain Networks, eToys, and VA Linux.

The economic flow of funds becomes systematically distorted during bubbles, leading to inflationary pressures on the prices of investments in companies. The system is impossible to stop because the actors are fragmented and uncoordinated—following their own frenzied impulses and failing to realize that their collective actions are increasingly making their hot investments very bad bets.

BUBBLE DEMAND

As much as investment bubbles create frothy enthusiasm detached from fundamental business metrics, they also distort real business fundamentals. Revenues, profits, and strategic opportunities become temporarily inflated during bubbles because they are earned from "bubble demand." Even start-ups that shouldn't exist need to buy computers and advertising, hire consultants, and hire staff, and rent office space. Profits of all businesses grow, enabling the start-ups to invest more and spend more. Unfortunately, business managers expect this level of consumption to continue into the foreseeable future. They don't realize that the bubble will burst, destroying their rosy projection for future sales growth. Eventually, the bubble bursts, proving these projections dramatically wrong.

The railway mania, for example, produced massive demand for products and services in related industries. Steel, iron, and construction workers all benefited tremendously from the real business spending during that mania and suffered greatly when it collapsed.

Among the Internet companies started by venture firms that were publicly traded, spending for the goods that they sell (costs of goods sold) reached $13 billion in 2000. Their spending on general administration reached $15 billion, and working capital was clocked at $16 billion in that year. Spending on advertising alone reached nearly $2 billion. These publicly traded firms employed 117,000 people and had sales of $24 billion that year. These figures represented real economic metrics, not eyeballs or inflated bubble expectations. Moreover, they represent just the tip of the iceberg. Many more firms never made it to the public market, making their business data invisible. Their stimulative effect in the economy, however, was no less important.

According to one study by the Federal Reserve Bank, spending by new economy firms overall, not just public dot.coms, on things other than software rose from $83 billion in 1995 to $177 billion in 2000.[7] This represented a rise from 13 percent of all capital spending to 18 percent.

By 2000, final sales of computers, software and telecommunications contributed 1.48 points to the growth rate of 5 percent. This was a steady rise from 1995 of just 0.51 points.[8]

The rapid growth in spending generates real economic growth, but it can't last because many of the companies doing the spending are unsustainable. They can exist only in a bubble. All of the spending that went to pay for hardware, people, services, and office space was very vulnerable to the bubble bursting.

By 2002, 31,000 people were laid off from these venture-backed publicly traded firms alone. Sales declined by $1.4 billion, working capital plummeted by $7.4 billion, and costs of goods sold and sales and general administration expenses together dropped $5.3 billion.

In January 2000, only 1 Internet company had shut down, as reported by Webmergers, a research group that follows Internet companies. By May of that year, the pace started accelerating quickly, with 13 start-ups closing shop that month. By the end of the year, 283 had closed. Over the course of 2001, another 501 closed.[9]

Bubbles create demand for real things. As a result, it is not always easy to determine what business activity is related to bubble markets and what is related to sustainable business growth.

ECONOMIC CONTEXT

The overall economic context plays an important role in shaping the potential of bubbles. Bubbles tend to emerge in very positive economic growth and market conditions.

The broader economic context during the Internet bubble period created a foundation on which the bubble could be formed. During the 1990s, the economy grew for the longest continuous period in history. The international economic instability stemming from the Asian economic crisis in 1997, the Mexican and Russian debt crisis in 1998, and Long Term Capital and Management debacle of 1998, remarkably, did not have deep sustained impact on the US economy or the stock market. These events temporarily dented the market enthusiasm, but in the end, they did very little to stop the bubble.

The declining government deficit and a schedule to pay off all of the national debt entirely by 2015 helped create low interest rates that further fostered strong business investments. When businesses invest, they create future productivity gains. They also help create jobs, which improves consumer spending, which improves business revenues. In the past, rising inflation emerges, creating a dilemma for policymakers. If inflation gets too high, the economy suffers dramatically. In response, the Federal Reserve Bank typically raises interest rates, which makes various forms of borrowing and investment more expensive, thus slowing down the economy and lowering prices. But judging exactly how much to raise interest rates given the pace of inflation is impossible to know for certain, especially since there is a lag of about 6 to 9 months when any interest rate change ripples through the economy in any noticeable fashion. As a result, the Federal Reserve usually raises rates too much, thus making borrowing much more expensive than needed and sending the economy into a recession. The Federal Reserve left interest rates unchanged during most of the bubble. There was no sign of inflation.

But during this period, the economy demonstrated remarkable record-breaking measures. In 1999, core inflation was just 2.1 percent the lowest since 1965. The unemployment rate reached 4.0 percent in 2000, the lowest since 1969. The poverty rate dropped to just 11.3 percent in 2000, a low not seen since 1970. After nearly 30 years of continuous budget deficits, there were 2 years in a row of budget surpluses.[10]

During the period there was a growing focus in the economy on information technology—the shift to a New Economy was real. Business investment in equipment and software grew from 5 percent of GDP in 1990 to 9.4 percent in 2000, for a total of $919 billion. Between 1995 and 2000, roughly 30 percent of the growth in domestic income came from the information technology sector. Perhaps most compelling, was the growth in the trend of productivity. Between 1995 and 2000, the annual average productivity was 3.1 percent compared to just 1.4 percent between 1973 and 1995.[11]

The approaching millennium also lead to fears of the Y2K bug, resulting in substantial spending by business to upgrade computer systems. The Telecom Deregulation Act of 1996 also generated large-scale spending as firms emerge to compete in the more open marketplace.

Finally, the role of the Federal Reserve during the period remains a source of controversy during and since the bubble. Chairman Alan Greenspan issued cautionary remarks about irrational exuberance in 1996 and continued to wonder about the repetition of bubbles in history. Despite these statements, he is widely criticized for making other comments about productivity improvements and the New Economy that seemed to some observers to justify the valuations. He is also criticized for not taking stronger action to increase interest rates sooner in order to pop the bubble. Much of the debate revolves around the question of whether the

Federal Reserve should be concerned with stabilizing inflation exclusively, whether it should also deal with stock bubbles, or even whether it should also be responsible for insuring stable economic growth overall.

A key factor in the debate is how good a job the Fed could do in correcting bubbles. Trying to raise interest rates or increasing margin requirements for banks may play a critical role in dampening investment momentum, but it may also result in overreaction or poor timing, creating a far deeper downturn than would have occurred otherwise. In the end, the actions of the Federal Reserve may not be sufficiently targeted mechanisms to efficiently correct many kinds of bubbles.

The details of the role the Fed should have played are complex, riddled with uncertainty, and best left for another book.

FOUR

REALITY RETURNS

It's not what we don't know that hurts us, it's what we know for certain that just ain't so.

—Mark Twain

EVENTUALLY ALL BUBBLES COLLAPSE. ONLY THEN, UNFORTUNATELY, does everyone undeniably see that a bubble existed in the first place. In general terms, bubbles burst because the investors who believed in the vision realize that they have been investing based on inflated expectations and reality becomes inescapable. Similarly, the investors who have been playing a speculative game at the expense of naïve retail investors lose confidence in the enthusiasm and hype and realize that the game is over.

Bubbles end in different ways. Some bubbles crash and lead to a protracted bear market. On Monday, October 19, 1987, the Dow Jones Industrial Average fell 508.32 and closed at 1,738.40 points. The Dow didn't recover to its October level until January 24, 1989.

More dramatically, during the roaring 1920s, the US stock market and economy boomed and peaked in September 1929. On September 3, the Dow Jones Industrial Average reached 381, up from 100 in 1926. The stock market crashed in October 1929, with frantic selling on Black Thursday, October 24; Black Monday October 28; and Black Tuesday, October 29. Stock prices fell to 145 by November, a decline of 62 percent. Despite this collapse, the market didn't stop there and the slide continued. On July 8, 1932, the market reached a record low of just

41.2. The Dow did not return to its September 1929 peak until November 22, 1954—*25 years later*.

Other bubbles, like the Internet bubble, slide in a "rolling blackout," as Michael Moritz called it. The personal computer bubble ended in a sliding decline rather than a crash, the go-go years of the 1960s also ended in a gradual but precipitous deflation.

The more detailed causes and timing of collapses are far more mysterious. Why did the Internet bubble end in March 2000, and not in July or December? Why not November 1999 or May 2001? The accounts of the crash of the Internet bubble are more fragmented and varied than accounts of the emergent bubble.

DOUBT

The momentum was still gaining in 1999. The number of venture deals and IPOs continued to grow, and private investors put more money into tech funds. However, close watchers of existing Internet stocks began to have growing doubt. The creepy presence of reality was lurking ever closer. Sara Zeilstra of Warburg Dillon Read started coverage of Amazon.com and eBay in January 1999 with a neutral recommendation. "People are realizing that a lot of these e-commerce companies aren't virtual anymore," she said "Investors thought this was a gold mine and nothing would go wrong."[1]

As the bellwether for numerous Internet stocks, Amazon.com was one of the first to reveal that the New Economy was far more complex and far less virtual that enthusiasts had imagined. The company revealed very strong results in 1999 that far outpaced expectations. They were also announcing continued significant spending plans on necessary infrastructure and logistics. "People started realizing it would be expensive," Zeilstra said. "People started to think that if Amazon has to do it, then some of these other companies must have to do it as well."[2]

This did not dampen overall enthusiasm for the Internet, indeed, despite the emerging concern, 1999 proved to be one of the frothiest in terms of IPOs, venture deals, and corporate acquisitions. In select quarters, however, and for those few whose ears were attuned to the change in tone, what was shifting, albeit slowly, was the sense that everything was possible.

In December 1999, Mary Meeker told *Barron's,* "There is good chance that the capital markets will remain robust, in large part because there are a lot of new market opportunities for new Internet players that are truly changing the way business is done. The lesson I've learned with Microsoft and AOL is that if the market opportunity is large enough and the company is executing well enough, they will surprise you on the upside."[3] But even Meeker was becoming more cautious, adding, "That said, there is an overlay of extremely high valuations. And we wouldn't be surprised at all to see a lot of dislocations among individual stocks because of high valuations. I think there will be an e-commerce shakeout in the first quarter of 2000. And that's because there is so much money being thrown at getting customers. I lived through the early days of the PC business in the early 1980s when every PC business was going to go to the moon."[4] Sure enough, just as she said, a shakeout of e-commerce companies began in March of 2000. However, the shakeout didn't stop there. Through the subsequent months the collapse would sweep across all Internet companies, all tech companies, the entire market—across the world.

Emerging doubt turned to deep concern in March 2000, when *Barron's* Jack Willoughby published some hard data that demonstrated systemic dangers. Willoughby, in collaboration with Pegasus Research International, showed that at least 51 Internet firms would run out of cash within 12 months. Three-quarters of the 207 companies studied had negative cash flows—and many had no realistic hope of profits in the near term. Even Amazon, had only 10 months of cash left. Another, Digital Island, with a tremendous market value of $7 billion, only had 3 and half months of cash. CDNow, a hot stock for downloading digital music, with a market value of $239 million, had *less than a month* of cash, given its historical spending patterns.[5]

In response to the article and growing awareness of the cash problem, public markets began looking for profit—*for the first time.* Joe Flint, general partner of Polaris Venture Partners, remarked on the shift in focus: "the two biggest investor concerns have now become cash and the business model. If companies don't have enough cash for at least 15 months or can't show significant progress by then, private investors are not going to buy in."[6]

The effect of the Willoughby article was profound. Bill Hambrecht and Alan Patricof remembered it as the beginning of the shift in psychology both in the public markets and among private equity funds. It brought to light the hidden underbelly, the decline of discipline, that had created systematic weakness in hundreds of start-ups.

Internet companies spent $1.52 billion in the fourth quarter of 1999. But the new environment put the pressure on start-ups to cut exuberant spending. By the first quarter of 2000, their burn rate had dropped to $1.15 billion. By October, the list of companies on the danger list, those with just 12 months of cash left, rose to 86 companies—35 more than in March.[7] Between March and October companies were scrambling for survival.

BAD APPLES VS. HOUSE OF CARDS

Despite this rocky period, a common view among many seemed to be that the crisis was due to some bad apples, not that the whole market had become an overvalued house of cards. Eddie Sanchez, vice president and portfolio manager with Citigroup Investments was at the Morgan Stanley Dean Witter Software and Networking & Internet Conference in Scottsdale Arizona in January 2000. "You'll get some reshuffling of names," he said, "you'll get some people talking about profits, and then I think the market goes higher." He viewed the business to business companies such as Ariba, CommerceOne, Mercury Interactive, and Veritas Software as leading the way.[8]

Christine Nairne, an analyst at Eoffering, remarked, "I would rather call this a bifurcation rather than a real correction. Rather than indiscriminately piling on IPOs, investors will employ a higher quality filter when making investment decisions."[9]

As it turns out, analysts' highly rated stock picks outperformed their lowest-rated stock picks every year during the bubble. During the bust, in a reversal of this good track record, the stocks that analysts thought would do poorly did better than the stocks they thought would do well. In 2000, the stocks receiving the most favorable recommendations *declined* by 7.1 percent while the stocks receiving the least favorable recommendations *rose* by 17.6 percent. In 2001, analysts also got it wrong, but by a slightly lesser amount. Their top picks still declined by 7 percent, but those they didn't expect to perform still grew by 9.3 percent.[10] You just can't time a bubble.

Even seasoned venture capitalists who were perhaps best positioned to know what lay under the hoods of rickety dot.coms liquidated their personal stock holdings selectively. Many kept their positions in the bellwethers—Cisco, Microsoft, Intel, and even Amazon, and Yahoo!—thinking these were the sound picks in a basket of rotten apples. This belief would be proven wrong, and in the end the whole market would fall.

Insider trading by individual firms revealed that some senior managers were bailing out of their own firms. But in other start-ups, top managers were buying as their stock was falling, deluding themselves that their firm would recover and that the dip represented a chance to buy low.

Many big investment banks still viewed the Internet as maintaining strength and positioned themselves to serve the future growth of the market. Morgan Stanley launched the Morgan Stanley Internet Index on March 24, 2000. By October 25, 2000, over 165,000 contracts had been traded but the index had declined 49 percent.[11]

Morgan Stanley High Tech 35 Index Fund, and Street Tracks Morgan Stanley Internet Index Fund, were launched by State Street Global Advisors on September 29, 2000. By October 25, 2000, each fund had assets of about $100 million and the funds still anticipated over a billion dollars by the end of the year. But over the previous 7 months the NASDAQ had declined by 14 percent. Citigroup also started a fund late in October 2000.

Analysts continued to look for a recovery. Each dip was viewed by many as a buying opportunity. Edward Kerschner, the influential market strategist of Paine Webber, was reported by *Barron's* to consider the market cheap. Thomas Galvin of Credit Suisse First Boston thought the NASDAQ could go up 20 to 25 percent from the October 2000 slump.[12]

A number of economists have found evidence that investors systematically tend to hang on to their losing stocks too long. In one such study of this idea, Leroy Gross, an investment advisor, articulated the decision-making process this way: "Many clients, however, will not sell anything at a loss. They don't want to give up the hope of making money on a particular investment, or perhaps they want to get even before they get out. The 'getevenitis' disease has probably wrought more destruction on investment portfolios than anything else. Investors are also reluctant to accept and re-alize losses because the very act of doing so proves that their first judgment was wrong."[13]

Focus on Survival Ends the Capital Spiral

Whatever the impact on the broad markets and investors' existing hold-ings, the capital spiral was ending. It became much harder to launch IPOs for existing companies. While there was some diversity in opinion about whether the market turn represented a long-awaited return to ra-tional valuations or a temporary correction, there appeared to be univer-sal belief that the IPO window had closed. For many years, the public market had been willing to accept fairly conceptual companies with lit-tle or no history and bestow great valuations. Now, it was not going to accept any kind of start-ups—regardless of the viability.

During bubbles, public markets are very bad at sifting the legitimate from illegitimate firms on the way up. They are equally bad at separating them when bubbles collapse. The tsunami of negative sentiment crashed through many start-ups that held intriguing promise. Firms in the IPO lineup postponed their plans. Start-ups that were considering going pub-lic dug in. Even large incumbent firms like Verizon, which was consider-ing spinning off its wireless division, shelved plans for their IPOs.

The effect of the negative sentiment went far beyond the firms in the IPO pipeline. The IPO represented the most effective "exit strategy" for venture capitalists to turn their investments into disbursable stock and thus cash. The closing of the IPO window meant that new investments might take years instead of months to become liquid. It also meant that without a hot IPO market that would accept practically any kind of business with dot.com in its name, VC would have to create real suc-cessful companies to generate significant returns. With the IPO decline went the VC decline. Company creation that drove so much excitement virtually stopped.

"After a huge sell-off like the one we're in right now, it's a big gamble for companies to issue, when they could wait three weeks and see if this is a correction on the magnitude of October 1987, when it took three-and-a-half years for the IPO window to open again—or whether it's like the

August-through-September slide in 1998 when issues slowed for just a short while," said Jay Ritter, an economist who studies the IPO markets.[14]

Venture capitalists also had to dig in and focus on their existing investments in a desperate attempt to weed through the firms that might make it and those that wouldn't. As Willoughby's article demonstrated, many of the start-ups would have quickly died. But many were artificially maintained by the venture capitalists who already had their investments stuck in them.

"Companies stayed in business because the venture investors had so much at a stake in their first rounds," lamented Alan Patricof, "they had to protect the first round and therefore they were prepared to go into second and third rounds which ended up exacerbating their loses and keeping a lot of these companies alive longer than they would under normal circumstances. When you invest $10 million in an opening round it's a lot harder to walk away then when you have $1 million or $2 million."[15]

Despite the declines, the pressure to maintain strong results in order to sustain inflated valuations was incredible. Some viewed this as part of the reason why a number of accounting scandals emerged among telecommunications companies. As companies began to shift their position in the eye of the public markets and business operations, the focus changed to—*Forget the vision, justify the fantasy.*

"You can imagine the pressure," said one telecommunications consultant. "You literally will get foreclosed on if you don't show certain results. So a little creativity in gray areas is probably a natural human reaction. You can see how the system builds pressure. Particularly in things that aren't clear. The capacity swaps are not clear and the accountants all signed off."

As we now know, the bursting of the bubble was not limited to a select group of silly dot.coms or even high technology more broadly. The decline was comprehensive—in fact, it became global. As a sign of how far things could drop, by March 2003, 3 years after the beginning of the slide in March 2000, Internet Capital Group's stock had dropped 99.8 percent, Palm fell 99.2 percent, Priceline 98.6 percent, and JDS Uniphase 97.9 percent.

The standard bearers also dropped. Lucent fell 96.9 percent, Sun slid 93.2 percent, and Cisco dropped 80.6 percent. Intel dropped 73.4

percent. The effects were felt around the world. The Bovespa in Brazil dropped 70.7 percent over the same period. Argentina's Merval fell 69.9 percent. Germany's DAX 65.2 percent. Japan Nikkei 225 fell 62.5 percent. France's CAC-40 dropped 54.8 percent and Britain's FTSE 100 dropped 45.9 percent.[16]

The bubble demand for real goods and services meant that once the bubble began to deflate there were widespread ripple effects. The first to be hit hard were some of the more stable Internet companies. Yahoo!, for example, by most accounts was destined to be a significant company over the long haul. Despite this, it became clear that it was floating on the bubble demand of dot.coms. With 40 percent of its revenue coming from dot.com advertising sales, Yahoo! went through a very rough period as Internet ad spending disappeared.

EVOLUTIONS CONTINUE WHEN REVOLUTIONS FALL

Despite the claims made at the time, the end of the bubble never meant the end of the Internet. It just meant that the "digital revolution" would take a lot longer than enthusiasts had imagined. Innovations may arrive very quickly, but transformations can be deceptively slow.

Older computer systems, "legacy systems" as they are called, make up a tremendous part of existing computer systems in businesses around the world. In a survey by CIO Insight, CIO's said that 45 percent of their computer systems are legacy systems. The average age of those computer systems was 8.2 years and they spend about 30 percent of their IT budgets on updating those systems. About 60 percent of finance and accounting functions were said to be done with legacy systems. Why do they hang on to this old technology? Fifty percent say that it is because they are still reliable.[17]

When speculative bubbles burst, like a currency bubble, they wipe away savings, wealth, and leave nothing else behind. However, when investment bubbles burst they leave the foundation of new technologies that continue to evolve and contribute to the economy for many years.

A survey in *The Economist* found that after the bubble burst, global business pulled back from hiring start-ups but continued to deepen its use of information technology. In January 2001, 67 percent of global businesses surveyed said that their executives were enthusiastic users of information technology. Despite the crash, those who said that they were enthusiastic users *rose* to 80 percent by July 2002. In 2003, the trend continued. In a survey by A. T. Kearney, the share of corporate IT budgets that would consist of e-business projects rose to 26.8 percent in 2003 from 18 percent in 2002. Only 6 percent of the 758 executives they surveyed said that their firms were *not* starting any e-business projects in 2003. As much as 70 percent said that they would be rolling out some kind of web services.[18]

While long-term use of technology grew, support for start-ups declined with the bursting of the bubble. According to one survey, while 45 percent said that their company was willing to experiment with new and unproven technologies in 2001, by July 2002 only 23 percent said so.[19]

Revolutionary innovations seem to overbuild infant experiments with the more important benefits coming years later. "There is a fairly common cycle where on the front end of this is the gilded age and the back end is the golden age," reflected Bob Kagle, "During the front end it's mostly about separating investors from their money and on the back end it's more about separating customers from their money. It turns out that it's a lot harder to do that latter than the former in an ebullient environment."[20]

A number of economists have conducted some remarkable and instructive studies of the adoption of electricity at the turn of the century.[21] Prior to the arrival of electricity, factories ran on water or steam-powered engines. Pulleys, leather belts and "line shafts" connected the engine to machinery. They stretched across each floor of a factory, though holes in the ceiling and walls to reach all the machines that needed to run, and sometimes they extended outside to deliver power to another building. The entire network of pulleys, belts and shafts, and machinery throughout the whole complex was inextricably interconnected. As a result, the whole operation was turned on in the morning and off at night—regardless of which machines were actually in use. If one part of the factory broke down, the whole factory had to be shut in order to make repairs. The whole system had to be constantly oiled and carefully maintained. A single plant often required thousands of feet of shafting and belts.

The first D.C. electric generator became available in 1870. It was first used in manufacturing in 1883, when it was marketed by Thomas Edison. By the early 1890s, D.C. motors were readily available for industrial use and first adopted in textiles and printing manufacturing, where the key benefits turned out to be cleanliness, steady power, speed, and ease of control. The new technology smoothed operations but did not change the process in any significant way. The electric engines simply replaced the existing water or steam powered energy source, leaving the network of pulleys, belts, and shafts in place. The system offered marginal cost savings, but often not enough to justify costs associated with the transition when companies would have to pull out the old technology and install the new one. By 1900, nearly 20 years after it became available, electricity still accounted for only 5 percent of the power used. Far-sighted engineers understood the tremendous potential to transform factories, stores, and homes. But the implementation of that technological visionvision had to first work itself though complex *human* systems.

With experience, managers learned that they could separate the interconnected parts of the factory by adding electric motors to each machine rather than one engine for the whole factory. The machines no longer needed to be placed according to the pattern of the belts and shafts; they could be arranged in a more efficient assembly line according to the manufacturing process. As a result, the materials did not need as much handling, and the factory floor space could be used much more effectively. The location of a specific machine could also be easily moved since it was no longer tethered to the network of shafts, enabling a far more flexible production process. Portable electric power tools also emerged and further increased flexibility. Similarly, factory expansion was made much easier because managers no longer had to rearrange or even replace the complex network of line shafts under the old paradigm. Quality also improved. The conveyor belts in the old system often slipped, creating irregular machine operations, but with electric power operations became more consistent.

This big shift occurred as managers recognized that electricity offered not only cost savings and smoother processes, but new ways of running a factory that could dramatically increase productivity. In 1901, Professor F. B. Crocker commented on the early results from a number of reports on productivity gain from electricity use. "It is often found that this gain [in output] actually amounts to 20 or 30 percent or even more, with the same floor space, machinery and number of workmen," he said.

"This is the most important advantage of all, because it secures an increase in income without any increase in investment, labor, or expense."

It was only over time that enough experience was gained and disseminated that the benefits of electrical power became clear. Eventually by 1914–1917 its adoption gained momentum. Electricity reached 50 percent penetration in 1919, more than 30 years after it became commercially available.

Another key factor necessary for widespread adoption was broader changes in the marketplace for complementary services and technology. For example, electricity supply from power plants had to be built up to serve the factories. Machines also needed to be completely redesigned. In the old system the machines were connected to the engine through the line shaft. Now, each machine required its own internal engine. It wasn't until after World War I that such machines became widely available.

What the electricity story reveals about the speed of technology innovation is that while the technology can become available very quickly, it can take a long time to make a substantial impact in human organizations, much less the economy as a whole. Technological transformation depends on many large and small changes among individual managers and the marketplace as a whole. The human process of realizing the benefits can take awhile. Numerous other developments in the marketplace are required to enable the new technology to spread.

In the frenzy created by extraordinary new innovations, investors' attention focuses on how great—how cool—the new technology is. What investors do not typically recognize is that transformative change does not occur just with the arrival of a new technology; it occurs with the slower development of a whole new system of human behavior and marketplace dynamics, and that takes a long time.

In a similar but more recent story, the personal computer revolution posed a quandary to economists for nearly 20 years. For all the improvements the computer was alleged to deliver, there was no evidence of any benefit in the official economic statistics of productivity. The "productivity paradox," as it was called, pointed to an apparent contradiction: huge amounts of money had been invested in the early years of the computer revolution ushering in the dawn of the information age—yet the results of that investment could not be measured in productivity statistics where they expected it to appear. Some economists began to wonder whether computers really provided any benefit to the economy. Others thought the data was flawed. Finally, by the mid-1990s, productivity figures began improving and in the subsequent years continued to grow at a frantic pace—despite a recession. A number of economists bicker over how much this productivity improvement is real versus statistical artifact and how much is really related to computers. But the majority opinion remains impressed with the strength of the productivity improvements and believes that these improvements have significantly contributed to the gradual adoption of and adaptation to these new technologies.

Robert Noyce was vice chairman of Intel and one of the two inventors of the integrated circuit that is the heart of the microchip. At the end of the PC bubble in the 1980s, as reality was returning to the personal computer industry, he provided insight into how we tend regularly to misjudge technology build-out: "The usual futurist projections are too optimistic in the short term and too pessimistic in the long term."[22]

The story of the personal computer is expected to be the same as the story of electricity and the Internet. The biggest and most powerful changes wrought by technology often seem to be evolutionary not revolutionary. It takes time for people to adopt and adapt to the new technologies and to learn how to use them, how to make them effective, how to make them worth what they cost.

In organizations, new technologies are typically met with resistance to change, turf battles, and outright hostility, as employees worry about losing their jobs or their stature, or even just doing things differently. Change is hard, and when the proposition for a new technology is to change the workings of an entire economy, it takes a long time. A lot of people need to do things differently to change an economy. A lot of entrenched habits and preferences need to be replaced with new daily behaviors.

John Fontana, a former management consultant and venture capitalist who has worked extensively with manufacturing firms, commented on the shift required by the arrival of the personal computer in the 1980s and then 15 years later the arrival of the Internet in the 1990s: "we were just figuring out how to use a hammer when they gave us a laser."[23]

One example is particularly instructive during the Internet bubble. One of the most intriguing opportunities offered by the Internet was business-to-business marketplaces and supply chain management systems across companies. The idea of these marketplaces was that companies would be able to connect online to a giant bazaar of hundreds of businesses to find the best prices for the things they need from staplers to engine turbines. The full vision imagined that the technology would not only be able to execute the transaction between companies at a good price, but that the entire processing of those transactions, from billing, to taxes, to legal paperwork, to logistical shipments, would also be integrated online into the marketplace. Think of the hundreds of pages of documentation, phone calls, delays, and hiccups that can occur through all the stages of a transaction. All of that would become digitized and automated over the Internet. The result would be a seamless, fluid, supply chain across the economy. That is a lot of efficiency. Companies offering this vision, such as Ariba and Commerce One, became among the most highly valued Internet companies. They proposed that they would be able to get a small percentage of every transaction that ran through the system as revenue. Since their system would include large parts of the $10 trillion US economy if not the global economy, those figures added up quickly.

Technologically, it seemed entirely possible. The speed of executing this change was imagined to be very fast. In reality, however, execution was hampered by deeply human, political, and organizational challenges. First, the marketplaces effectively squeezed the prices of all suppliers since the marketplaces put the prices on a level playing field, eliminating many advantages that leading firms use to create price premiums. As a result, few suppliers ended up joining, making the marketplaces pretty barren for buyers. Secondly, changing the very deep and broad purchasing decision making throughout big organizations proved extremely difficult. Resistance was intense, because jobs were on the line.

Fontana explained that the human dimension in supply chains is so deep that it will take years to really make supply chain software usable on mass scale and fulfill the vision. He described it this way: "If you are a purchasing manager and you buy stuff, you know who you typically buy from personally. You go out. You do sales meetings and get drunk together. There is so much chaos in organizing supply chains [that] you need that human relationship. Trucks break down, so you need a back up. The shipment gets lost so you need a new order to be put ahead of everyone else in an emergency. You know who will pull through for you in a crunch. The Internet comes along and as great as it is, it doesn't do any of this complex work at the human relationship level. Someday it will, but that will take a long time."[24]

Scott Bertetti worked for Wingspan, an early effort at Internet banking. Online banking also faced far slower customer adoption than anticipated. "Trying to change people's sense of trust is hard," he pointed out after Wingspan failed to gain enough customers. "I don't think that this is something you can accelerate. Getting people to make the leap of faith—we underestimated the challenge. At the end of the day people feel more comfortable with a retail branch. They may never walk into it. They may not have for the last 6 years, but they want it there."[25]

Dave Dorman calls this the "impedance of learning," referring to the resistance that electrical current faces when it runs through a wire and slows its movement, "If one of these [technology innovations] occurs and technology runs way ahead, you can't learn it that fast—there is impedance that is time based. It takes awhile for you to catch up. If technology is still moving, you have to learn at a faster rate to gain ground."[26]

In the fullness of time, much of the Internet vision will likely prove itself correct and probably with some surprises along the way. "We've entered a period of experimentation and refining," reflected Hal Varian, dean of the Berkeley Business School and notable professor who has written about technology and the Internet. "I think we'll see a fair amount of tinkering with business processes to get them working more smoothly, and that's going to be a slow, steady process. We're past the era of the category killer. Now we're in an era of relentless improvement, where a lot of small things will accumulate to be tremendously significant."[27]

Bubbles as R&D

While evolutionary learning generates lasting benefits, bubbles accelerate the pace of learning in the early stages of innovation. The Internet created a new medium for business and consumer interaction. Learning the details of how to deploy this technology effectively is no simple task, and certainly during the bubble a lot of people got it wrong. But they were trying to figure it out and were being paid a lot of money to do so by venture financing and the public markets.

"These businesses were being built by entrepreneurs who were learning about an industry overnight," commented Habib Kairuz about efforts to sell goods to consumers online. "They were backed by people who understood technology, but not retailing. Over time we hired top people with retailing experience. But given that the technology was so new, we also asked them to forget the way they did things. You couldn't do it all, you couldn't do it all at the same time."[28]

In some ways, the Internet bubble, and technology bubbles in general, are akin to oversized R&D efforts by the economy—not only technology R&D, but also business R&D, marketing R&D, and strategic R&D— all testing what will work. Over the 1990s, billions were spent by venture firms effectively on Internet R&D on behalf of the national economy. Some six thousand start-ups were created. With a budget so large, it should not be a surprise that massive amounts of it were squandered on greed, bad decisions, and even corruption. But many poorly executed ideas and failed dot.coms provided valuable learning for others to succeed and for everyone to gain a more sophisticated appreciation for the integrations of this new technology into daily life and organizations.

With so much uncertainty about new technologies, it takes a lot of failures to get it right. This leads to overproliferation of start-ups, most of which fail. But over time, the successes emerge. In the early days of the auto, it wasn't clear whether the "horseless carriage" would be steam, electric, or gas powered. It wasn't clear whether they would remain a recreational vehicle for the rich or reach a broader market.

Like the beginning of so many technological bubbles, the auto craze began with tinkerers taking different approaches at similar goals. Early interest was sparked among enthusiasts by seeing races between Paris and

Rouen in July 1893, among others. Carl Benz and Gottleib Dailmer were the European leaders in experimentation.

The races captivated many in the United States. By September 1895, over 500 applications related to the automobile were sent to the U.S. Patent Office for approval. The barriers to entry were low. Between 1900 and 1908, almost 500 manufacturers entered the industry. By some accounts, as many as 1,500 start-ups emerged over the 20 years following 1895. Many of these were suppliers to the industry and empty speculative shells who raised capital but produced little more than a concept. But, as usual, the markets had a hard time distinguishing the legitimate from illegitimate firms.

In the early days, the capital markets were in a slump during the 1890s, creating some early resistance among investors. But that would not last. The toughest challenge in the early days was demonstrating minimal mechanical knowledge to pull it off or the ability to convince investors that the fledgling entrepreneur had the knowledge. Among the entrepreneurs were William Chrysler, Alexander Winton, James Packard, Ransom Ols, the Studebaker family, Frank and Charles Duryea, and of course, Henry Ford.

The demand for automobiles also verged on a craze. In 1900, 4,100 cars were sold. By 1910, the figure rose to 181,000 and 10 years later in 1920, the number would reach 1.9 million.[29]

How much of bubble investments are wasted compared to money spent on learning compared to directly generating real economic returns is impossible to quantify. Moreover, as with any R&D effort, the boundaries between these would be extremely fuzzy.

The events that precipitate the demise of bubbles are mysterious and varied, which is why it is so hard to predict their end and get out of the market before they burst. Whatever specific forces are at work, in the end, investors lose confidence and collectively realize that they have been gambling on inflated expectations.

In the market whiplash backward, good companies as well as bad are swept away. When bubbles do burst, those expensive assets, stocks, companies, and company assets become very cheap, and those well positioned with cash can reap great benefits from the fire sale.

What gets proven wrong when bubbles burst is not that the visionaries were wrong but that investors had exaggerated ideas of the profits that could be derived and how long the process would take. Over the long haul, the vision of the new opportunities is proven largely true—it just takes far longer than anticipated. Furthermore while the value to the economy and to society are all apparent, profits for investors can be more complex and elusive.

Partial List of Bubbles of the Past

Early 2000	China opening market, privatizing
Early 2000	Hedge Funds
Early 2000	Biotechnology
Late 1990s–2000	Internet bubble
Early 1990s–1997	Asian Tigers (Thailand, Indonesia, Korea), opening market, privatizing, directed lending
Mid 1990s–1997	Russian Debt
Mid 1990s	Long Term Capital Management
Mid 1990s	China opening market, privatizing
Early 1990s	Biotechnology
1980s	Japan stock market, real estate
1982–October 18, 1987	US Stock market
Early 1980s	Personal Computers and related hardware, software in US
Late 1970s–1980	OPEC 1979 price rise in oil
Late 1970s –1982	Third world syndicate bank loans
Mid 1970s	REITs, office buildings, tankers, Boeing 747s
1960s	Go-Go years: technology companies ("onics"), color television
1920s–1929	Stock market, radio, autos, telephone
Late 1910s–1921	Postwar boom, stocks, ships, commodities
Early 1900s–Oct 1907	Coffee, Union Pacific
Early 1890s–May 1893	Silver, Gold
1840s–1945	British Railway mania II
1840s–1850s	US Railway mania
1830s–1936	British Railway mania I
1820s	Latin American bonds, mines, cotton in England
Late 1790s–1810s	Various waves in commodities, securities in England, Hamburg
1790s	Canal mania
1770s	East India Company in Amsterdam. Canals, turnpikes in Britain
1770s	Commodities in Amsterdam
1720s	South Sea Company, company stock in England
Late 1600s	East India company, new companies, lotteries, in England
1630	Tulipmania in Dutch Republic, real estate, canals
1810s	Coins in Holy Roman Empire

Source: Charles Kindleberger, *Manias, Panics and Crashes;* and author's additions.

FIVE

WE'VE BEEN
THERE BEFORE

The four most dangerous words in investing are—It's different this
time.

—Sir John Templeton

THE INTERNET BUBBLE WAS JUST THE LATEST IN A LONG and rich history
of bubbles. Despite these variations, bubbles are not unusual events.
They occur all the time. It is comforting to view business and economic
behavior as a rational process that periodically runs into fits of irrational
enthusiasm, only to return to rationality when bubbles burst. In reality,
bubbles are regular features of economic activity.

Since the 1950s, there is hardly a period of normal economic growth
that does not show some kind of bubble somewhere. Charles Kindleberger's definitive book on financial manias provides a list of recent bubbles: During the 1950s and 1960s, there was speculation in numerous
currency markets in France, Canada, Italy, Britain, and the United
States. In addition to these mentioned by Kindleberger there were also
bubbles during go-go years of the late 1960s, which generated a mania
for numerous "concept stocks" that had little underlying business rationale and overvalued anything that seemed to relate to high technology
and early computing with names ending in "onics." Kindlerberger also
outlines the enthusiasm for stocks, real estate, tankers, and Boeing 747s

that peaked in 1973 and crashed in 1974–1975. In 1979, there was an investment craze in third-world syndicated bank loans, oil stocks, real estate in the Southwest, and U.S. farmland. He also describes manias for the stock market overall, luxury housing, office buildings, and the U.S. dollar in the 1980s. In addition to these mentioned by Kindleberger there were also bubbles in personal computers, software and related peripherals, and biotech. Japan faced a stock market bubble in 1990. The period from 1994 to 1995 saw investment enthusiasm in Mexico, while the years leading up to 1997–98 saw investment enthusiasm in the newly emerging markets of Thailand, Indonesia, Malaysia, Korea, Russia, and Brazil. Forgetting quibbles about exactly when each of these might have started and ended, this list leaves very few years since 1950 that did not experience a bubble in some market.

Investment bubbles that deeply affect the way business and the economy function are quite different from purely speculative asset publics that operate exclusively in an abstract marketplace. The tulip mania of 1634 was, for example, a purely speculative asset bubble.

Tulips were first imported into northern Europe from Turkey in the 1550s. Trade in tulips grew and by the end of the century they became available in Holland. Even in the early days of their arrival tulips were viewed as a status symbol. The nobility of Europe were eager to have increasingly uncommon varieties of these plants. The most coveted were those that had been afflicted with a virus that caused strange mutations to the tulip's inner petals, creating new shades of pinks, mauves, yellows. Demand was dramatically growing by the 1620s. The semper Augustus in 1624 was worth 1,200 florins. Its large calux was white, the base lightly flecked in blue and trimmed with bright red vertical stripes.

Horticulturalists and collectors were the primary traders until 1633, when the public became swept up in frenzy and prices started to rise rapidly. Rare tulips were worth more than their weight in gold. Skeptics called these investors Kappisten, meaning "the hooded ones," because madmen of the day wore hoods.

In the final hours of the mania in 1936–37, foreign funds swamped the country, and people from all classes liquidated other assets to participate in the tulip market. The frenzy suddenly terminated in early 1637. Rare tulip bulbs could not be sold for even 10 percent of their previous prices.

Throughout the period, obviously, the flowers themselves did not affect any deeper aspects of how people interacted or businesses functioned nor did they induce fundamental changes in existing economies. There was not even lasting effects on the tulip market. By contrast, investment bubbles, despite the hype, do end up forcing dramatic transformations.

The bubbles of the past featured some differences, but they also demonstrated some striking similarities. The historical record is better for some than for others, but even for those manic waves for which historians have plumbed the daily papers and available records, there are limits to how much insight can be gleaned about the thought processes without directly asking the participants. This is why the Internet bubble provides such useful information and insight, because we can document in detail, through interviews, many aspects that are not fully covered in written histories.

Whereas this book has explored, so far, a number of drivers that motivate individual investment decisions during bubbles, historians have looked at more sweeping trends that help put these forces and events in perspective. Carlotta Perez focuses her historical study on technological innovations. She found that over the major revolutions throughout history, each featured four similar stages: irruption, frenzy, synergy and maturity.[1]

Perez found that the irruption phase features a love affair of the financial community with the new technology, intense funding in new technologies, and disdain for anything connected with the old. The frenzy period arises with a decoupling of the way financial markets are valuing the technology and its actual productive value. The financial markets attract increasing and potentially excessive investments into the new technology. As a result, this investment frenzy becomes a driving force for change as firms emerge to seize the opportunity the financial markets are creating, while other "old economy" firms are forced to play along due to market pressures. During this phase the financial markets drive much of the pace of company formation and technology build-out—but the process is likely based on irrational terms. Once investors realize that they have overbuilt the new technology, the panic brings the valuations proposed by the financial markets back in line with the real productive capacity and value of the new technologies. The synergy phase is a more sensible deployment of the new technology throughout the economy. The financial markets return to the traditional role of enabling and financing corporate development rather than driving technology frenzy. Returns on investments become better founded on the real value generated by business projects. During the maturity phase, productivity begins to slow, returns to financial markets moderate further, and investors become restless. "Idle" money starts looking for the next new big wave of growth.

Kindleberger's famous macro-study describes several larges stages within bubbles. He found 5 sweeping stages of bubbles that occur within these transformative periods: displacement, euphoria, mania, financial distress, and revulsion. Displacement occurs because of some outside shock to the system. In technology bubbles, this consists of the widespread adoption of an invention with pervasive effects. The result is that new profit opportunities open up and displace existing ones. Business managers and investors shift their strategic focus, rush in to get a piece of the action in the new, and abandon the old.

Over time, growing demand stretches the capacity of production or existing financial assets and fuels inflation. Those rising prices create further profit opportunities and more investors and producers. Emerging from this growing activity is "euphoria." Mania or the bubble emerges as increasingly naïve investors and business people enter the fray. With so many ignorant investors trying to become rich quickly, swindlers flourish. "Financial distress" begins as insiders decide to sell off and price increases begin to level off. As a growing number of people realize that the party is over, they leave, precipitating falling prices. Finally, there is a backlash against the period and everything associated with it as the populous and investors feel "revulsion" for the excesses they helped create.

For all the references here to bubbles involving grand, transformational change in technology or the opening of new markets, it is worth noting that bubbles can be focused on a specific product as well. Long-Term Capital Management (LTCM) appeared to be driven by similar patterns of behavior and certainly became an unsustainable opportunity. The hedge fund was started in 1994 by John Meriwether, a former bond trader at Salomon Brothers, and Nobel Prize winners Myron Scholes and

Robert Merton. The partners were using complex *statistical* models to take advantage of arbitrage deals and manage their portfolio.

Not only did Long-Term Capital bet the wrong way, it had also leveraged its bets to an astonishing degree. The fund had less than $2.5 billion in capital, which it used as collateral to purchase as much as $125 billion in securities. Using these securities as collateral, the firm was able to engage in complex financial transactions, mostly involving derivatives and forward contracts, with notional amounts of as much as $1.25 trillion in securities.

The models they developed detected and traded on temporary anomalies in price spreads. The fund took substantial positions believing that the anomalous spreads they discovered would be corrected in an efficient market. It was stunningly successful for a while. The frenzy among big banks to participate was tremendous. Few people outside this industry knew what was going on, but for those who operated in global arbitrage the bubble was unavoidable.

Fueling this stunning accumulation of capital were some familiar characteristics of frenzy. The decline of discipline in evaluating how LTCM operated was central. The banks had no idea how these high-flyers were trading. Indeed the partners of LTCM prevented anyone from looking at their books and were free to operate in unprecedented secrecy. All of the investors were contributing tremendous amounts of capital based on blind trust in a classic trust pyramid. "We had no idea they would have trouble—these people were known for risk management. They taught it; they *designed* it," Dan Napoli, the Merrill Lynch risk manager told Lowenstein. "God knows, we were dealing with Nobel prize winners!"[2]

Investors gave the partners of LTCM tremendous latitude. They were extraordinarily successful for a period of time. As a result, like with any bubble, the pressure to play created a competitive cascade of poorly considered investments. "The whole market was pressuring us," Richard Dunn, the head of Merril's debt markets in Europe and the United Kingdom told Lowenstein. "To suffer the organization telling you that you are losing business—it takes a tremendous amount [of courage] to stand up and say, 'I'm not going to do it.' The street all got that collectively wrong."[3]

The flood of money also led to increasingly bad investment practices within LTCM. Gradually, they strayed from their core models and took increasingly speculative bets—they had to do *something* with all their money.

A succession of economic crises, starting with Mexican debt, then the Asian economic crisis, then the Russian debt default, created a global capital flight to safety. The temporary distortions, instead of narrowing as in the past, actually ballooned as worried investors around the world poured their funds into the safest possible investments, such as U.S. government bonds. None of these individual crises were modeled, much less their succession, much less how it would affect systemic appetites for risk that created lasting spreads between asset classes that were theoretically unsustainable in the long term. Their model predicted a return to "normalcy" and in the end they were correct—but the anomalies lasted over a far longer time period than they anticipated; or were able to sustain. The banks that made incredibly generous investments in the fund's highly leveraged positions eventually had to take large losses.

Perhaps one of the most remarkable issues highlighted in the LTCM case is how much money such a small entity can capture once the frenzy set in.

While the stock market bubbles of the 1920s, the 1960s, and the 1980s were the biggest in the twentieth century, two other bubbles are worthy of particular attention here. The personal computer bubble of the early 1980s serves as an excellent case study. For one, it resulted in critical building blocks of the Internet bubble. More important, the press accounts and the individuals involved are far more accessible, making some key features visible.

One old bubble that is worth noting is the railway mania. The railway mania is important because it was most likely larger relative to the national economy of the day than the Internet bubble. It also built an infrastructure for the industrial age similar to the way that the Internet created the infrastructure of the information age. Finally, it is an excellent illustration for the proposition that bubble dynamics are remarkably similar even 150 years apart, and even without venture capital funds, CNNfn, and other features of the Internet bubble that seemed so important. In reality those are merely features of a bubble. The core driver of bubbles is human psychology that, for now, appears essentially immutable.

RAILWAYS IN BRITAIN

The first commercially successful railway ran between Liverpool and Manchester. It opened on September 15, 1830, and was built by George Stephenson, a leading engineering innovator of the day. Similar to the canal networks that already existed, the railways connected industrial businesses such as coal suppliers and users. In fact, previous railroads did not compete with canals but acted as short-haul feeders to and from the wide-spread and intricate canal systems. They were meant to support the existing canal system in places where canals could not be built, not to supplant it. The Liverpool-Manchester line was the first to directly compete with canals.

Soon, the interest in railways rose to a frenzy. Capital was plentiful, and one of the biggest challenges facing investors, as we have observed repeatedly, were the vast sums of money chasing too few companies. Between 1836 and 1837, railway prices doubled and 44 new companies were granted Parliamentary authorization.[4] (Parliamentary authorization was required prior to construction of any new railroad.)

Prior to 1843, parliamentary authorizations for investment in railroads averaged £4 million (or about $3 billion in 2002 dollars) per year. In 1844 alone, £20 million was authorized; in 1845, £60 million; in 1846, £132 million or $95 billion in 2002 dollars—a growth of 3,200 percent in just over 4 years.[5] Actual net investments reached £20 million per year, about 5 percent of GDP. In the United States, that would be equivalent to spending over $500 billion per year.[6] Share prices rose for a long period. Rail share prices doubled between 1843 and 1845. By 1844, investment in transport and communication reached 40 percent of total domestic fixed capital formation in the entire country.[7]

In proportion to the economy at the time, the scale of the railway bubble may have been larger than the Internet bubble. According to one account, the 1,200 railways were projected to cost over £560 million. Their liabilities reached £600 million—*more than the national income* of the day. By 1846–48, railway construction accounted for half of total investment in Britain and employed 250,000 people in construction alone.[8] By comparison, investment in software and equipment accounted for just under 10 percent of GDP in 2000.

George Hudson, the best-known entrepreneur, quickly became infamous as the Railway King. His first railway investment linked the emerging industrial sector of the North to urban London. He expanded from there to acquire the strategically important main routes through the country. By 1844, he controlled some thousand miles of track, over 30 percent of all the track in Britain.

Many of the railways that were proposed to the Board of Trade were not based on sound business analyses of their potential growth. Amidst the frenzy, discipline collapsed and there was little attempt to assess anticipated returns on invested capital. Companies that made no economic sense flourished. The poet William Wordsworth observed, "The country is an asylum of railway lunatics. The Inverness patients, not content with a railway to their hospital from Aberdeen, insist on having one by the Highland road from Perth. They admit that there are no towns, or villages, no population, and no chance of many passengers. But then they will dispatch such flocks of sheep and such droves of nowt."[9]

Boosting the investment spiral further was an overall strong economy and low interest rates. People who never heard of the stock exchange were spurred on by explosive press coverage and jumped into the game. The gains seemed quick and easy, and for a period for time, they actually were. By 1844, the three largest railway companies were paying dividends of 10 percent, several times the prevailing interest rate.

Prices spiraled upwards, but despite that, investors were willing to pay even higher prices for anything connected to railways. The frenzy to reap these seemingly competitive but unknowable returns became particularly clear in October 1844 when Hudson was able to raise £2.5 million without telling the shareholders what he was going to do with the money. He was even bold enough to declare "I have got my money and I have not told a soul what I am going to do with it."[10] Discipline had been tossed away thoroughly.

In the same way that Netscape created the platform on which entrepreneurs could create their own web-businesses, the early years of railways also seemed to offer the potential for anyone willing to pay the fees to create their own train on the railway tracks that were being laid down.

The railway mania was a land grab in far more literal terms than was ever true of the Internet bubble. In 1844 alone, 66 applications were sent to Parliament. Numerous proposals emerged for the same line, even though it was obvious that only one could survive to provide service. But all their shares gained substantial premiums.

There was a continuous raft of observable data illustrating tremendous returns that reinforced the vision of a future with wondrous opportunities. Hudson played a strong role in amplifying the sentiment: "All railways are yet in their infancy, and day after day, week after week, and month after month, they will go on increasing their resources." Importantly, he also helped maintain this image as immeasurable by closing many of his books from public scrutiny and saying "I will have no statistics on my railway!"[11]

New journals emerged to broadcast numerous stories declaring that railways represented the most significant revolutionary advance ever in the history of the world. One journal hailed, "the length of our lives, so far as regards the power of acquiring information and disseminating power, will be doubled, and we may be justified in looking for the arrival of a time when the whole world will have become one great family, speaking one language, governed in unity by like laws, and adoring one God."[12] Even more specific echoes of the Internet bubble can be discerned in the talk that human life would now operate on "railway time" and at "railway speed." The public spoke in awe of the "railway revolution." The new technology would change *time*. New technologies always appear to have that power—they speed up human existence.

The media outlets reporting on the railway mania exploded. By 1845, some 14 weekly papers were in circulation—some coming out twice a week—along with 2 daily papers. Interestingly, along with the media puff pieces, there was coverage of fraud as well as concerns among many that speculative excess had seized the masses with disastrous and inevitable results. But, similar to subsequent bubbles, these warnings were never heeded. Investors listened only to what they wanted to hear.

Railways were built all over the country with little evaluation of how they fit together into a national network. Copycat lines running between the same locations meant that many would turn out to be unprofitable. But capital *seemed* so cheap at the time that it didn't these poor business decisions did not matter.

Similar to the structure of many Internet IPOs, the insiders of new rail scrip retained large ownership percentages for themselves and released relatively few shares to the public, creating significant scarcity amidst enthusiastic demand. The retained ownerships not only ensured fabulous wealth but also became key sources of capital to purchase property along the proposed rail line. The press hyped these new stock issues.

Scams of every sort emerged as tremendous profits attracted the vipers. Vapor companies could easily be flipped into the public market and then liquidated. In October 31, 1845, the *Times* reported that a new rail company made £25,000 from selling overpriced shares, only to be quickly dissolved. The initial deposits were returned, but the premium went to the schemers.[13] Promoters faked their qualifications or improperly claimed that dignitaries were involved in their plan in order to attract investment.

Conflicts of interest were also rife. During the Internet bubble, investment bankers were the gatekeepers who provided Internet companies access to the public markets through IPOs. The banks faced conflicts of interest because they were also providing research that advised the markets about the value of companies they were taking public. Similarly, at the height of the railway mania, the gatekeepers who approved the railway plans in Parliament were almost all involved in the new companies as committeemen or significant shareholders. In some cases, members of Parliament sold their votes for approval of rail line plans. There was an active debate about whether everyone was playing a speculative game or whether a group of insiders was preying upon another group of naïve investors.

A historian of the period, P. J. Ransom, described the railway mania in a way that parallels many of the key drivers for the Internet bubble. With so little information available about how to locate good investments in railways, investors were forced to rely on the trust pyramid. "For a railway company promoter, a judiciously spread rumor that Hudson 'The Railway King' was interested could send the price of shares soaring," Ransom noted. Hudson's investment decisions were the stamp of approval, the signal of quality, with the logic seeming to be, "Well if *he's* interested, it's got to be good."

The railway mania also featured the steady deterioration of new companies being created. Eventually, railways were being built to flip. According to Ransom, "Railway promotion, originally a matter for routes where the need was evident and the engineering practicable, had spread first to routes where demand was doubtful and the engineering full of problems. . . . But then promotion had spread still further . . . with the public clamouring for railway shares, companies now were being formed solely so that promoters might in due course unload their shares at a premium, leaving others to hold their unlikely babies."[14]

The *Economist* described the market dislodging from business fundamentals this way: "The market value [of railway scrip] . . . depends not on the opinion as to the ultimate success of the undertaking, but rather how far the circumstances will tend to sustain or increase the public appetite for speculation. Nothing can show this more powerfully than the fact that we see nine or ten proposals for nearly the same line, all at a premium, when it is well known that only one can succeed."[15]

The end of the railway bubble was triggered by surprisingly familiar causes. The financial projections proved to be wildly overoptimistic. In particular, the costs of building extensive rail lines proved to be far higher than expected—sometimes double the initial projections. To sustain investor enthusiasm, rail companies continued to maintain high dividend payments at substantial premiums over the market interest rate, thus squeezing cash flows even further. As it became clear that the high asset prices were not going to produce extraordinary returns, capital dried up. Investor confidence was further undermined by growing awareness of fraud throughout the businesses. Many investors were also highly leveraged and the declines in expectations forced them to liquidate positions quickly. The trigger may have been an increase in interest rates by the Bank of England on October 16, 1845. This increase may have signaled that the party was over. But financial shenanigans sent the stocks plummeting. Euphoria quickly turned to disgust at all that had transpired.

By 1850, railway scrip had declined by more than 85 percent on average, and the total market value of the railroads was less than half the total money that had been spent on building the lines. Overconstruction and competition created massive overcapacity and very poor returns. Dividend payments dropped to 2 percent from the 10 percent during the bubble.

The London *Times* of April 10, 1849, reported, "In 1845 respectable men did monstrous things, and were thought very clever. Thousands rejoiced in premiums which they believed to have been puffed up by mere trickery, collusion and imposture."

The broader economic conditions also deteriorated. In the public eye, George Hudson was transformed from a hero of the railway revolution who made so many people feel rich to a notorious crook.

By 1850, there were about six thousand miles of track with operating rails connecting all major cities. Reflecting widespread dismay at the apparent failure of railways to deliver on the hype, in 1857 the *Economist* lamented, "it is a very sad thing unquestionably that railways, which mechanically have succeeded beyond anticipation and are quite wonderful for their general utility and convenience, should have failed commercially."[16]

But as in many bubbles, evolution succeeds when revolutions fall short. By 1900, railway mileage reached 20,000 miles. Passenger trips grew ten times over the period from 1850 to 1900. Furthermore, along the way, and despite the excesses, the railway did transform the British economy. The railway lines became a critical infrastructure component of the modern industrial economy, much as current analysts believe that the Internet will be the foundation of an emerging digital economy. It became far more efficient to transport goods and people within the country, and it provided Britain some competitive advantage over Germany and France. To a significant degree, the vision of the lunatics came true, the value of railways was tremendous. What failed was the idea that individual businesses could guarantee great wealth and profits.

RAILWAYS IN THE UNITED STATES

The American economic boom originated at roughly the same time as the British boom and was also fueled by innovation in transportation. The Erie Canal, finished in 1825, gave rise to a host of imitators and attracted British capital. As railroads pushed to the forefront, foreign capital flowed to finance the rail boom of 1860–1873. This ended abruptly when the Northern Pacific Railroad and the bank Jay Cooke and Company collapsed amidst scandals.

The number of miles of railroad built rose from 2,665 in 1878 to 11,569 in 1882, a growth of 334 percent. This period of growth was the extension of the initial efforts of rail building that had started before the panic of 1873. The panic itself interrupted construction and led to a focus on feeders and branches of main lines. This boom then, was powered primarily by existing firms that already had some experience rather than by new start-ups. The transformative effects of these rail lines were immense, enabling not just the transport of goods but also allowing a significant population expansion west of the Mississippi.

Money flowed in just about anything that seemed connected to railways, just as it would do later with the Internet. The *Chicago Tribune* worried at the time, "why is it that in such a time as that, funds are contributed by all classes of people for almost any enterprise whose promoters promise great returns?" The article provided answers that echoes a number of key forces of the Internet mania. Huge profits were evident everywhere, as the *Tribune* article commented: "It is because they see business active all around them, people in enterprises already established winning large profits and everything apparently inviting them to be rich." Discipline declined: "They are seized with the craze of money-making and become incapable of reasoning on any project that is presented for their consideration." Fraud emerged: "It is easy for unscrupulous men to humble them at such a time." And magical thinking took hold, "Even the promoters of enterprise half believe the lies they tell and partake of the prevailing mania"[17]

The explosive increase of rail construction had also increased the demand for iron and steel. The mills expanded their capacity dramatically, benefiting from bubble demand. The railway enthusiasm "stimulated over-production in all the industries contributing to, or allied with, railroad property, which in turn affected every other branch of business. Every railroad which is constructed, and especially in the West and South, creates fresh opportunities for investment in agriculture, mining, mills and foundries."[18]

Supporting this growth were low interest rates, spurred in part by an emerging surplus of the federal government. Unemployment dropped to remarkable lows. However, optimism dropped in 1881 in part due to a realization that profits were waning. New issues were hard to bring to the public market. While railroad construction continued, trust was shaken by emerging evidence of fraud, poor management execution, and growing sense that not all of these railroads could become profitable, as well as "some apprehension as to the effect of the opening of so many new lines of road." The public market sagged and the funding stream shut off.

As the railroad began to decline, it took with it many of the industries relying on its growth: "blast furnaces were blown out; rail mills were shut down; wages were reduced, hands were discarded. Other branches of mining and manufacturing suffered increasingly."

In 1884, a bank panic struck in New York, initiated by the failure of the brokerage firm Grand and Ward and the Marine National Bank, which was significantly dependent on brokerage. The Second National Bank also failed when it became known that the president had stolen $3 million. The metropolitan banks closed a day later from a more general run on the banks. Despite the upheaval, the contraction was short-lived, indicating a robust economic foundation.

PERSONAL COMPUTERS

The first personal computers were introduced as kits for electronics enthusiasts in 1975. They did not have keyboards to input data or programming instructions. They did not have a monitor to see the results. They were programmed by flicking toggle switches on and off. The results were meager flashing red lights. In 1977, Apple Computer and Radio Shack launched preassembled machines for the first time and began the early stages of broadening the interest in these quirky devices. It wasn't for another 4 years that IBM would feel its turf threatened enough to launch its own personal computers. By 1982, the installed base of personal computers reached 1 million and was forecast to grow by 50 percent for the next decade.

Early experimentation took place in dorm rooms and garages. Steve Wozniak literally built the Apple computer in his garage. Bill Gates and Paul Allen first got the idea to develop a programming language when Gates was at Harvard in January 1975. A friend showed him an issue of *Popular Electronics* that featured the first personal computer, called the Altair. He teamed up with Allen to develop a programming language that people could understand. Early on their oft-stated mission was putting "a computer on every desk and in every home, running Microsoft software." Remarkably, such an audacious goal was accomplished.

In 1978, Dan Bricklin was getting his MBA at Harvard when he had an idea for a program that would make financial analysis easier. He teamed up with Bob Frankston, and they started Software Arts, Inc. In 1979, they launched VisiCalc, which at the time turned into the best-selling software application in history and transformed the possibilities of the personal computer into something that people could actually use. The VisiCalc launch crystallized the burgeoning sense of possibilities among entrepreneurs and, perhaps more powerfully, the media who set the enthusiastic presses running. The crystallized consensus may have been similar to the way Netscape transformed the Internet from a primarily academic enterprise into a mass market business. In both cases, the potential market grew from a group of top tier clients to millions of consumers everywhere, and the race was on to serve them all. Along with this new big market came the frenzy of enthusiasm.

Start-ups emerged from many sources. Paul Lutus wrote Apple Writer, a popular word processing program, in a wood cabin atop a mountain in Oregon, 23 miles from the closest town (a 1,300-foot extension cord powered his computer from the nearest outlet).

Mitch Kapor was the founder of Lotus Development Co., one of the most successful software firms in the 1980s. (But initially, he was getting his Ph.D. in psychology and dropped it when he started Micro Finance Systems from his apartment.) He sold that company to Personal Software for $1 million and started Lotus. At the time his comment on the entrepreneurs of the day could equally have applied to the hotshots of the 1990s: "A number of pioneers in this industry have gotten rich in the past few years by being merely competent and very lucky."

No one knew where real profits could be made, or, ultimately, what the PC was actually good for. An early merchandising effort by Macy's in 1978 to sell the $500 VideoBrain by Umtech Inc. met with a mix of enthusiasm and confusion. According to Robert Frey, Macy's consumer electronics buyer, "There was an intense desire on the part of a lot consumers, and our own personnel, to be involved with the machine. But when people stopped and asked what it could do for them, we found that we couldn't explain it."[19]

The high-tech boom of the 1980s consisted of many mini-waves starting with the personal computer and software and then moving into related items like disk drives, printers, and video monitors.

Despite the lack of a real business case, the distorted valuations reflected the bubble. In 1980, Apple Computer had profits of $12 million but a market capitalization of $1.7 billion, more than Chase Manhattan Bank, the third largest bank in the United States at the time.

Money poured in faster than the already fast pace of concept creation. "We financed Apple in 1977, took it public in 1980. If you're in another venture firm you don't have one of those. What do you do?" reflected Don Valentine. He saw the copycat start-ups of the Internet era following the same patterns as those of the PC era. "You go and get one. You finance one. And what happens with the inflation of value in companies, in part because Apple went public, [is that] everyone can now see how terrific this business is. But it didn't do anything. The first memory device was an audio tape player. Part of the issue at Apple was creating what became called the killer applications. When that momentum builds, other investors, other venture firms want to invest in PC companies. The whole world then looked at DEC's product with the VT 100 tube that costs $250,000. When you could buy one for $4000—no one knew what people would do with it. There was no answer. The answers that people served up were humorous at best."[20]

Apple Computer was taken public by Morgan Stanley. With so much uncertainty and so few people who really understood this new technology, investors needed to look to other experts for insight. Don Valentine saw the Apple IPO as a critical event in generating market enthusiasm. Morgan Stanley became part of the trust pyramid that made Apple computer viable for so many other investors. Don Valentine remembered its role, saying it was the "imprimatur that there must be something fabulous here—that was very carefully orchestrated to get Morgan to do that."[21]

The market effects of connecting start-ups to the public markets further fueled the overdrive generation of copycats that saturated the market. "These things tend to be categories in which a small number of companies could be financed, and fit and do well in a time when you truly had inadequate funding in the venture community. Once you had these public markets with the tourists having access to large amounts of money, then you could no longer limit the number of start ups in a category to a rational number," said Valentine.[22]

The success of Apple, like the success of Netscape, set the standard. Both companies crystallized in people's imagination the possibilities of getting very rich very fast and changing the world. After each start-up went IPO, the hunt was on for the next one. Judy Myer, who invested in Apple two years before it went public, observed at the time, "That's the name of the game—to find more Apples."[23]

An entertaining account of the history of the personal computer by Robert Cringely, speaks of the PC clone wave that followed in the latter half of the 1980s and software copycat companies. "After the success of the Compaq Computer, every venture capitalist in the world wanted to fund a PC clone company. After the success of Lotus Development, every venture capitalist in the world wanted to fund a PC software company. They threw tons of money at anyone who could claim anything like a track record. Those people took the money and generally failed. . . . VCs love to do me-too products and have the tendency to fund simultaneously twenty-six hard disk companies that all expect to have 8 percent of the market within two years."[24]

This vision of grand transformations fed the hype. In 1983, *Time* magazine made Adam Osborne the "Man of the Year." Adam Osborne, who founded Osborne Computer Corporation and made portable computers, was quoted as saying, "I liken myself to Henry Ford and the auto industry."[25] The Osborne computer was launched in the summer of 1982 and folded into the size of a suitcase and weighed "just" 24 pounds, as one news account mentioned. The Osborne sold for $1,795 and in the first 4 months showed sales of $1 million and had a 25 month backlog of orders. The company claimed it would sell $200 million by the end of the next year (half the revenues of Apple Computer after 5 years of production.) Instead, it went bankrupt the next summer.

The media joined the frenzy, creating the familiar echo chamber by hyping the market and generating ad revenues. According to the Television Bureau of Advertising, money spent on TV network and spot advertising by the computer industry jumped from about $26 million in 1981 to more than $262 million in 1984. By one account, in 1984 the computer industry's share of magazine advertising accounted for 56.7 percent of the total.[26] *Byte* was the largest magazine. The November 1983 issue was 728 pages. *PC* magazine switched to twice a month, but the March 6, 1984, issue was still 525 pages. Postal workers refused to deliver the telephone-book-sized periodical. By one account there were as many as 400 computer magazines on the market.

Mike Belling of Stoneware Inc. noted at the time that the discipline had declined dramatically in the bubble environment, "The software business is growing so fast that all you've got to do to stay in business is hang on to your tail. Other people are making mistakes too, so you can afford to run a company by the seat of your pants."[27]

Apple computers did not have a company budget until 1982—five years after it started. No one knew how much money was coming in or going out, but there was so much money coming in, it didn't seem to matter.

The young entrepreneurs of the day were also 20-somethings creating a new computer and software industry from scratch. The lack of any history, benchmarks, or reliable information created both excitement as well as uncertainty in valuing these young enterprises. "It's a tremendous business to be a part of," said Mike Belling, who bought a software company in 1980. "But it has its pitfalls like cars used to. It's all so brand new that there's nothing to go by yet. There's no history to tell you how many copies of a program to produce."[28]

In an effort to get closer to the profits generation, traditionally conservative banks altered their traditional ways of doing business and began finding ways to participate in the high returns of start-ups. The Small Business Investment Corporation estimated that 28 of the largest 50 banks had arrangements to get into investing in start-ups through Small Business Investment Companies.[29]

Large corporations felt significant pressure to jump into the consumer market. The standards of the day such as Texas Instruments, Atari, and IBM all tried. But surprising firms also tried to contort themselves to get a piece of the action. Both Mattel and Timex launched efforts, as they succumbed to the temptation to stretch beyond their core competence to get a piece of the action.

The public markets were increasingly primed for infant companies. Seagate, for example, raised $26 million in the public market in September 1981, having introduced its first product in only July 1980. After the IPO the company was valued at $185 million, worth over 18 months of sales.

Between 1978 and 1985 there were about 40 personal computer/microcomputer companies funded by venture capitalists. While Apple was the first high-flyer, first funded in 1978 with half a million dollars from Sequoia Capital, it ushered in many followers. Altos, Eagle Computers, Franklin Computers, Cosmos Computers, Compaq, Corona, and many others all made their best efforts.

During the same period some 30 printer companies were started by venture capitalists. And most famously between 1977 and 1984, 43 different manufacturers of Winchester disk drives were funded with almost $400 million.[30]

The investment community was also captivated. The MBAs understood the new tool because they saw the real benefit of the spreadsheets to do financial analysis. Continually on the search for the next big investment opportunity, they collectively decided the PC was it. But they made the same conceptual leap about consumer adoption, made by many Internet analysts—If I want to use it today, so will everyone else. Thus they created the vision of a huge market that would grow practically *instantly*. The combination of Apple Computer and VisiCalc was a powerful mixture that ignited the imagination and the markets. For the first time, many corporate middle managers saw what the computer could do on their desktops. It became a powerful tool for day-to-day financial analysis, scenario planning, and complex systems calculations.

In 1981, Fidelity launched sector funds specializing in electronics, computers, telecommunications, and software and computer services. By 1985, their size grew to $1.34 billion. The funds performed very well, capturing 3 of the top 5 spots in the Lipper Analytical Services, Inc survey of annual performance.[31] At the time, Lipper counted some 21 science and technology sector funds in operation.

The sense that the young people got it and the older managers would have to adapt or die was also apparent as the headline of one *Wall Street Journal* article illustrated: "Finished at Forty: Rising Stars Can Become Obsolete Has-Beens If They Can't Come to Grips with the Computer." The article asserts, "They're becoming the lost generation of American business." The president of Roy Walters Associates, a management con-sulting, firm was quoted as saying that technology "is scaring the hell out of these 35 to 45 year old middle managers. A lot either get shoved aside with younger people getting their jobs or they get fired."[32]

In reality, the speed of adoption was far slower than analysts had antici-pated. Adoption was slowed by cumbersome software that forced non-tech-nical people to grapple with the tool rather than find it useful. Productive payroll packages were abandoned because they were not easy enough to use and not worth the conversion. One manager said at the time, "probably 75 percent of our employees still have no reason to buy a PC."[33]

While resistance to the hype may have been appropriate, outright skepticism of the potential of personal computers now seems ridiculous. "Our surveys over the past two years found that a preponderance of Americans cannot imagine any way they could use a personal computer, either at home or at work," said William Cogshall, president of Software Access, in 1985.[34]

"You have to use common sense, says Dennis Whitaker, a Radio Shack computer salesman and another skeptic. "Some things, like bal-ancing a checkbook, you don't need a computer for. There are people who think computers will solve every problem and that's not true."[35] But in the end the optimistic vision would be proven correct.

The market slid sharply in 1984, hurting investors who had viewed the personal computer as the fastest road to riches. Hambrecht & Quists technology index representing 152 stocks peaked at 940.21 in June 1983. By the end of 1984 it dropped by almost one half to 480. The market was very poor at distinguishing legitimate companies from ille-gitimate ones on the way up, and, just as during the Internet bust, it was very bad at separating them on the way down. "The market has been throwing the babies out with the bath water," says Otis Bradley, a per-sonal computer analyst with Alex Brown & Sons.[36] The wipeout left all companies beaten, but a select few emerged as survivors. At the time they were Apple, Lotus, Compaq, Tandy, and Commodore.

By the first quarter of 1985, the industry as a whole, from mainframes to minis to personal computers, became sluggish. The slowdown dashed expectations that 50 or 60 percent increases in PC sales would continue through the decade.

According to one analyst, the revenue and profit of the five largest producers were not just slowing down but lagging the overall economy for the first time in its 30-year history. IBM, Digital Equipment, Hewlett-Packard, Burroughs, and Apple all saw revenue growth of just 6 percent in the first quarter of 1985 compared to 17 to 19 percent between 1981 and 1984. Profits shrank 16 percent in the same quarter compared to growth of 16 to 25 percent in the preceding 3 years.[37]

In the late 1980s, after the collapse, people remarked on the excesses and the lessons learned. Bill Hambrecht said at the time, "They've all come to Jesus as far as cash management is concerned."[38] The lack of discipline and the overoptimistic projections fed poor spending habits. "If a company thought it would sell 100 computers, it would buy supplies for 110," said an analyst who worked for Hambrecht.[39]

John Doerr, one of the most high profile VCs during the Internet bubble and a partner at Kleiner Perkins Caufield & Byers, said after the PC collapse, "Venture capital has financed far too many me-too companies, and now we are beginning to see the consequences."[40]

Illegitimate companies also emerged producing what was called "Vaporware." But separating these from the real thing became difficult because so few people understood this new industry. "All the vaporware and hype and over-promotion have been the electronic equivalent of crying wolf," said Lawrence Brilliant, chairman of Network Technology International. "It's frightening new users."[41] Robert McClellend, a computer industry analyst with Solomon Brothers, warned investors in July 1984, "if you cannot understand a company's business, beware; it is probable that the company's management doesn't either."[42]

Kevin Landry, managing partner at T. A. Associates, commented after the bust, "It's been too easy. We were taught that the economy punishes weak companies, but for the last couple of years we have made money even on bad investments."[43]

New models were being rushed out, creating chaos in the marketplace and confusion among consumers. "Five years ago, the industry said that if you could make it, you probably should. It was a technology-driven mentality," said Robert Brownstein, vice-president of Regis McKenna, a PR firm whose clients included Apple Computer. "Now the companies want to see that there are specific markets and customers for the technology.

They're not just throwing spaghetti against the wall and seeing which strands stick."[44]

John Sculley, Apple's CEO, reflected on the bubble period, "people were buying without knowing what they wanted."[45]

The decline of discipline also led computer manufacturers to produce for the frontiers of technology rather than for genuine customers. "The problem in the computer industry today is both sides of the house are entirely driven by computer engineers," said Richard Koffler, a consultant who studied how people work with computers.[46]

The seemingly endless supply of capital was also apparent during the PC bubble. "We build capacity and staff as though the boom would never end," said Ray McNulty spokesman for GenRad, "We thought 30 percent and 40 percent growth was the norm. Now we expect 10 percent to 20 percent."[47]

But as with the end of the bubble of the 1990s, the end of the PC bubble took many participants by surprise. "They got blindsided by the slowdown in market growth rate," said Bob Lefkowitz at InfoCorp.[48]

"There may have been a hiatus for a while, while customers tried to learn to integrate the various options they had," said IBM vice president Ed Lucente.[49] After the PC boom ended, the optimists would end up being proved correct and the pessimists wrong. The mistake was not in perceiving the potential but in projecting the speed of growth and profits.

SIX

MANAGING THE BUBBLE BATH AHEAD

True genius resides in the capacity for evaluation of uncertain, hazardous, and conflicting information.

—Winston Churchill

THESE BUBBLE-MAKING DRIVERS OF HUMAN NATURE are immutable for the foreseeable future. We will create many more bubbles. Most will not be as large as the Internet bubble that spread through large parts of the U.S. and global economy. The next one may be an industry bubble or a product bubble. It may not be related to technology. In 2004, we are probably witnessing a new market opportunity bubble in China. Bubbles are inevitable.

Four years after the Internet bubble burst in March 2000, insiders and outsiders continued to worry about many smaller bubbles in hedge funds, exchange traded funds, biotechnology, outsourcing, nanotechnology, social networking platforms, oil prices, real estate in numerous parts of the world, and plasma screens. In each of these cases, participants have said *this is like the Internet in 1999*. The frenzy operates similarly in small and big market opportunities. The economy, business managers, and investors are awash in bubbles. This means that the risks and opportunities of bubbles are ever present. It does not mean that *all* managers and investors must confront the frenzy, but it does mean that *some* managers and investors *always* face the frenzy.

One of the important lessons from the history of bubbles is that they have been created in a wide range of countries, with substantially different financing institutions, economic structures, technologies, and governments. Bubbles are not dependent on venture capital funds; they do not need CNNfn. Entrepreneurs are always experimenting and tinkering, often clustering around common efforts—nanotechnology, biotechnology, and bioinformatics seem to be the latest. Big breakthroughs will get noticed, and those will always attract financing from somewhere. If there is a sufficient number of confirming signals, a consensus crystalizes and then the bubble cycle begins. Investors are always looking for the next hot thing. The media is always poised to hype it up. The markets are always looking for the highest returns.

Bubbles are self-reinforcing systems that are hard to escape. In the broadest sense, bubbles are created by mania or irrational exuberance that seizes the markets. At one level more nuanced, they are also driven by the reinforcing tugs of fear and greed. At yet a finer level of detail we see that bubbles occur when there is systematic distortions in the perception of investors amidst wild uncertainty as well as competitive incentives and pressures that over time compel more and more investors to join the momentum. The information distortions are the power of positive stories, the decline of discipline, the shunning of the skeptics, the failure to distinguish value from profit, peer pressure, confirmation bias, information manipulation, and trust pyramids. The competitive distortions feed the competitive cascade that compels investors to seize the great opportunities and avoid the risks of being left behind leading to too many investors funding too many start-ups. The perception of endless money further distorts investors' ability to assess risk and manage business functions normally.

As we have seen, during bubbles three kinds of bad investments far outweigh the good investments. There are too many copycat investments that saturate the market, there are too many investments in poor business opportunities, and even the legitimate businesses suffer from excessive valuations. Each of these collectively means that more and more money is spent on unsustainable and unprofitable targets, ultimately insuring that the bubble will end in wreckage for most investors while a few lucky ones walk away very rich.

THE BUBBLE BATH AHEAD?

Changes in technology and financial markets may end up increasing the frequency of bubbles in the future.

SIZE AND SPEED OF GLOBAL CAPITAL

Global capital moves faster and in greater volume now than at any time in measurable history, enabling investors to chase the greatest returns anywhere in the world, increasing volatility, and contributing to bubble formation.

The percentage of U.S. stocks owned by foreign residents has grown steadily over the decades. In 1960, just 2 percent of U.S. equities were owned by those abroad, about $9 billion. The share grew to almost 5 percent in 1980 and to 7 percent by 1990. The share of U.S. equities owned by foreign residents peaked in 2002 at 11 percent, amounting to $1.4 trillion.

More importantly, the movement of global capital, the inflows and outflows, has been accelerating. At the turn of the millennium, the *quarterly* inflows from abroad were $194 billion and represented 1 percent of the total market value of the U.S. stock market, a record level since the Federal Reserve started collecting data in 1952. This was more than total inflows into mutual funds. To put this in historical perspective, the only previous period in which foreign inflows surpassed *half this* inflow was the brief period before the end of the last bubble of 1986 and 1987. The global growth in both the size and speed of capital movement has brought powerful benefits to businesses and investors to many parts of the world. At the same time, the trend also poses challenges to investors and governments that need to be recognized and analyzed. Now that capital flows are not just attracted to sectors that show remarkable returns, capital floods those sectors with astounding speed.

LARGER VENTURE CAPITAL INDUSTRY

Another development that will help fuel future bubbles is that the venture capital industry is now far larger than in the past. Through each new wave of technology funding, from 1960, 1980 to 1990, the former cottage industry has deepened not only its expertise in financing new companies but also become a substantial global industry reaching $100 billion. This tremendous size means that there is significant "pent up" capital always looking for extraordinary returns. The need to create large returns on so much money, will create powerful incentives to fuel the next bubble.

Despite the Internet bust, limited partners continue to invest heavily in venture funds. It is hard to know for sure how this will affect the industry dynamics. The venture funds will ultimately have to put that money to work. Without a bubble available to create money making opportunities, it is likely that the returns to those limited partner investors will be low. Alternatively, a bubble may arrive to channel that pent up capital.

A common lesson that many investors and venture capitalists seemed to draw from the Internet bubble as well as the PC bubble was not to stay away from bubbles the next time but to time them better in the future. The next time, many hope, they will get in and out earlier. Others hope that they will be able to maintain better discipline in their investment decisions but are fairly realistic about holding up against the momentum.

In addition, the growth of the venture industry may help spur the pace of innovation, which can also foster bubble formation. According to a study by Samuel Kortum and Josh Lerner, venture capital activity in an industry significantly increases the number of patents it produces. In the years leading up to 1998, when the study was done, the VC industry was an average of just 3 percent of the size of the R&D spending. However, the study finds that venture capital accounts for 15 percent of industrial innovations.[1] So with far less spending they are able to generate many more innovations. As the venture industry grows, this may spur innovation further.

ACCELERATING INNOVATION

Investment bubbles related specifically to technology may increase in frequency because a growing share of the U.S. and global economy is driven by this sector. Communications across borders and research disciplines may also be increasing the speed of innovation. Each new innovation seems to have multiplied the areas for further innovation. Consider the semiconductor: Within a few decades it enabled the computer, the PC, the Internet, wireless, and so forth. Each of these innovations spawns further innovative ideas and investment possibilities.

According to the U.S. Patent Office, 157,495 patents were granted in 2000, up from 90,365 in 1990 and 61,819 in 1980. Looked at another way, in 2000 there were 560 patents per 1 million people in the population of the United States, compared to 363 in 1990, 273 in 1980, and 317 in 1970.[2]

One sign of this accelerating innovative process is that the life-cycle of existing technology is shrinking. New technologies become obsolete in shorter and shorter periods. Scott McNealy put it humorously when he said, "The nice thing about technology is that is has the shelf-life of a banana. It's going to wear out, it will get used up."[3] A study by the Federal Reserve determined this to be true statistically: the depreciation of goods, and particularly computers, has been accelerating dramatically over time, leading to an increasing need to invest.[4]

Corporations also increasingly view perfecting innovation as their only way to survive. According to Michael Cox, chief economist of the Federal Reserve Bank in Dallas, from 1917 until 1977 it took an average of 30 years to replace half the companies in the top 100. But between 1977 and 1998 it took just 12 years to replace half the firms. Of the 100 largest public companies in 1999, only five are survivors from the top 100 of 1917. Half the firms in the top 100 are newcomers, entering the list in just the past two decades.[5] That is a remarkable acceleration in "creative destruction."

These three factors—global capital movement, growing venture capital industry, and accelerating innovation—are not stand alone forces. They can reinforce each other as venture capital continues to fuel innovation and global capital movement is poised to flood the next sector that appears to generate frenzied returns. The interaction between these forces will certainly add strong pressures and will likely increase the frequency of bubbles. In the past there was hardly a year of economic growth that did not feature a bubble in some sector somewhere since 1950. In the future there may be multiple bubbles occurring at any one time. The bubbles of the future may compete with each other for attention and for capital. We will live in interesting times.

INSTITUTIONS FOR MITIGATING BUBBLES

One of the important lessons to draw from the persistent occurrence of bubbles is that investors are still pretty bad at evaluating innovative opportunities in new technologies or markets. Free markets are the best system available to allocate investments, but unfortunately, that is still a fairly messy process with the potential for many mistakes along the way. The core reason should not be a surprise: The new opportunities that create bubbles are based on the unknowable future. Markets need information to work efficiently. For all our progress, there are still no crystal balls to see the future clearly. Free markets also create the need for competitive returns, which progressively encourages investors to let go of discipline and follow the momentum.

With bubbles being an inevitable and ultimately valuable part of innovation, a key focus then is to manage them effectively as investors, business managers, and policy makers. It remains imperative to ensure that institutions play a productive role in improving the effectiveness of businesses and economies to continue to innovate while avoiding catastrophe. Institutions cannot prevent bubbles, but they can play an important role in mitigating bubbles negative consequences.

Regulatory agencies must maintain vigilance over all forms of market manipulation that distort information and access to the market. The Internet analysts who lied about their true thoughts and analyses of company prospects undermined the ability of markets to function well during an already confusing period. Efforts to warp the competitive playing field in favor of selected individuals or businesses further distort efficiency and exacerbates bubbles. Throughout history, scams emerge during bubbles. As a result, constant vigilance is essential.

Emerging markets face much tougher institutional challenges during bubbles. In general, the information about any business or market activity is far less available. The banking systems in most emerging markets are relatively weak, making recovery far more difficult when bubbles burst. Labor markets are also more delicate. When the Asian economic crisis hit in 1997, the economies affected had been effectively full-employment economies. When the bubble burst, the employees were laid off for the first time ever. But, the countries had no system to deal with this, no unemployment insurance, no job training, no assistance to help people find other jobs. As a result, the burst bubble led not just to a financial crisis but to widespread social unrest. In order for smoothly functioning economies to weather the ups and downs, stabilizing financial and labor markets mechanisms need to be in place.

The United States learned this through the Great Depression. Afterward we made important changes in the banking system. The Federal Reserve Bank improved its understanding of how to use interest rates to stabilize the economy. We created unemployment insurance systems to cushion individuals during downturns.

A stunning feature of the U.S. economy today is that one of the biggest bubbles in history did not do more financial, economic, and social damage when it burst. It is a testament to the strong market structures we have built so far.

All of these institutional mechanism and policy lessons will not stop the next bubble, since bubble dynamics are driven by human nature. Hopefully, however, over time, with constant refinement, we can lesson the negative consequences.

A CALL TO ACTION: REFORM MBA CURRICULUM

In the United States, the core institutions exist and need monitoring. The next frontier for reform is not regulatory or institutional—it is *ourselves*. Individual decision-making needs to be improved. MBA's are trained to be the educated elite of business management. Well-trained MBA's should have been an important source of *resistance* to the poorly thought through business plans, investment decisions and collective insanity. As they swarmed into young start-ups, venture capital firms, and investment banks over the course of the 1990s, they should have been among the first to sound the alarm bells that basic business practices and economics were being violated at the risk of everyone involved. They should have been able to provide better insight into where the real opportunities lay. Instead, they were more caught up in the frenzy than most. Some point to a lack of experience needed to complement the classroom lessons. But many of the mistakes made were fundamental mistakes in basic business analysis and would have led to failing grades on any exam. Indeed, the curriculum may have done more harm than good because it fed arrogance and overconfidence without providing enough intellectual substance to cut through the mania and identify the real opportunities.

MBA programs should provide their graduates with a far better understanding of how bubbles function and how the frenzy distorts decision-making. Bubbles are a standard feature of business and investment decision-making. Thus, the history and dynamics of bubbles should be a standard part of MBA curriculum, taught right along side discounted cash flow and other basic topics in corporate finance classes.

Current curriculum is lopsided even in the top-tier schools, focusing on some basic valuation techniques without providing students a more comprehensive understanding of how financial modeling and markets frequently run amok and what to do about it. This is not just a benefit MBA programs can offer their students and employers, but a responsibility.

WARNING SIGNS

It is impossible to know when a bubble begins. Among many others, Alan Greenspan worried about irrational exuberance in 1996. Even after the crash, none of the overall market indexes returned to the level that raised his concern. Once bubbles burst, there is even no clear way to know when they began. There are no tell-tale signs that can clearly signal "a bubble is here." But there are warning signs that should set off an alert that a bubble may be arriving or already sweeping the marketplace. Bubbles are more apparent in patterns of behavior than in specific numbers.

Not all of these are visible to the general public. Some are discernable only to those who are inside the investment decision-making process in venture capital firms, corporations, or investment funds.

BLOCKBUSTERS

The fist sign that a bubble may be on the way is the break-away blockbuster that crystallizes investors imagination and solidifies the idea that investors can become rich very quickly. When the fragmented marketplace becomes synthesized into a wondrous money-making story, investors may be very close to setting a full-fledged bubble in motion. When investors start chasing or perhaps more accurately trying to create the next Netscape, the next Apple Computer, the next Genentech, trouble is on the way. This eye-catching event is not a sign that a bubble has arrived. It is a sign that a bubble might emerge as investors become enamored of the frontier of the new opportunity. As the opportunities increase with successive stellar IPOs or investment returns, the probability that a bubble will emerge deepens because investors will be increasingly tempted to focus on stock price movement, new metrics, and the image of a wondrous new world rather than sustainable business opportunities.

COPYCATS

Once the copycat opportunities emerge, there is a strong probability that a bubble is in full swing. It is a sign that investment decisions are no longer looking for innovative opportunities that can succeed in producing incredible returns, but rather jealously emulating past successes in the hopes of reaping the same returns. Copycat successes are likely to be brief at best. Timing is everything, as the vast majority will fail. Picking the winners would be equivalent to picking the right number on the roulette wheel.

CHEAP MONEY

Another important sign that a bubble is in full swing is when money seems to be endless and can be effortlessly raised for the "hot opportunity." Cheap money is a sign that investors are evaluating investment opportunities based not on real business potential but rather on the enthusiasm and momentum of the marketplace. As a result, money is spent indiscriminately on bad investment opportunities. The metric for "cheap money" is hard to define clearly and may be harder for the public market to notice. Venture capitalists may be the first to see cheap money emerging in a bubble market, as they find it easier to raise money from limited partners on more advantageous terms. There is no publicly available data point that quantifies this, but experienced venture capitalists see it clearly. Similarly, corporate budgeting for hot initiatives also loosens. Employees see the policy shift. The public may notice their press releases announcing grand new initiatives. The key is to reverse the human tendency to see the increasing valuations and IPOs and signs of growing opportunity and instead see them as growing signs of a bubble that may feature short-term opportunities for speculators but are destined to collapse over time for everyone.

SECTOR FUNDS

One extremely visible signal that a bubble may be in full swing is the growth in the number of investment funds focused on a targeted sector. When investors start plowing their money into highly targeted funds in great numbers, it is likely that the environment is unsustainable for decent returns on that money.

Sector funds emerge only when demand for a specific investment category is high enough. It is when sector fund creation *accelerates* that there is real danger. When investors are attracted to startling returns in a specific sector, that that they are probably inappropriately misbalancing their investment portfolio. When an increasing number of funds are being created year after year to capture this demand, investors are probably chasing past returns rather than likely future returns. They are become swept away by the frenzy piling their money into funds created just before the crash.

Venture capital allocation to different emerging industries also become out of balance during bubbles. As the chart in Chapter 3 shows, each of the last 3 venture financed bubbles shows venture capital disbursements in computer hardware, biotech, and the internet becoming a large percentage of total venture spending—generating bubbles. Computer hardware peaked at 35 percent, biotech also at 35 percent while the Internet topped out at nearly 50 percent of all venture investments. Industries that never experienced bubble rarely rise above 10 percent of total venture allocations. This recent history suggests a pattern that can be used to identify future emerging bubbles: When venture capital allocation rises above 15–20 percent of all venture investments a bubble is likely emerging. The good news for investors is this threshold may be the early signs with years left before the crash.

MANAGING BUBBLES OF THE FUTURE

Management Issues

The process of managing bubbles effectively should begin before the next bubble starts. Being prepared for the next technology bubble means understanding the innovative frontiers before they become distorted by hype. Insight into core technological change is central to managing innovation. Obtaining expertise early and regularly, through R&D and strategic partnerships, will help reduce the uncertainty that so many investors suffered from during bubbles. However, ongoing expertise will not eliminate uncertainty.

As result, individuals and organizations that make investment decisions must be able to cope with unexpected change. That means building an internal culture capable of avoiding many of the disastrous mistakes we've surveyed over the course of this book.

At the core of this culture must be unrelenting integrity and analytical discipline. Far too many investment decisions in innumerable organizations during bubbles are made based on hype, momentum, and excitement, without any serious thought process. Too many individuals try to sway others through bravado and charisma rather than deliberation. Creating a culture that can assess the ambiguities and recognize the risks and opportunities is an ongoing process of culture development. That requires a culture of disciplined deliberation. Effectively thinking through strategic and investment ambiguities during frenzied periods is frighteningly scarce especially given how important it is to avoid disastrous investments during bubbles. Building a culture that can maintain this discipline through the whirlwind of change means establishing standards early and deep in the organization.

Embrace the skeptics.   One method of doing this is embracing the skeptics. Skeptics are extremely valuable because they serve as important counterweights to enthusiasm and frenzy. Skeptics may be wrong, but their commentary should be debated and considered, not shunned. Through this process, the final investment decision will be deeper and safer. This will help avoid the human tendency to seek information that confirms our existing beliefs. If a natural skeptic is not present to play a critical role, a "devil's advocate" should be appointed to challenge the prevailing thinking.

Part of the challenge to maintaining these standard good business practices during bubbles is that other businesses appear to become far more exciting and cutting-edge to employees. Key staff start defecting to those organizations that seem to be so successful, so dynamic, so sexy, and offer the possibility of becoming fabulously rich. During the Internet bubble, a number of businesses launched Internet initiatives primarily to maintain their staff and boost morale.

Philosophy of bubbles. One way to maintain organizational stability through these dramatic periods is to create a philosophy of bubbles—"stay out" or "ride the wave" should be a decision made before the bubble starts so that a culture can be created to effectively respond. Some of the businesses that were most torn apart during the Internet bubble were those who *switched* orientation from resistance and skepticism to embracing the Internet mania and jumping in late, just in time for it to collapse. The effect of switching can be devastating financially, strategically, and organizationally.

Some organizations may chose to be "bubble-seekers," meaning they are always ready to seek and inflate the next bubble, whatever it is, whenever it is. These organizations foster hype internally and externally. For these organizations, success will largely depend on luck or laying as many seeds as possible early enough in the hopes of striking gold early in the bubble and timing everything else correctly.

For everyone else, it is always important to know that "bubble-seekers" will always exist in the market and their investment decisions will have dramatic ripple effects on everyone else. Organizational incentives need to be properly aligned to this approach to bubbles. This means that compensation packages such as bonuses, and options can be calibrated to have extremely short term (bubble chasing) incentives or longer term incentives that promote sustainable growth.

No amount of pre-bubble preparation will make bubbles easy to manage. Organizations that find themselves in a bubble market are torn by intense pressures. Decision-making is very hard. The common mistakes that we have seen over the course of this book serve as a partial guide on what to do instead.

ANALYTICAL ISSUES

By now it is obvious that one of the most important responses to a frenzied environment is to maintain disciplined analysis. The stronger the pressure grows to follow the market trend, the more important it is to remain firm. Investments made in 1999, when so many were piling in almost indiscriminately, lost significantly. Those investors were chasing the past returns, not the future opportunities. They were chasing the returns that only those lucky enough to be in the market several years earlier had reaped. It is when this pressure to capitulate is strongest and investors are most likely to bend, that it is already probably too late to capture the great returns that appears to be rewarding bad investments. The bubble will quickly end, leaving these late-comers with staggering losses. No matter how well poor companies seem to be doing, the key is to view their success as a symptom of the bubble market, not as a reflection that traditional discipline needs to be evaluated with fresh eyes.

Separate speculation vs. Investments.   Investors may, in the end, wish to make speculative investments even if their disciplined analysis shows that the opportunity is not a good business investment in the traditional sense. However, it will serve all investors to acknowledge this speculative approach explicitly, rather than trying to conduct analysis that makes speculative investments look like good business investments. Speculative investments, if undertaken at all, should be relegated to a separate pool in any investment portfolio. The most important question for this segment is what and when is the opportunity to cash out before the bubble collapses.

Use probabilistic analysis not point estimates.   One analytical tool for handling uncertainty is to avoid point estimates and use probabilities. Uncertainty pervades all business decisions and it is better when doing forecasts of revenues, costs, and stock prices, to use probability distributions than single point estimates. During bubbles, when uncertainty is so much greater, using point estimates becomes nearly meaningless. To illustrate, consider a stock price target of $110. That figure, in most cases, depends on estimates of future revenues, various expenditures, and the risk of the business to derive and estimate of how profitable the business may become and how much cash it may generate that could go to shareholders. In reality, each of these inputs are subject to significant uncertainty, especially for new technologies and business in emerging markets. As a result, each input should not be estimates as a single data point such as revenue in 2007 will be $100 million; but rather a probability distribution where the average is $100 million but some probability that it may also be $10 million, $200 million and everything in between. If each of the key inputs have ranges like these, then the final stock price also will have a range with an expected probability that of $100 but also a probability that it will be just $20. The probability distribution helps determine the risks. For example, stock prices that have a 95 percent probability of laying between $60 and $150 is safer than one that may lay between $20 and $180. It is similarly helpful to know, for example, that there may be a 5 percent probability that the stock is work only $5 if you are betting that it will be worth $120. This doesn't necessarily mean you always want the safer investment, but this focus on probabilities helps understand more clearly the risks.

Wall Street reports that stipulate specific price targets, are in effect, ill serving their readers. They should all provide probability distributions to improve the information to their clients. This approach also reinforces and acknowledges that all investments especially in new technologies and new markets are betting on various layers of uncertainty, not expectations of a specific target.

Separate the risk of an investment and the risk of the market momentum. Numerous investors will face intense competitive pressures to play. Investors will capitulate once they perceive that it is less risky to be wrong with the crowd than right alone. All investors, however, should be able to separate the two types of risk and evaluate them separately. There is the investment risk of a specific business opportunity, and there is the strategic risk associated with participating or avoiding the market momentum during bubbles.

Fully understand the decision-making process of the experts. It is important to understand that investment bubbles are generated amid significant uncertainty, and emerging experts have an effect on the marketplace disproportionate to the true insight they provide. When observing the actions of "experts," investors must fully appreciate their full decision-making process, especially their approach to risk. It is not enough to assume that their investment decision is a good one because they are experts. They may have specialized approaches toward risk and opportunity. As a result, it is important to understand how these individuals' positions differ from ours so we can appropriately understand the signal and not be deceived by the noise.

Be wary of information manipulation.   Bubbles always bring in scams. As a result, investors must be especially wary of the information being provided and the terms of any deals being offered.

Strategic Issues

Find a strategy to manage risk through the full arc of the bubble. No one knows when bubbles begin or when they will end. But bubbles do have an arc, and the big investment opportunities appear at the early stage of bubbles and after it has all ended. Everything else will do poorly once the bubble bursts.

Investing during this early period usually requires an ongoing effort to be at the innovative cutting-edge so that your investments are already in place once the rest of the market is captured by frenzy. Investors that miss the beginning are advised to wait until the end. Those who resisted the momentum and were skeptical, and waited too long, will be better off staying out of the market altogether rather than jumping in, because it is likely that they will make this conversion right at the end. Unfortunately, it is impossible to know when the beginning is over and it's time to quit.

Throughout bubble environments it is critical always to know that investments will be cheaper once the bubble bursts—especially during the period when markets overreact in revulsion. Bubbles are the worst times to invest, even though they appear to offer the most compelling, exciting, and seemingly lucrative possibilities. Investments during bubbles are buy-high/sell-low investments—whether they involve financing a start-up, buying stocks, or acquiring a business.

Passing on investments may look dumb to many observers and may be hard to resist the pressure to play, but in the end waiting can save a lot of money; money that can be used later to focus on investments in the likely winners rather than getting lost in a blizzard of indistinguishable companies and opportunities. Resisting the pressure to play may be the most effective strategy for protection against overpaying for business opportunities.

While private companies in particular and certain other investment decisions may be able to resist successfully, for many there is little underestimating how difficult it would be to resist the onslaught from Wall Street, clients, staff, the media, practically everyone.

Minimize "real" exposure to downturn.   For those who are forced to participate in the bubble for competitive reasons, it is best to minimize real exposure. That means avoiding real cash whenever possible. If you are planning a trip to Europe and the dollar is very low compared to the euro, it would be great to have a bank account already there from which you can draw euros to spend there rather than converting your money from cheap dollars to expensive euros and getting killed on the exchange rate.

Using cash to pay for investment during bubbles is like converting your cheap dollars to expensive euros rather than paying for them in the inflated currency. Use inflated stock to purchase inflated stock whenever possible. Cisco did a great job in its acquisitions by making primarily stock transactions. Alternatively, use strategic partnerships deals and barter. GE used barter arrangements for a long time during the bubble. This helps avoid inflated prices.

Hedges and insurance investments may be necessary to protect core business in the face of the uncertainty of the new technology. But they should be viewed explicitly with this mindset and valuations methods.

Remain diversified.   Opportunities do exist during bubbles, just as opportunities exist when people buy lottery tickets—however, the odds are not in most people's favor. Those with deep insight or competitive positioning have a better chance than anyone else. The odds are stacked in their favor. Everyone else is scrambling to pick the right deal that happens to create the timely money making event. Given that so much of anyone's portfolio of investment decisions will be largely based on luck during bubbles, don't bet the farm and don't be greedy. It is more important than ever to remain diversified. While diversification will mute returns that many hope for during bubble mania, that protection will be worth a lot when things crash. Consider AOL/Time Warner, Vivendi, and WebVan as looming warning signs.

The effects of bubbles are profound and typically have created dramatic and systematic improvements in business, economics and social interaction. The railroad, radio, cars, television, computers, and the Internet have all thoroughly transformed the economy and social interaction. The bubbles in emerging markets such as the Asian Tiger Countries and now China have lifted millions of people from poverty and created powerful global businesses.

Bubbles usher in momentous change, but they do not represent the entire journey. It is the road to get there that is so bumpy and it is our driving skills that need improving to avoid continuing wreckage.

NOTES

INTRODUCTION

1. Remarks by Chairman Alan Greenspan, "New Challenges for Monetary Policy," before a symposium sponsored by the Federal Reserve Bank of Kansas City in Jackson Hole, Wyoming, August 27, 1999.

ONE

1. Author interview with Thomas Perkins, July 22, 2003.
2. Jim Clark, *Netscape Time,* St. Martin's Griffin, New York: 1999, p. 8.
3. Author interview, July 3, 2003.
4. The Herring Takes an in-depth look at the hottest topic in the venture capital community: the risks and opportunities of investing in the Internet," April 1994.
5. Author interview with Michael Moritz, August 26, 2003.
6. George Gilder, *Microcosm,* Simon & Schuster: New York: 1989, p. 17.
7. Anthony Perkins and Michael Perkins, *The Internet Bubble,* HarperBusiness: New York, 2001, p. 173.
8. Chris Freeman and Francisco Louca, *As Time Goes Buy: From the Industrial Revolution to the Information Revolution,* Oxford, Oxford University Press, 2002.
9. Edward Chancellor, *Devil Take The Hindmost,* New York, Plume, 2000, p. 124.
10. Freeman and Louca, *As Time Goes Buy.*
11. Author interview with Habib Kairuz, May 14, 2002.
12. Joseph Schumpeter, *Capitalism, Socialism, and Democracy,* HarperPerennial, New York, 1975.
13. Robert Shiller, "Conversation, Information and Herd Behavior," *The American Economic Review,* Vol. 85, No. 2 May 1995.
14. Gretchen Morgenson and Jonathan D. Glatter, "$1 Billion Settlement in I.P.O. Price-Fixing Case," *New York Times,* June 26, 2003.
15. Jay Ritter, University of Florida, http://bear.cba.ufl.edu/ritter/RUNUP750.pdf

16. Sarah O'Brien, "Fighting to hop the IPO express," *Crains,* January 24, 2000.

17. Author interview with Paul Johnson, March 20, 2004.

18. "Wall Street's Spin Game," *Business Week,* October 5, 1998, p. 148.

19. Office of the Attorney General, Morgan Stanley Findings.

20. Brett Trueman; M.H. Franco Wong; Xiao-Jun Zhang "Back to Basics: Forecasting the Revenues of Internet Firms," *Review of Accounting Studies* Vol. 6, 2001: 305–329. 2000.

21. *Business Week,* "Investing in 2004," December 29, 2003.

22. Thomas Mauet, "The Psychology of Jury Persuasion," *American Journal of Trial Advocacy,* Spring 1999.

23. Mauet, "The Psychology of Jury Persuasion."

24. Jack Willoughby, "Paper Tigers," *Barron's,* September 13, 1999.

25. Author interview September 28, 2002.

26. Author interview with Bob Kagle, December 17, 2003.

27. David N. Dreman, *Psychology and the Stock Market,* Amacon: New York 1977.

28. Author interview with Steve Dow, January 23, 2003.

29. Author interview with Tony Sun, October 9, 2003.

30. Author interview with Bill Hambrecht, October 2, 2003.

31. Author interview with Ken Barbalato, February 13, 2003.

32. Author interview with Geoff Yang, October 9, 2003.

33. Author interview with Steve Dow, January 23, 2003.

34. Author interview with Peter Sisson, February 1, 2003.

35. Author interview with John Bogle, February 10, 2004.

36. Author interview with Ken Barbalato, February 13, 2003.

37. Brad Barber and Terrence Odean, "The Internet and The Investor," *Journal of Economic Perspectives,* Vol. 15, No. 1, Winter 2001, pp. 41–54.

38. Fred Giufrida, "Back to the Future ? Or Is Asset Allocation the End of Private Equity?," Presentation to Limited Partners Summit 2003.

39. Author interview with Gene DeRose, December 20, 2002.

40. Author interview with Gene DeRose, December 20, 2002.

41. Author interview with Gene DeRose, December 20, 2002.

42. Author interview with Ken Barbalato, Feb 13, 2003.

43. Brad Barber and Terrance Odean, "All that Glitters: The Effect of Attentionand News on the Buying Behavior of Individual and Institutional Investors," http://faculty.gsm.ucdavis.edu/~bmbarber/research

44. Jeffrey Busse and Clifton Green, "Market Efficiency in Real Time," *Journal of Financial Economics,* 65, 415–437 (2002).

45. Author interview with Kan Barbalato, February 12, 2003.

46. Gretchen Morgenson, "How Did They Value Stocks? Count the Absurd Ways; Those Lofty 'New Economy' Measures Fizzle," *New York Times,* March 18, 2001.

47. Morgenson, "How Did They Value Stocks?

48. Bret Trueman, M.H. Franco Wong; Xiao-Jun Zhang, "The Eyeballs Have it: Searching for the Value in Internet Stocks," *Journal of Accounting Research:* 137–162 (2000).

49. Chancellor, *Devil Take The Hindmost*, p. 195.
50. Brad Barber, and Terrence Odean, "The Internet and The Investor," Journal of Economic Perspectives. Vol 15, No. 1, Winter 2001, Pages 41–54.
51. Author interview with Tim Draper, August 28, 2003.
52. Author interview with Dave Dorman, January 23, 2004.
53. Author interview with Don Valentine, August 25, 2003.
54. Author interview with Jim Lessersohn, March 13, 2003.
55. Author interview with Jim Lessersohn, March 13, 2003.
56. Author interview with Rob Shepardson, April 16, 2002.
57. Author interview with Lenny Stern, April 16, 2002.
58. Author interview with Rob Shepardson, April 16, 2002.
59. Author interview with Mark Walsh, July 26, 2002.
60. Author interview with Thomas Perkins, July 22, 2003.
61. Stanley Milgram, *Obedience to Authority*, New York: Harper & Row, 1974.
62. Author interview with Thomas Perkins, July 22, 2003.
63. Author interview with Alan Patricof, December 1, 2003.
64. Author interview with Tony Sun, October 9, 2003.
65. Author interview with Bob Kagle, December 17, 2003.
66. Brad DeLong, "The NASDAQ's Round Trip," April 2001,
67. Eli Ofek, and Matthew Richardson, "Dotcom Mania: The Rise and Fall of Internet Stock Prices, " *NBER Working Paper 8630*, December 2001.
68. Stephen Penman, "Fundamental Analysis: Lessons from Recent Stock Market Bubble," Speech to Japanese Association of Security Analysts, October 26, 2001.
69. Author interview with Mark Walsh, July 26, 2002.
70. Author interview April 3, 2003.
71. Author interview with Tony Sun, October 9, 2003.
72. Author interview with Ken Barbalato, February 13, 2003.
73. Author interview with Mike Moritz, August 26, 2003.
74. Author interview with Alan Patricof, December 1, 2003.
75. Author interview with Strauss Zelnick, July 7, 2003.
76. Author interview with Strauss Zelnick, July 7, 2003.
77. Alasdair Nairn, *Engines That Move Markets: Technology Investing from Railroads to the Internet and Beyond*, New York: John Wiley & Sons, 2002, p. 254.
78. Susan Douglas, *Inventing American Broadcasting, 1899–1922*. Baltimore: Johns Hopkins University Press, 1989.
79. Alasdair, *Engines That Move Markets*, p. 258.
80. Ibid. p. 63.
81. Author interview with Scott Bertetti, April 4, 2002.
82. Author interview with Scott Bertetti, April 4, 2002.
83. Author interview April 3, 2003.
84. Author interview April 3, 2003.
85. Author interview with Mark Walsh, July 26, 2002.
86. Floyd Norris, "Biotechnology: Great Science, Greater Fools," *New York Times*, April 7, 1991.

87. Hal Varian, "Economic Scene: Comparing Nasdaq and Tulips Unfair to Flowers," *New York Times,* February 8, 2001.
88. Suzanne Woolley, *Money,* New York: Jan 1999, Vol. 28, Iss. 1; p. 94.
89. Susan Pulliam, "Analyst Warns of Price War As Internet Stocks Lose Ground," *Wall Street Journal,* January 25, 1999, pg C1.
90. Nelson D Schwartz. "Have Net Investors Lost Their Minds?," *Fortune,* June 8, 1998.
91. Greg Ip, "There's No Mania Like Internet Mania—Historically, This May Take the Cake," *Wall Street Journal,* December 30, 1998. p. C.1.
92. "Internet mania," *Time,* New York: Jan 18, 1999. Vol. 153, Iss. 2; pg. 91, 1 pgs
93. "Net Worth: interview with Mary Meeker," Barron's, December 20, 1999.
94. Author interview with Bill Hambrecht, October 2, 2003.
95. Author interview with Strauss Zelnick, July 7, 2003.
96. *New York Times,* September 1, 1929.
97. Author interview with Don Valentine, August 25, 2003.
98. Author interview with Chip Morris, June 1, 2004.
99. Press Release from Attorney General Eliot Spitzer, "Conflict Probes Resolved At Citigroup and Morgan-Stanley," April 28, 2003.

TWO

1. Charoles Rolo, "The Market a Go Go," the *New York Times,* May 8, 1966.
2. Author interview with Tom Perkins July 22, 2003.
3. Author interview with Paul Johnson, March 20, 2004.
4. Author interview with Dan Estabrook, April 10, 2002.
5. Author interview with Mark Walsh, July 26, 2002.
6. Author interview with Ken Barbalato, February 13, 2003.
7. Author interview with Michael Moritz, August 26, 2003.
8. Author interview with Tony Sun, October 9, 2003.
9. Author interview with Steve Dow, January 23, 2003.
10. Author interview with Bob Kagle, December 17, 2003.
11. Author interview with Bob Kagle, December 17, 2003.
12. Nicole Harris, Nick Wingfield, Andrea Petersen, Evan Ramstad and Khanh T. L. Tran, "Digits," *Wall Street Journal,* June 15, 2000, p. B6.
13. Sandra Sugawara, "Biotech Firms Stocks Dazzle Wall Street; Investors are Looking for Next Big Discovery," *Washington Post,* April 15, 1991.
14. Author interview October 8, 2003.
15. Author interview with Thomas Perkins, July 22, 2003.
16. Don Valentine quoted in *Electronic Business,* Anniversary Issue, October, 2000.
17. Author interview with Chip Morris, June 1, 2004.
18. Author interview with Geoff Yang, October 28, 2003.
19. Author interview with Tony Sun, October 9, 2003.
20. Author interview with Alan Patricof, December 1, 2003.

21. Author interview October 8, 2003.

22. Author interview with Tony Sun, October 9, 2003.

23. Author interview, October 28, 2003.

24. Iris Stuart and Vijay Karan, "eToys Inc: A case examining Pro Forma financial reports, analysts' forecasts and going concern disclosures," *Issues in Accounting Education,* Vol. 18.2 pg. 191 2003.

25. Greg Ip, Susan Pulliam, Scott Thurm, Ruth Simon, "How the Internet Bubble Broker Records, Rules, Bank Accounts," *Wall Street Journal Interactive Edition,* July 14, 2000.

26. Author interview with Geoff Yang, October 28, 2003.

27. Author interview October 8, 2003.

28. Author interview with Geoff Yang, October 28, 2003.

29. Author interview with Alan Patricof, December 1, 2003.

30. Author interview with Tom Perkins, July 22, 2003.

31. Author interview April 3, 2003.

32. Author interview April 3, 2003.

33. Peter H. Lewis, "Yahoo Gets Big Welcome On Wall Street," *New York Times,* April 13, 1996.

34. Author interview April 3, 2003.

35. Author interview with Ken Barbalatto, February 13, 2003.

36. Dave Kansas, "Lone Bear on Wall Street," *Wall Street Journal,* December 5, 1995, C.

37. Patrick McGeehen, "A Lumbering Street Bear is Getting Out of the Spotlight," *Wall Street Journal,* January 14, 1998, C1.

38. McGeehen, "A Lumbering Street Bear is Getting Out of the Spotlight," C1.

39. Alan Lavine, "Closer Look—Friess Framed," *Financial Planning,* January 1, 2000, p. 1.

40. Author interview with portfolio manager.

41. Author interview with Bill Hambrecht, October 2, 2003.

42. Roger Lowenstein, "Manager's Journal: The Tiger Fund Is Gone; Who's Next?," *Wall Street Journal,* April 3, 2000. p. A48.

43. Gregory Zuckerman and Paul Beckett, "Tiger Makes It Official: Hedge Funds Will Shut Down—Value-Investing Chief Decided He Couldn't Make Sense of Market," *Wall Street Journal,* March 31, 2000. p. C1.

44. Robert McGough, "Bears Will Be Right On Stocks Someday, Just You Watch," *Wall Street Journal,* July 17, 1997. p. A1.

45. Author interview with John Bogle, February 10, 2004.

46. Robert McGough, "For Some Price Doesn't Matter," *Wall Street Journal,* March 16, 1999, p. 1.

47. James M. Clash, "Henry Blodget Debates Jeremy Grantham," *Forbes,* http://pages.stern.nyu.edu/~adamodar/New_Home_Page/darkside/articles/blodget.html

48. Author interview with Bill Hambrecht, October 2, 2003.

49. Mary Meeker and Chris DePuy, *The Internet Report,* Morgan Stanley, February 1996.

50. Judith Chevalier and Glenn Ellison, "Career Concerns of Mutual Fund Managers," gsbwww.uchicago.edu/fac/judith.chevalier/research/

51. Charoles Rolo, "The Market a Go Go," the *New York Times,* May 8, 1966.

52. Victor Hillary, "Abreast of the Market," *The Wall Street Journal,* December 29, 1969.

53. Hillary, "Abreast of the Market."

54. Robert Metz, "Market Place: A 'Super Bear' Tells His View,'" the *New York Times,* April 22, 1970.

55. A. B. Kennickell, M. Starr-McCluer, and Brian Surette "Recent Changes in U.S. Family Finances: Results from the 1998 Survey of Consumer Finances," *Federal Reserve Bulletin,* January (2000).

56. Author interview April 3, 2003.

57. Anthony Perkins and Michael Perkins, *The Internet Bubble,* HarperBusiness: New York, 2001, pp. 163–4.

58. "Online Trading: Better Investor Protection Information Needed on Broker's Web Sites," U.S. General Accounting Office, May 2000.

59. "Online Trading: Investor Protections Have Improved but Continued Attention is Needed," US General Accounting Office, June 2001.

60. Brad M. Barber, and Terance Odean. "The Internet and The Investor." *Journal of Economic Perspectives,* 15 (1) pp. 41–54, 2001.

61. Perkins and Perkins, *The Internet Bubble,* p.48.

62. Brad Barber and Terrance Odean, "Trading Is Hazardous to Your Wealth: The Common Stock Investment Performance of Individual Investors," *Journal of Finance,* 55.2 April 2000.

63. Author interview with Chip Morris, June 1, 2004.

64. Author interview with John Bogle, February 10, 2004.

65. Author interview October 8, 2003.

66. Mani Subramani, and Eric Walden, "The Impact of E-Commerce Announcements on the Market Value of Firms." *Information Systems Research,* Vol. 12, No. 2, pp. 135–154, 2001.

67. Michael Cooper, Orlin Dimitrov, Raghavendra Rau, "A Rose.com by Any Other Name," *Journal of Finance,* November 2000.

68. Calmetta Y. Coleman, "K-Tel Stock Soars 45% as News of Plan To Sell Music Over Internet Proves a Hit," *Wall Street Journal,* April 21, 1998, p. 1.

69. Author interview September 28, 2002.

70. Author interview with Habib Kairuz, May 14, 2002.

71. Mark Veverka, "Get Ready for Dow.com," *Barron's,* December 20, 2000.

72. Author interview with Edmond Sanctus, August 2, 2002.

73. Author interview with Strauss Zelnick, Monday, November 3, 2003.

74. Author interview with Strauss Zelnick, Monday, November 3, 2003.

75. Alec Klein, *Stealing Time,* New York: Simon & Schuster, 2003.

76. Klein, *Stealing Time.*

77. Klein, *Stealing Time.*

78. Author interview with Jim Lessersohn, March 13, 2003.

79. Holman Jenkins, "Business World: How A Telecom Meltdown Will Cause the Next Recession," *Wall Street Journal,* September 27, 2000.

80. Author interview with Dave Dorman, January 23, 2004.

81. Author interview with Michael Armstrong, January 26, 2004.

82. Author interview with Maziar Dalaeli, January 23, 2003.

83. "Now its electron Jack," *Fortune,* September 27, 1999.

84. Daniel McGinn, "Jack Welch Goes Surfing," *Newsweek,* December 25, 2000.

85. Author interview with Jim Lessersohn, March 13, 2003.

86. Author interview with Dave Dorman, January 23, 2004.

87. Author interview with Edmond Sanctus, August 2, 2002.

88. Author interview with Geoff Yang, October 9, 2003.

89. Documents released by Attorney General Eliot Spitzer, "Conflict Probes Resolved At Citigroup and Morgan-Stanley," http://www.oag.state.ny.us/press/2003/apr/apr28a_03.html

90. Documents released by Attorney General Eliot Spitzer, "Conflict Probes Resolved At Citigroup and Morgan-Stanley," http://www.oag.state.ny.us/press/2003/apr/apr28a_03.html

91. Author interview, April 3, 2003.

92. Robert Burgleman and Philip Meza, "Vivendi Universal," *Case Number SM-96,* Graduate School of Business Stanford University, November 2001.

93. Author interview with Thomas Perkins, July 22, 2003.

94. Author interview with Geoff Yang, October 9, 2003.

95. Author interview with Geoff Yang, October 9, 2003.

96. Author interview with Geoff Yang, October 9, 2003.

97. Author interview with Bob Kagle, December 17, 2003.

98. Author interview, October 8, 2003.

99. Author interview with Bill Hambrecht, October 2, 2003.

100. Author interview with Bob Kagle, December 17, 2003.

101. Linda Himelstain and Gerry Khermouch, *Business Week,* July 17, 2001.

102. Author Interview with Michael Mortiz, August 26, 2003.

103. Author interview with Peter Sisson, February 1, 2003.

104. Author interview with Don Valentine, August 25, 2003.

105. Author interview with Bob Kagle, December 17, 2003.

106. Author interview with Alan Patricof, December 1, 2003.

107. Author interview with Habib Kairuz, May 14, 2002.

108. John Byrne, "The Fall of a Dot-Com," *Business Week,* May 1, 2000.

109. Author interview with Alan Patricof, December 1, 2003.

110. Greg Ip, Susan Pulliam, Scott Thurm, Ruth Simon, "How the Internet Bubble Broke Records, Rules, Bank Accounts," *Wall Street Journal,* July 14, 2000.

111. Author interview with Mark Walsh, July 26, 2002.

112. Author interview with Thomas Perkins, July 22, 2003.

113. Author interview with Bob Kagle, December 17, 2003.

THREE

1. Author interview with Marty Yudkovitz, March 3, 2003.
2. Joseph Stiglitz, *Economics,* W.W. Norton & Co, New York: 1993.
3. Author interview with Bob Kagle, December 17, 2003.
4. Paul Gompers and Josh Lerner. "Money Chasing Deals? The impact of fund inflows on private equity valuations," *Journal of Financial Economics, (*55) February 1999, 281–325.
5. Mark Mowrey, "Net IPO Pipeline Floods," *Industry Standard,* September 25, 2000.
6. Gretchen Morgenson and Jonathan Glatter, "$1 Billion Settlement in I.P.O. Price Fixing Case," *New York Times,* June 26, 2003.
7. Rochelle Antoniewicz, "Financing of Publicly-Traded 'New Economy' Firms in the United States," Federal Reserve Board Preliminary Draft (April).
8. Steven Landefeld and Barbara Fraumeni, "Measuring the New Economy," *Survey of Current Business, Bureau of Economic Analysis,* Department of Commerce, March 2001.
9. Webmergers.com.
10. Economic Report of the President, February 2000.
11. Economic Report of the President, February 2001.

FOUR

1. Jacqueline Doherty, "E-Commerce Stocks: Waiting for Value," *Barron's,* September 13, 1999.
2. Doherty, "E-Commerce Stocks."
3. "Net Worth: An Interview with Mary Meeker," *Barron's,* December 20, 1999.
4. Ibid.
5. Jack Willoughby, "Warning: Internet Companies are running out of cash-fast," *Barron's,* March 20, 2000.
6. Jack Willoughby, "Up In Smoke: Dot.coms are still burning cash, but the market has forced big changes," *Barron's,* June 19, 2000.
7. Jack Willoughby, "Smoldering Internet Companies, Still burning cash, try to conserve their tinder," *Barron's,* October 2, 2000.
8. R. Scott Raynovich, "Market Turbulence: Bubble Popping?" *Red Herring,* January 6, 2000.
9. Gracian Mack, Red Herring, April 6, 2000.
10. Brad Barber, Reuven Lehavy, Maureen McNichols, Brett Trueman, "Profits and Loses: Reassessing the Returns to Analysts Stock Recommendations," *Financial Analysts Journal.*
11. Documents released by Attorney General Eliot Spitzer, "Conflict Probes Resolved At Citigroup and Morgan-Stanley," http://www.oag.state.ny.us/press/2003/apr/apr28a_03.html
12. Lauren R. Rublin, "What Now? Some Street Seers Say the Halcyon Days of the Market Are Over," *Barron's,* October 16, 2000.

13. Hersh Shefrin, and Meir Statman, "The Dispositition to Sell Winners too Early and Ride Losers Too Long: Theory and Evidence," *Journal of Finance* 40.3. (1985) 777–790.
14. Prof. Jay Ritter quoted in *Red Herring,* April 6, 2000 by Gracian Mack.
15. Author interview with Alan Patricof, December 1, 2003.
16. *New York Times,* March 10, 2003.
17. CIO Insight, "Legacy Systems: Are Your Older Systems Slowing You Down?" December 13, 2002.
18. A.T Kearney, "Line56 E-Business Outlook 2003," August 2002.
19. "IT grows up," *The Economist,* August 24, 2002.
20. Author interview with Bob Kagle, December 17, 2003.
21. Warren Devine. "From Shafts to Wires: Historical Perspective on Electrification," *The Journal of Economic History* 43:2, January 1983, 347–372. Paul David. "The Dynamo and the Computer: An Historical Perspective on the Modern Productivity Paradox," *American Economic Review* 80:2, May 1990, 355–361.
22. Paul David and Gavin Wright. "General Purpose Technologies and Surges in Productivity: Historical Reflections on the Future of the ICT Revolution," Paper Presented to the International Symposium on Economic Challenges of the 21st Century in Historical Perspective, Oxford, England, July 2–4, 1999.
23. Dennis Kneale, "Technology in the Workplace—The Unfinished Revolution: Before it Lives Up to Its Enormous Potential, the Computer Revolution Has a Long, Long Way to Go," *Wall Street Journal,* September 16, 1985.
24. Author interview, July 13, 2002.
25. Author interview, July 13, 2002.
26. Author interview with Scott Bertetti, April 4, 2002.
27. Author interview with Dave Dorman, January 23, 2004.
28. Hal Varian quoted in *Fortune,* June 11, 2002 by Anna Bernasek.
29. Author interview with Habib Kairuz, May 14, 2002.
30. U.S. Census Bureau, Historical Statistics of the United States Colonial Times to 1970, U.S. Department of Commerce, 1975. Series Q148–162.

FIVE

1. Carlotta Perez, *Technological Revolutions and Financial Capital,* Edward Elgar, Northhampton, MA, 2002.
2. Roger Lowenstein, *When Genius Fails,* Random House, New York, 2000, p. 179.
3. Lowenstein, *When Genius Fails,* p. 130.
4. Alasdair Nairn, *Engines That Move Markets: Technology Investing from Railroads to the Internet and Beyond,* New York: John Wiley & Sones, 2002, p. 9.
5. Alasdair Nairn, p. 9.
6. Andrew Odlyzko, "Pricing and architecture of the Internet: Historical perspectives from telecommunications and transportation," http://www.dtc. umn.edu/~odlyzko/doc/recent.html

7. Peter Temin, "The Anglo-American Business Cycle, 1820–60," The Economic History Review, Vol. 27, No. 2, May 1974, p. 212.
8. Chris Freeman and Francisco Louca, *As Time Goes By.* Oxford Press: London. (2002)
9. Edward Chancellor, *Devil Take the Hindmost,* New York: Plume: 2000, p. 134.
10. Chancellor, *Devil Take the Hindmost,* p. 128.
11. Chancellor, *Devil Take the Hindmost,* p. 128.
12. Chancellor, *Devil Take the Hindmost,* p. 126.
13. Chancellor, *Devil Take the Hindmost,* p. 131.
14. P. J. G. Ransom, *The Victorian Railway and How it Evolved,* quoted in Chris Freeman and Francisco Louca, *As Time Goes By,* London: Oxford Press, 2002.
15. Chancellor, *Devil Take the Hindmost,* p. 136.
16. Andrew Odlyzko, "The Many Paradoxes of Broadband," www.dtc.umn.edu/~odlyzko
17. Rendigs Fels, "The American Business Cycle of 1879–85," *Journal of Political Economy,* 60.1, February 1952, 60–75.
18. Fels. "The American Business Cycle of 1879–85."
19. "The Push For Computers As Home Appliances," Business Week, March 13, 1978.
20. Author Interview with Don Valentine, August 25, 2003.
21. Author Interview with Don Valentine, August 25, 2003.
22. Author Interview with Don Valentine, August 25, 2003.
23. Karen Slater, "Banks Seek Profits in Venture Capital Arena," *The American Banker,* October 31, 1983.
24. Robert Cringely, *Accidental Empires,* HarperBusiness, New York, 1996.
25. "Big Plans for Little Computer," *New York Times,* February 15, 1982.
26. Steve Daley, "Media Feel the Pinch as Computer Ads Shrink," *Chicago Tribune,* July 12, 1985.
27. Steve Ditlea, "The Birth of an Industry," *New York Times,* January 1982.
28. Ditlea, "The Birth of An Industry."
29. Slater, "Banks Seek Profits in Venture Capital Arena."
30. William Sahlman and Howeard Stevenson, "Capital Market Myopia," *Harvard Business School,* December 1998.
31. "Fidelity Investment Offers More Specialized Funds" Wall Street Journal, August 22, 1985.
32. Terence Roth, "Technology in the Workplace: Finished At Forty: Rising Starts Can Become Obsolete Has-Beens If They Can't Come to Grips With the Computer," *Wall Street Journal,* September 16, 1985.
33. Dennis Kneale, "Computer Industry's Rapid Growth Is Slowing," *Wall Street Journal,* May 24, 1985.
34. "Home Computers Go Beyond Needs: Survey," *Associated Press,* October 1, 1985.
35. Carolyn Phillips, "Personal Computing: The Home—Who Needs It ?," *Wall Street Journal,* June 16, 1986.

36. William Buckley, "Analysts Select Attractive Survivors of Shakeout in Personal Computers," *Wall Street Journal*, December 26, 1984.

37. Kneale, "Computer Industry's Rapid Growth Is Slowing."

38. Lazza Reschi, "High-Tech Boom Finds an Industry That's Matured," *Los Angeles Times*, May 15, 1988.

39. Reschi, "High-Tech Boom Finds an Industry That's Matured."

40. Richard Shaffer, "Venture Capitalists Pay Less to Invest in High-Tech Firms," *Wall Street Journal*, May 4, 1984. p. 1.

41. Kneale, "Computer Industry's Rapid Growth Is Slowing."

42. Ronald Bailey, "Business Bookshelf: Showdown in Silicon Valley," *Wall Street Journal*, July 6, 1984.

43. Shaffer, "Venture Capitalists Pay Less to Invest in High-Tech Firms," p. 1.

44. Reschi, "High-Tech Boom Finds an Industry That's Matured."

45. Bailey, "Business Bookshelf: Showdown in Silicon Valley."

46. Dennis Kneale, "Technology in the Workplace—The Unfinished Revolution: Before it Lives Up to Its Enormous Potential, The Computer Revolution has a Long, Long Way to Go," *Wall Street Journal*, September 16, 1985.

47. Reschi, "High-Tech Boom Finds an Industry That's Matured."

48. John Eckhouse, "Computer Firms Recover from Rough Ride in '85," *San Francisco Chronicle*, December 9, 1985.

49. Paul Carroll, "Personal Computers for the Office Begin to Rebound—But Not All the Way Back," *Wall Street Journal*, November 5, 1985.

SIX

1. Samuel Kortum, and Josh Lerner, "Does Venture Capital Spur Innovation?" *NBER Working Paper No. 6846*, December 1998.

2. U.S. Patent Activity, 1790–Present, U.S. Patent Office and Census Bureau.

3. Steve Liesman, "Economy Faces Constant Force of Its 'Creative Destruction'," *Wall Street Journal*, September 19, 2002.

4. Stacy Tevlin and Karl Whelan, "Explaining the Investment Boom of the 1990s," *Journal of Money, Credit and Banking* 35, February 2003, pp. 1–22.

5. Michael Cox, "The Churn Among Firms," *Southwest Economy*, Dallas Federal Reserve, 1999.

COMPETITIVE CASCADE
Investors play the game

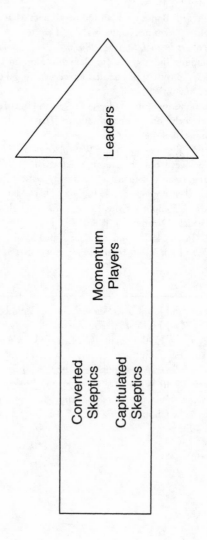

Converted
Skeptics

Capitulated
Skeptics

Momentum
Players

Leaders

Leaders in the new market opportunity succeed first. Their success attracts momentum players who are chasing fast money. As time passes, and successes seem to accumulate, skeptics are forced to play. Some are converted, the become believers in the new opportunity. Others capitulate, they remain skeptical, but play along because they need to generate competitive returns for investors.

COMPETITIVE CASCADE
Creates Distorted Business Bubble Market

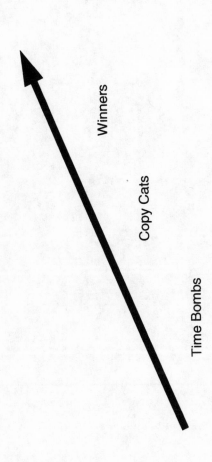

Time Bombs   Copy Cats   Winners

Winning start-ups attract copy cats who try to seize the same market opportunity and time bombs that are illegitimate businesses marketed to the public frenzy. Proliferation of copy cats saturate the market opportunity. Time bombs lay in wait, ready to explode and destroy the party. Most investors cannot distinguish the winners, copy-cats and time bombs making all of them overvalued. This insures that the amazing opportunities become an unsustainable bubble that will bust.

BIBLIOGRAPHY

Atkeson, Andrew and Kehoe, Patrick J. "The Transition to A New Economy After the Second Industrial Revolution" *NBER Working Paper 8676*, December 2001.

Baily, Martin and Lawrence, Robert. "Do We Have a New Economy?" *NBER Working Paper 8243*, April 2001.

Barber, Brad and Odean, Terrance. "The Internet and the Investor," *Journal of Economic Perspective*, Vol. 15, No. 1, Winter 2001, pp. 41–54.

Barber, Brad and Odean, Terrance. "Trading is Hazardous to Your Wealth: The Common Stock Investment Performance of Individual Investors," *The Journal of Finance*, April 2000.

Bikhchandani, Sushil and Sharma, Sunil. "Herd Behavior in Financial Markets: A Review," *IMF Working Paper WP/00/46*, March 2000.

Bikhchandani, Sushil. Hirshleifer and Welch Ivo "Learning from the Behavior of Others: Conformity, Fads and Information Cascades," *Journal of Economic Perspectives*, Vol. 12, Issue 3, Summer 1998, pp. 151–170.

Blanchard, Olivier. "Consumption and the Recession of 1990–1991," *The American Economic Review*, Vol. 83, No. 2, May 1993, pp. 270–273.

Blinder, Alan and Yellen, Janet. *The Fabulous Decade: Macroeconomic Lessons from the 1990s*, New York, A Century Foundation Report, 2001.

Brooks, John. *The Go-Go Years: The Drama and Crashing Finale of Wall Street's Bullish 60s*, New York, John Wiley & Sons, 1998.

Brynjolfsson, Erik and Hitt, Lorin. "Beyond Computation: Information Technology, Organizational Transformation and Business Performance," unpublished, April 2000.

Bureau of Economic Analysis. "Benchmark Input-Output Accounts of The United States, 1992," Department of Commerce, September 1998.

Casidy, John. *dot.con: The Greatest Story Ever Sold*, New York, Harper Collins, 2002.

Chari, V. V. and Hopenhayn, Hugo. "Vintage Human Capital, Growth, and the Diffusion of New Technology," *The Journal of Political Economy*, December 1991, Vol. 99, No. 1, pp. 1142–1165.

Chauvet, Marcelle and Potter, Simon. "Recent Changes in the US Business Cycle," *Journal of Economic Literature*, April 2001.

Chancellor, Edward. *Devil Take the Hindmost*, New York, Plume, 2000.

Christensen, Clayton. *The Innovator's Dilemma: When Technologies Cause Great Firms to Fail,* Boston, MA, Harvard Business School Press, 1997.

Clark, Jim. *Netscape Time: The Making of the Billion Dollar Start-up That Took on Microsoft,* New York, St. Martins Griffin, 1999.

Crafts, N. F. R. "British Economic Growth, 1700–1831: A Review of the Evidence," *Economic History Review,* Vol. 36, No. 2, May 1983, pp. 177–199.

Cringly, Robert. *Accidental Empires,* New York, HarperBusiness, 1996.

DeRose, Gene. "How far can consumer online services go?" *Red Herring,* April 1994.

Dash, Mike. *Tulipomania: The Story of the World's Most Coveted Flower and the Extraordinary Passion it Aroused,* New York, Three Rivers Press, 1999.

David, Paul. "The Dynamo and the Computer: An Historical Perspective on the Modern Productivity Paradox," *The American Economic Review,* Vol. 80, No. 2, May 1990, pp. 355–361.

David, Paul and Wright, Gavin. "General Purpose Technologies and Surges in Productivity: Historical Reflections on the Future of the ICT Revolution," Paper Presented to the International Symposium on Economic Challenges of the 21st Century in Historical Perspective, Oxford, July 2–4, 1999.

DeLong, Bradford. "Macroeconomic Vulnerabilities in the Twenty-First Century Economy: A Preliminary Taxonomy," Conference Draft, 2002.

DeLong, J. Bradford and Froomkin, A. Michael. "Speculative Microeconomics for Tomorrow's Economy," unpublished draft, November 14, 1999.

DeLong, Bradford, Shleifer, Andrei, Summers, Lawrence and Waldman, Robert. "Noise Trader Risk in Financial Markets," *The Journal of Political Economy,* Vol. 94, No. 4, December 1989, pp. 703–738.

Derman, Emanuel. "The Perception of Time, Risk and Return During Periods of Speculation," *Goldman, Sachs & Co,* January 2002.

Devine, Warren. "From Shafts to Wires: Historical Perspective on Electrification," *The Journal of Economic History,* Vol. 43, No. 2, January 1983, pp. 347–372.

Dremam, David, *Psychology and the Stock Market,* New York, Amacom, 1977.

Edison, Hali and Slok, Torsten. "New Economy Stock Valuations and Investment in the 1990s," *IMF Working Paper WP/01/78,* May 2001.

Evans, Philip. *Blown to Bits: How the New Economics of Information Transforms Strategy,* Boston, MA, Harvard University Press, 2000.

Flynn, Laurie. "A corner turns for Yahoo and other Internet search concerns," *New York Times,* February 11, 1997, p. D8.

Freeman, Chris and Louca, Francisco. *As Time Goes Buy: From the Industrial Revolution to the Information Revolution,* Oxford, Oxford University Press, 2002.

Fuhrer, Jeffrey and Schuh, Scott. "Beyond Shocks: What Causes Business Cycles? An Overview," *Federal Reserve Bank,* 1998.

Galbraith, John Kenneth. *A Short History of Financial Euphoria,* New York, Penguin Books, 1990.

Galbraith, John Kenneth. *The Great Crash 1929,* New York, Mariner Book, 1997.

Garber, Peter. "Tulipmania," *The Journal of Political Economy,* Vol. 97, No. 3, June 1989, pp. 535–560.

Gilder, George, *Mircocosm,* New York, Touchstone, 1989.

Gimein, Mark and Koudsi, Suzanne. "Meet the dumbest dot-com in the world," *Fortune,* July 10, 2000.

Gompers, Paul and Lerner, Josh. "Short Term America Revisited ? Boom and Bust in the Venture Capital Industry and the Impact on Innovation," *Innovation Policy and the Economy,* Vol. 3, 2002.

Gompers, Paul and Lerner, Josh. "Money Chasing Deals? The impact of fund inflows on private equity valuations," *Journal of Financial Economics,* Vol. 55, February 1999, pp. 281–325.

Gompers, Paul and Lerner, Josh. "What Drives Venture Capital Fundraising?" *Brookings Papers on Economic Activity—Microeconomics,* 1998, pp. 149–192.

Gordon, Robert J. "U.S. Economic Growth since 1870: One Big Wave?" *American Economic Review,* May 1999.

Gordon, Robert J. "Does the 'New Economy' Measure up to the Great Inventions of the Past?" Draft of paper for *Journal of Economic Perspectives,* April 28, 2000.

Gordon, Robert J. "Explaining the U.S. Economic Miracle" Presentation at *OECD Jobs Conference,* January 27, 2000.

Gordon, Robert J. "Panel Discussion on the New Economy" Presentation at *Annual Meeting of the American Economic Association,* January 6, 2001.

Gordon, Robert J. "Technology and Economic Performance in the American Economy," *NBER Working Paper 8771,* February 2002.

Greenspan, Alan. "The Challenge of Central Banking in a Democratic Society," Francis Boyer Lecture of The American Enterprise Institute for Public Policy Research, Washington, D.C., December 5, 1996.

Haacker, Markus and Morsink, James. "You Say You Want A Revolution: Information Technology and Growth," *IMF Working Paper WP/02/70,* April 2002.

Haimowitz, Joseph. "Has the Surge in Computer Spending Fundamentally Changed the Economy?" *Economic Review Federal Reserve Bank of Kansas City,* Second Quarter 1998.

Helpman, Elhanan and Trajtenberg, Manuel. "A Time to Sow and A Time to Reap: Growth Based on General Purpose Technologies," *NBER Working Paper 4854,* September 1994.

Helpman, Elhanan. "Diffusion of General Purpose Technologies," *NBER Working Paper 5773,* September 1996.

Hobun, Bart and Jovanovic, Boyan. "The Information-Technology Revolution and the Stock Market: Evidence," *American Economic Review,* December 2001.

Jackson, Tim. "Inside Track: Boldness Bar None," *Financial Times,* July 4, 2000.

Jorgenson, Dale and Stiroh, Kevin. "Raising the Speed Limit: U.S. Economic Growth in the Information Age," *Brookings Papers on Economic Activity,* Vol. 1, 2000.

Jovanovic, Boyan and MacDonald, Glenn. "Competitive Diffusion," *The Journal of Political Economy,* February 1994, Vol. 102, No. 1, pp. 24–52.

Jovanovic, Boyan and Rousseau, Peter. "Why Wait? A Century of Life before IPO." *NBER Working Paper 8081,* January 2001.

Kaplan, Philip. *F'd Companies: Spectacular Dot-Com Flameouts,* New York, Simon & Schuster, 2002.

Kindleberger, Charles. *Mania, Panics and Crashes: A History of Financial Crises,* New York, John Wiley & Sons, 2000.

Klein, Alec. *Stealing Time: Steve Case, Jerry Levin and the Collapse of AOL Time Warner,* New York, Simon & Schuster, 2003.

Kurtz, Howard. *The Fortune Tellers: Inside Wall Street's Game of Money, Media and Manipulation,* New York, Touchstone, 2000.

Lamoreaux, Naomi and Sokoloff, Kenneth. "Inventive Activity and the Market for Technology in the United States, 1840–1920," *NBER Working Paper 7107,* May 1999.

Landefeld, J. Steven and Fraumeni, Barbara. "Measuring the New Economy," *Survey of Current Business, Bureau of Economic Analysis, Department of Commerce,* March 2001.

Leamer, Edward E. "The Life Cycles of US Economic Expansions," *NBER Working Paper 8192,* March 2001.

Levine, Rick, Locke, Christopher, Searls, Doc and Weinberger, David. *The Cluetrain Manifesto: The End of Business as Usual,* Cambridge, MA, Perseus Publishing, 2000.

Levitan, Lauren and Benjamin, Keith. "Etoys, Inc: Initiating Coverage of eTailing Category Killer with a Buy Rating," *BancBoston Robertson Stephens,* June 1999.

Levitan, Lauren and Cibula, Michael. "Etoys, Inc: Worst Case Scenario Plays Out for eToys," *BancBoston Robertson Stephens,* December, 2000.

Lewis, Michael. *Next: The Future Just Happened,* New York, Norton, 2001.

Lewis, Peter. "Yahoo Gets Big Welcome on Wall Street," *New York Times,* April 13, 1996, p. 33.

Litan, Robert and Rivlin, Alice. "Projecting the Economic Impact of the Internet," *AEA Papers and Proceedings,* May 2001, pp. 313–317.

Lowenstein, Roger. *When Genius Failed: The Rise and Fall of Long Term Capital Management,* New York, Random House, 2000.

Lowry, Michelle and Schwert, William G. "IPO Market Cycles: Bubbles or Sequential Learning?" *NBER Working Paper 793,* October 2000.

Lum, Sherlene and Yuskavage, Robert. "Gross Product by Industry, 1947–96," *Survey of Current Business,* Bureau of Economic Analysis, Department of Commerce, November 1997.

Lynch, Aaron. "Thought contagion in the stock markets: A general framework and focus on the Internet Bubble," *Derivatives Use, Trading & Regulation,* Vol. 6, No. 4, September 2000.

Mackay, Charles, *Extraordinary Popular Delusions and the Madness of Crowds,* New York, MetroBooks, 2002.

Mahar, Maggie. *Bull! What Drove the Breakneck Market—And What Every Investor Needs to Know About Financial Cycles,* New York, Harper Business, 2003.

Malik, Om. *Broadbandits: Inside the $750 billion Telecom Heist,* New York, John Wiley & Son, 2003.

Mandel, Michael. *The Internet Depression: The Boom, the Bust, and Beyond,* New York, Perseus Books, 2000.

Meeker, Mary, and DePuy, Chris. *The Internet Report,* Morgan Stanley, 1996.

Miller, Ross. "Can Markets Learn to Avoid Bubbles?" *The Journal of Psychology and Financial Markets,* January 2002.

Moore, Gordon. *Inside the Tornado: Marketing Strategies from Silicon Valley's Cutting Edge,* New York, Harper Business, 1995.

Moran, Larry and McCully, Clinton. "Trends in Consumer Spending, 1959–2000," *Survey of Current Business, Bureau of Economic Analysis, Department of Commerce,* March 2001.

Motavalli, John. *Bamboozled at the Revolution: How Big Media Lost Billions in the Battle for the Internet,* New York, Viking, 2002.

Mullainathan, Sendhil and Thaler, Richard. "Behavioral Economics," *NBER Working Paper 7948,* October 2002.

Nairn, Alasdair. *Engines That Move Markets: Technology Investing from Railroads to the Internet and Beyond,* New York, John Wiley & Sons, 2002.

Negroponte, Nicholas. *Being Digital,* New York, Vintage, 1995.

Norris, Floyd. "Exuberant, You Bet. Irrational? Not Now," *New York Times,* July 27, 1997, p. E6.

Ofek, Eli and Richardson, Matthew. "Dotcom Mania: The Rise and Fall of Internet Stock Prices," *NBER Working Paper 8630,* December 2001.

Patrick, Kennith. "Comparing NIPA Profits with S&P Profits," *Survey of Current Business, Bureau of Economic Analysis,* Department of Commerce, April 2001.

Perez, Carlotta. *Technological Revolutions and Financial Capital: The Dynamics of Bubbles and Golden Ages,* Cheltenham, Edward Elgar, 2002.

Perkins, Anthony and Perkins, Michael. *The Internet Bubble: The Insight Story on Why It Burst- and What You can Do to Profit Now,* New York, Harper Business, 2001.

Planting, Mark and Kuhbach, Peter. "Annual Input-Output Accounts of the U.S. Economy, 1998," *Survey of Current Business,* Bureau of Economic Analysis, Department of Commerce, December 2001.

Rabin, Matthew. "Psychology and Economics," *Journal of Economic Literature,* Vol. 36, No. 1, March 1998, pp. 11–46.

Ritter, Jay and Welch, Ivo. "A Review of IPO Activity, Pricing and Allocations," *The Journal of Finance,* August 2002.

Ritter, Jay. "Initial Public Offerings," *Contemporary Finance Digest,* Vol. 2, No. 1, Spring 1998, pp. 5–30

Sahlman, William and Stevenson, Howard. "Capital Market Myopia," *Harvard Business School Cases,* August 1987.

San Francisco Chronicle, "Dot-Coms Lose Millions By Giving Money Away for Surfing the Internet," August 7, 2000.

Scharfstein, David and Stain, Jeremy. "Herd Behavior and Investment," *The American Economic Review,* Vol. 80, No. 3, 1980. pp. 465–479.

Schumpeter, Joseph. *Capitalism, Socialism and Democracy,* New York, Harper Perennial, 1950.

Schumpeter, Joseph. *The Theory of Economic Development,* New Brunswick, Transaction Publishers, 2002.

Schwert, G. William. "Indexes of U.S. Stock Prices from 1802 to 1987," *The Journal of Business.* July 1990, Vol. 63, No. 3, pp. 399–426.

Shiller, Robert J. "Measuring Bubble Expectations and Investor Confidence"

Shiller, Robert J. *Irrational Exuberance*, New York, Broadway Books, 2000.

Shiller, Robert J. "Conversation, Information and Herd Behavior," *The American Economic Review*, Vol. 85, Issue 2, May 1995.

Shiller, Robert J. "Market Volatility and Investor Behavior," *The American Economic Review*, Vol. 80, Issue 2, May 1990.

Siegel, Jeremy. *Stocks for the Long Run*, New York, McGraw-Hill, 1998.

Sohl, Jeffrey. "The US Angel and Venture Capital Market: Recent Trends and Developments," *Journal of Private Equity*, Vol. 6, No. 2, 2003.

Stevenson, Richard W. ,"" *New York Times*, December 7, 1996, p. 35.

Stross, Randal. *eBoys: The True Story of the Six Tall Men Who Back eBay and Other Billion Dollar Start-ups*, New York, Ballantine Books, 2000.

Subramani, Mani and Walden, Eric. "The Impact of E-Commerce Announcements on the Market Value of Firms," *Information Systems Research*, Vol. 12, No. 2, 2001, pp 135–154.

Teplin, Albert. "The U.S. Flow of Funds Accounts and Their Uses," *Federal Reserve Bulletin*, July 2001.

Tevlin, Stacey and Whelan, Karl. "Explaining the Investment Boom of the 1990s," *Federal Reserve Bank*, March 2000.

Temin, Peter. "Steam and Waterpower in the Early Nineteenth Century," *The Journal of Economic History*, Vol. 26, No. 2, June 1966, pp. 187–205.

Temin, Peter. "The Causes of American Business Cycles: An Essay in Economic Historiography," *NBER Working Paper 6692*, August 1998.

Tvede, Lars. *The Psychology of Finance*, Oxford, Norwegian University Press, 1990.

White, Eugene. "The Stock Market Boom and Crash of 1929 Revisited," *Journal of Economic Perspectives*, Vol. 4, No. 2, Spring 1990, pp. 67–83.

World Economic Outlook, International Monetary Fund, October 2001.

World Economic Outlook, International Monetary Fund, May 2000.

Yuskavage, Robert. "Improved Estimates of Gross Product by Industry, 1959–94," *Survey of Current Business*, Bureau of Economic Analysis, Department of Commerce, August 1996.

Zarnowitz, Victor. "What is a Business Cycle?" *NBER Working Paper 3863*, October 1991.

Zarnowitz, Victor. *Business Cycles, Theory, History, Indicators, and Forecasting*, Chicago, University of Chicago Press, 1992.

INDEX